TABLES *of* CONTENT

Tables of Content has received the following awards:

2006 South Regional Winner, Tabasco Community Cookbook Awards,
sponsored by the McIlhenny Company

2006 Finalist, *Foreword Magazine*'s Book of the Year Awards

2007 Winner of the "Home" Category, Eric Hoffer Awards,
sponsored by Hopewell Publications

2007 Winner of the "Cookbook" Category, National Indie Excellence Book Awards,
sponsored by *PubInsider Magazine*

TABLES *of* CONTENT

SERVICE, SETTINGS AND SUPPER

The Junior League of Birmingham, Alabama

TABLES *of* CONTENT

SERVICE, SETTINGS AND SUPPER

Published by the Junior League of Birmingham
Copyright © 2006

Junior League of Birmingham, Inc.
2212 Twentieth Avenue South
Birmingham, Alabama 35223
205.879.9861
www.jlbonline.com

Photography: © Ralph Anderson
Food/Photo Stylist: Julia Dowling Rutland
Artist: Barbara Melson Lavallet

Library of Congress Catalog Number: 2006924081
ISBN: 978-0-9774688-0-5

Edited, Designed, and Manufactured by **Favorite Recipes® Press**
An imprint of

FRP

P.O. Box 305142
Nashville, Tennessee 37230
800.358.0560

Art Director: Steve Newman
Book Design: Craig Biddle and Phil Sankey
Project Manager and Editor: Debbie Van Mol

*Photograph for the cover was taken in the gardens of Cathy and Tom Adams.
Table and chairs provided by Frontera. Table setting supplied by Table Matters.*

Printed in China
First Printing: 2006   30,000 copies
Second Printing: 2007   20,000 copies

VISION

The Junior League of Birmingham—Building Partnerships for a Better Birmingham.

MISSION

The Junior League of Birmingham is an organization of women committed to promoting voluntarism, developing the potential of women, and improving the community through the effective action and leadership of trained volunteers. Its purpose is exclusively educational and charitable.

VALUES

As volunteers of the Junior League of Birmingham, we value the following:

- Honesty
- Integrity
- Compassion
- Respect for the individual
- Positive impact on the community through financial support
- Efficiency and professionalism within our organization and projects
- Personal responsibility and accountability
- Personal growth and training
- The spirit of camaraderie
- Leaving a legacy
- Financial stewardship

COMMUNITY FOCUS

The Junior League of Birmingham believes that proactive involvement in the health, education, and well-being of women and children strengthens the quality of family life.

The Junior League believes

- Food, shelter, housing, and employment are essential to the economic independence of families
- Primary and preventative health care should be accessible to all women and children
- Infants and children are entitled to a stimulating, healthful, and educational environment
- Individuals have a right to excellence in education
- Parents, educators, and the community have the responsibility to ensure that children are provided with effective education and enrichment opportunities
- Individuals who understand the needs of children are empowered to be more effective parents and caregivers
- Women and children have the right to live in safe, violence-free households

Contents

Foreword

As a native of Birmingham, I have a great appreciation for good food. I love it! The Junior League of Birmingham has put together this book and it is filled with recipes that remind me of home. *Tables of Content* is the kind of cookbook that will be cherished for generations.

Publishing this cookbook is just one small part of the League's mission. These industrious, talented women offer opportunities throughout Birmingham for women and children to improve their health, education, and overall well-being. It might be helping children complete schoolwork at the Junior League of Birmingham Sunshine School so they can keep up with their classmates while receiving necessary medical treatment at Children's Hospital. Sometimes it's as simple as putting books into the hands of people learning to read through the Hooked-On-Books project. The Junior League of Birmingham reaches out to its community through approximately thirty-seven different projects involving the efforts of more than 2,700 members. All that and great cooks to boot!

The sale of every copy of *Tables of Content*, as well as their other cookbooks, *Magic* and *Food for Thought*, generates a significant source of revenue to continue the League's positive impact on Birmingham.

Now, start cooking!

Courteney Cox

Preface

by Kathryn Tortorici and Nancy Bynon

Anyone who has worked on a cookbook realizes that the initial idea slowly evolves to become the final product after many, many hours of discussion, photo styling, and recipe testing. When we began, we knew we wanted to celebrate the dinner hour and to solicit family recipes that were both comforting and memorable, familiar but with a new twist. We encouraged contributors to include stories about the food and why their particular recipe was important to them. As these stories so often included conversations around the table, our title soon became obvious—*Tables of Content* and we knew it also had to include *Supper*—one of our favorite Southern words.

We also wanted to showcase Birmingham's landmarks and give a little more information about each one. So we decided to photograph each of our "tables" in a landmark local setting. We're proud of Birmingham and it was difficult to choose only nine settings as there is much, much more to see in what is truly a "Magic City." Hence, *Settings*.

Finally, we hoped to include a little information about the history of our Junior League, now one of the largest in the country. So we chose to include sidebars that would detail some highlights of the league over its eighty-year history, as well as some of the service projects of which we're particularly proud. And so, *Service*.

And that's how it happened…Our *Tables of Content* would include *Service, Settings and Supper*!

Along the way, we gathered interesting tips and menu ideas from our food editors, and tried to include them where they'd be helpful. We're especially grateful for our introduction by Rick Bragg, one of Alabama's finest writers, who knows lots about family, food, and memories—and can express it in a way familiar to all of us.

But for the other information, we're grateful to a large team of enthusiastic and very talented women who cheerfully tested and retested, wrote and rewrote, styled and restyled. We're also fortunate to have a large group of community advisors who offered suggestions, recipes, venues, provided props, and offered most importantly their support.

We hope the result is truly a representation of Birmingham, as well as an excellent and versatile cookbook. We had lots of fun! But most of all, we hope to encourage "tables of content" in everyone's home. Today's supper conversation may be tomorrow's favorite memory—don't let the opportunity pass you by!

Introduction

by Rick Bragg

TABLE

The tables were topped with pale yellow or seafoam green linoleum, or hammered and glued together from pine, scarred by generations of knife-wielding toddlers and dimpled by a million sweating Bama jelly glasses of sweet iced tea.

The settings were not of silver but stainless steel, which somehow was always a little stained. The plates were unmatched and heavy, the bowls chipped, and we drank from Mason and Ball jars long before we knew it was cool.

There I sat as a child, my legs dangling from the straight-backed chair, and knew that I was as close to heaven as perhaps I would ever be.

It might have been the food: the unbearably aromatic, brown-crusted mounds of fried chicken, the beef short ribs that melted into a pile of red-skinned potatoes and Spanish onion, the slabs of barbecued pork chops that would be just as good six hours later, when I tiptoed into the kitchen and liberated one from the refrigerator while all the rest of the world wasted its time with sleep. And it might have been the vegetables—the mountain of butter-heavy mashed potatoes, the miles of green beans, the vats of ham-seasoned pinto beans and stewed squash, and fried green tomatoes and hot corn bread. Or, of course, it might have just been the banana puddin'.

But as great as the food was—and it was great, the best in this world—it was the union of my people around that table that turned its surface into a great experience, that changed a straight-backed chair into a rocket ship that carried me beyond the limits of my child-life and into the broader one of work, of politics, of fist fights and dog fights, of droughts and snake killings and strikes and football and whose souped-up car would out-run who else's. The table was where the world was discussed, and even if the world sometimes seemed to stop at the county line, it was enough for me then, for a child.

Many, many days, it still is.

We still gather around tables, but not as much, still eat the wonderful food and tell the stories. The stories and the food are as one in my memory, like salt and pepper, like corn bread and buttermilk, and when I am an old man I will still have them, even if I am relegated to strained mush.

I will remember the stories around those tables and think of buttered biscuits and crab apple jelly, and even if I am a million miles away, I will be home.

Rick Bragg, author of the critically acclaimed and best-selling All Over but the Shoutin' *and a Pulitzer Prize-winning national correspondent for the* New York Times, *says he learned to tell stories by listening to the masters, the people of the foothills of the Appalachians. The book, a* New York Times *notable book of the year, won several awards and was selected as one of the best books of the year by several news organizations and reader groups.*

Bragg was born in Alabama, grew up there, and worked at several newspapers before joining the New York Times *in 1994. He has twice won the prestigious American Society of Newspaper Editors Distinguished Writing Award, and more than fifty writing awards in his twenty-year career. In 1992, he was awarded a Nieman Fellowship at Harvard University. He has taught writing in colleges and in newspaper newsrooms and currently teaches creative writing at the University of Alabama. He is also the author of* Somebody Told Me, *a critically acclaimed collection of his newspaper stories.*

http://www.randomhouse.com/ knopf/authors/bragg/

Cookbook Committee

EXECUTIVE STEERING COMMITTEE

Chairman: Kathryn Lavallet Tortorici
Co-Chairman: Nancy Bedsole Bynon
Photography/Production Chairman: Julie Grimes Bottcher

STEERING COMMITTEE

Editorial Assistant: Lena Clark Blakeney
Business Manager: Pat Sandlin Johnson
Recipe Testing Director: Lyda Helen Jones
Recipe Testing Co-Director: Holley Contri Johnson, MS, RD
Chapter Directors: Mary Spotswood Box
Allison O'Neal Skinner
Kelly Hooper Troiano
Christine McGrath Velezis
Copy/Production Director: Rebecca Bradberry Moody
Marketing Director: Jennifer Ruby McCain
Writer: Beaty Evans Coleman
Special Features Director: Barri White Murse

PHOTOGRAPHY COMMITTEE

Photographer: Ralph Anderson
Food/Photo Stylist: Julia Dowling Rutland
Photo Stylist: Cari Lorentz South
Food Stylist: Julie Grimes Bottcher
Lyda Helen Jones
Mary Spotswood Box
Photography Assistant: Elizabeth Lassiter Fitzpatrick

ASSISTING COMMITTEE

Special Events Director: Carolyn Amos Freeman
Sustainer Advisor/Editor: Susan Emack Alison
Sustainer Advisor: Pilar Caceres Taylor
Computer Assistants: Elizabeth Lawson Lyons
Mary Elaine Lark Jolly
Nancy Knight Wilson
Katherine Vengrouskie Allison
Proofers: Janet Curry Robinson
Christiana Dunn Roussel

Rise and Shine

BREAKFAST AND BRUNCH

Casting a watchful eye and clutching a spear from atop Red Mountain is Birmingham's most recognizable landmark—Vulcan, Roman god of fire and forge! Whether you are watching the sun rise or basking in the late afternoon sunset, the city's ten-acre park features spectacular panoramic views of Birmingham. While at Vulcan Park, celebrate the top of the morning from one of the tallest points in Birmingham.

Designed by Giuseppe Moretti and built in 1904, Vulcan was cast in Birmingham and sent to St. Louis to represent Birmingham at the World's Fair. After winning the grand prize, Vulcan was shipped home piece by piece and left atop Red Mountain until he moved to the Alabama State Fairgrounds, where he languished for almost thirty years. Today the park atop Red

Mountain includes the restored statue, picnic grounds, an open elevator to the foot of Vulcan, and a museum/exhibition hall housing the early industrial history of Birmingham. Re-opened in 2004, Vulcan welcomes more than 100,000 visitors annually.

And just what to prepare for that sunrise picnic? Try our Buttermilk Crumb Coffee Cake on page 31, which you can prepare the night before. For a crowd later in the day, the Blueberry Lemon Bread on page 33 is a good bet and can be doubled if you have unexpected numbers. For a special holiday treat, Baked French Toast on page 25 cannot be beat. And remember when you are frying those eggs in a cast-iron skillet to cast an eye upon Vulcan, the world's largest cast-iron statue!

Visit Vulcan at www.vulcanpark.org.

Vulcan Park

Homemade Waffles

Breakfast and Brunch

CONTENTS

VEAL CREOLE WITH GRITS

SERVES 8

3 pounds veal scaloppine, trimmed
Salt and pepper to taste
2/3 cup self-rising flour
2 green bell peppers, chopped
1 onion, thickly sliced
2 cups beef broth
1 (15-ounce) can no-salt-added tomato sauce
1 tablespoon chopped fresh garlic (about 3 cloves)
1 tablespoon Worcestershire sauce
1 teaspoon oregano
1 teaspoon basil
1 teaspoon thyme
1 teaspoon brown sugar
Hot cooked grits

Season the veal with salt and pepper and coat lightly with the self-rising flour, shaking lightly to remove any excess. Brown the veal in a large skillet coated with nonstick cooking spray over medium-high heat for 5 to 7 minutes per side. Remove the veal to a platter using a slotted spoon, reserving the pan drippings.

Add the bell peppers and onion to the reserved pan drippings and cook over medium heat for 5 minutes, stirring frequently. Stir in the broth, tomato sauce, garlic, Worcestershire sauce, oregano, basil, thyme and brown sugar.

Return the veal to the skillet and cook, covered, over medium-low heat for 30 to 45 minutes or until the desired consistency, stirring occasionally. Serve over hot cooked grits.

LENA CLARK BLAKENEY

Low Country Shrimp and Grits

SERVES 6 TO 8

6 cups water
1 teaspoon salt
1 1/2 cups quick-cooking grits
2 cups (8 ounces) shredded sharp Cheddar cheese
5 ounces prosciutto or country ham, chopped
1/8 teaspoon cayenne pepper
2 tablespoons butter
2 pounds medium shrimp, peeled and deveined
1 tablespoon chopped fresh garlic (about 3 cloves)
1/2 cup dry white wine
3 tablespoons lemon juice
1 cup sliced green onions

Bring the water and salt to a boil in a Dutch oven and gradually whisk in the grits. Cook over medium-low heat for 10 minutes or until tender, stirring frequently. Stir in the cheese, prosciutto and cayenne pepper. Remove from the heat and cover to keep warm.

Melt the butter in a large skillet over medium-high heat and add the shrimp and garlic. Cook for 3 minutes or just until the shrimp turn pink, stirring frequently. Mix in the wine and lemon juice and stir the shrimp mixture and green onions into the grits mixture.

Ruth Carpenter Pitts

GREEK OMELET

SERVES 4

1/4 cup (1/2 stick) butter
1/2 cup chopped red bell pepper
1/2 cup chopped onion
2 garlic cloves, minced
1/4 cup chopped pitted kalamata olives
1/4 cup chopped tomato
6 eggs
1/4 cup milk
1 teaspoon chopped fresh oregano, or
    1/4 teaspoon dried oregano
1/2 teaspoon salt
1/2 teaspoon pepper
1/2 cup (2 ounces) crumbled feta cheese

Melt 2 tablespoons of the butter in a 10-inch nonstick skillet over medium-high heat. Sauté the bell pepper, onion and garlic in the butter for 5 minutes or until tender-crisp. Remove from the heat and stir in the olives and tomato.

Whisk the eggs, milk, oregano, salt and pepper in a bowl until combined. Heat 1 tablespoon of the remaining butter in a 10-inch omelet pan over medium heat. Add 1/2 of the egg mixture to the hot pan, tilting to ensure even coverage.

Cook, gently lifting the edge of the omelet with a spatula and tilting the pan to allow the uncooked portion to flow underneath; do not stir. When the egg mixture is almost set sprinkle 1/2 of the sautéed vegetables and 1/4 cup of the cheese over half of the omelet. Continue cooking until set. Loosen the omelet with a spatula and fold over. Slide onto a heated serving plate. Repeat the procedure with the remaining 1 tablespoon butter, remaining egg mixture, remaining sautéed vegetable mixture and remaining cheese. Serve immediately.

RAMI MARIE PERRY

In 1922 the Junior League of Birmingham was established as a member of the Association of Junior Leagues of America with 131 charter members. Eighty-three years later the JLB has more than 2,700 members.

PIMENTO CHEESE EGGS

Buying your favorite pimento cheese spread will make this wonderful dish even easier.

SERVES 6

Pimento Cheese Spread
16 ounces extra-sharp Cheddar
    cheese, shredded
8 ounces Parmesan cheese, grated
1 (4-ounce) jar pimentos, drained
    and chopped
1/4 cup mayonnaise

Eggs and Assembly
12 eggs
1 tablespoon heavy cream or whipping cream
1 tablespoon butter
6 English muffins, split
Butter to taste
12 slices thick-cut bacon, crisp-cooked
    and drained
Salt and pepper to taste

For the spread, combine the Cheddar cheese, Parmesan cheese, pimentos and mayonnaise in a bowl and mix well.

For the eggs, whisk the eggs and cream in a bowl until blended. Melt 1 tablespoon butter in a nonstick skillet and add the egg mixture. Scramble the eggs over low heat until fluffy and cooked through.

Toast the muffins. Spread the cut sides of the muffins lightly with butter to taste and then spread with a heaping spoonful of the pimento cheese spread. Stack 1 slice of the bacon, broken into halves, over the pimento cheese and top evenly with the scrambled eggs. Season to taste with salt and pepper. Arrange on a baking sheet and broil on low for 2 to 3 minutes or until heated through and light brown.

MARY SPOTSWOOD BOX

The JLB believes that proactive involvement in the health, education, and well-being of women and children strengthens and improves the quality of family life.

The JLB supports and initiates projects that increase literacy, improve health care, curb domestic violence, ensure better child care, enhance school performance, and reduce homelessness.

BRUNCH EGGS

SERVES 6

12 slices ready-to-serve bacon
10 eggs
1/2 cup milk
1/2 cup (2 ounces) shredded sharp
    Cheddar cheese

1/4 cup chopped green bell pepper
1/4 cup chopped red bell pepper
1/4 cup chopped onion
1 teaspoon salt
1/4 to 1/2 teaspoon pepper

Preheat the oven to 350 degrees. Spray 12 muffin cups with nonstick cooking spray. Line each prepared muffin cup with 1 slice of the bacon. The slice should be place in a circle around the edges; do not cover the bottoms of the cups.

Whisk the eggs, milk, cheese, bell peppers, onion, salt and pepper in a bowl until combined. Pour enough of the egg mixture into each prepared cup to fill 2/3 full and bake for 40 to 45 minutes or until puffy and liquid is no longer visible on top. Cool in the pan on a wire rack for several minutes. Remove from the pan and serve immediately.

AIMEE SISK PRUITT

CRUSTLESS CHEESE AND SPINACH QUICHE

This is an easy but impressive dish to serve at your next get-together. It's a yummy way to sneak spinach in a dish that kids will enjoy.

SERVES 8

1 (10-ounce) package frozen chopped
    spinach, thawed and drained
1 1/2 cups (6 ounces) shredded
    mozzarella cheese
1/2 cup heavy cream or
    whipping cream

1/3 cup pesto
5 eggs, lightly beaten
1/2 cup (2 ounces) shredded
    mozzarella cheese

Preheat the oven to 375 degrees. Press the excess moisture from the spinach. Combine the spinach, 1 1/2 cups cheese, cream, pesto and eggs in a bowl and mix well. Pour the spinach mixture into a 9-inch pie plate sprayed with nonstick cooking spray. Bake for 25 to 30 minutes or until set. Sprinkle with 1/2 cup cheese and bake for 2 to 3 minutes longer or until the cheese melts.

LAUREN CASWELL BROOKS

FARMER'S FRITTATA

SERVES 6

1 tablespoon olive oil
2 cups frozen cubed hash brown potatoes
3/4 cup chopped green bell pepper
1/4 cup chopped onion
2 garlic cloves, minced
10 eggs
1/4 cup milk
1 1/2 cups chopped cooked ham
3/4 cup chopped tomato
1/2 teaspoon salt
1/2 teaspoon pepper
1 cup (4 ounces) shredded Cheddar
    Jack cheese

Preheat the oven to 350 degrees. Heat the olive oil in a 10-inch ovenproof skillet over medium-high heat. Sauté the potatoes, bell pepper, onion and garlic in the hot oil for 10 minutes or until tender.

Whisk the eggs in a bowl until blended and stir in the milk, ham, tomato, salt and pepper. Pour the egg mixture over the potato mixture and stir gently to combine. Bake for 12 minutes or until set. Sprinkle with the cheese and broil for 3 to 5 minutes or until golden brown. Cut into wedges and serve immediately.

LORI JOHNSON GOODSON

Photograph for this recipe on page 42.

In 2005 the Junior League of Birmingham is the sixth largest out of 294 Leagues across the United States, Mexico, Canada, and England.

In 2004–2005 the Junior League of Birmingham invested $932,105 in our community.

SUNDAY NIGHT CHEESE SOUFFLÉ

I have never figured out my husband's often repeated suggestion, "You don't need to cook on Sunday night, just make a cheese soufflé." With good bread and a green salad this is the ultimate simple comfort food.

SERVES 6 TO 8

1/4 cup (1/2 stick) unsalted butter
1/4 cup all-purpose flour
1 1/2 cups milk
2 cups (8 ounces) shredded sharp Cheddar cheese
1/2 cup (2 ounces) grated Parmesan cheese
1/2 teaspoon salt
1/4 teaspoon cayenne pepper
1/4 teaspoon dry mustard
Tabasco sauce to taste (about 4 drops)
4 egg yolks
4 egg whites

Preheat the oven to 375 degrees for a moist soufflé or 325 degrees for a drier soufflé. Melt the butter in a saucepan and stir in the flour until blended. Cook until bubbly, stirring constantly. Bring the milk to a boil in a saucepan and add all at once to the flour mixture, whisking constantly until smooth.

Cook until thickened and of a sauce consistency, stirring constantly. Remove from the heat and add the Cheddar cheese and Parmesan cheese, stirring until the cheese melts. Mix in the salt, cayenne pepper, dry mustard and Tabasco sauce.

Beat the egg yolks in a mixing bowl until blended. Add the hot cheese sauce 1 tablespoon at a time to the egg yolks until the egg mixture is warm, stirring constantly. Whisk the warm egg mixture into the cheese sauce. Beat the egg whites in a mixing bowl until stiff peaks form and fold into the cheese mixture. Gently spoon into a buttered 2-quart soufflé dish and bake for 30 minutes at 375 degrees or 50 minutes at 325 degrees. Serve immediately.

CATHY CRISS ADAMS

HOLIDAY FRENCH TOAST

Smells like Christmas!

SERVES 6 TO 8

1 cup packed light brown sugar
1/2 cup (1 stick) butter, melted
1 teaspoon ground cinnamon
3 Granny Smith apples, peeled and
    thinly sliced (about 1 3/4 pounds)
1/2 cup dried cranberries

1 (8-ounce) loaf French bread,
    cut into 1-inch slices
1 1/2 cups milk
6 eggs
1 tablespoon vanilla extract
2 teaspoons ground cinnamon

Combine the brown sugar, butter and 1 teaspoon cinnamon in a bowl and mix well. Add the apples and cranberries and toss to coat. Spread the apple mixture over the bottom of a 9×13-inch baking dish sprayed with nonstick cooking spray. Arrange the bread slices cut side down over the prepared layer. Whisk the milk, eggs, vanilla and 2 teaspoons cinnamon in a bowl until blended. Pour the milk mixture over the prepared layers and chill, covered with foil, for 4 to 24 hours. Preheat the oven to 375 degrees. Bake, covered, for 40 to 45 minutes or until brown and bubbly. Let stand for 5 minutes and serve with warm syrup.

LENA CLARK BLAKENEY

BAKED FRENCH TOAST

MAKES 10 (2 1/2×4 1/2-INCH) SLICE SERVINGS

1 (9-ounce) loaf dry French bread
3 eggs
3 tablespoons sugar
1 teaspoon vanilla extract
2 1/4 cups milk

1/2 cup all-purpose flour
6 tablespoons dark brown sugar
1/2 teaspoon ground cinnamon
1/4 cup (1/2 stick) butter or margarine
1 cup fresh or frozen blueberries

Cut the loaf diagonally into 1-inch slices and arrange cut side down in a single layer in a greased 9×13-inch baking dish. Beat the eggs, sugar and vanilla in a mixing bowl until smooth. Stir in the milk until blended and pour over the bread slices, turning to coat. Chill, covered, for 8 to 10 hours. Preheat the oven to 375 degrees. Mix the flour, brown sugar and cinnamon in a bowl. Cut the butter into the flour mixture until crumbly to form a streusel. Turn the bread slices and sprinkle evenly with the blueberries and then the streusel. Bake for 40 minutes or until golden brown. Cut into squares to serve.

KATHRYN LAVALLET TORTORICI

Nutritional Profile for this recipe on page 327.

HOMEMADE WAFFLES

*These buttery waffles melt in your mouth. This is a recipe handed down
from my great-grandmother, Georgia Bibb Miller.*

MAKES 6 TO 8 WAFFLES

1¹/₄ cups all-purpose flour
1¹/₄ teaspoons baking powder
1 teaspoon sugar
¹/₄ teaspoon salt
1¹/₃ cups buttermilk
¹/₂ teaspoon baking soda
¹/₂ cup (1 stick) margarine, melted
1 egg, beaten

Sift the flour, baking powder, sugar and salt into a bowl. Whisk the buttermilk and baking soda in a bowl until blended. Add the buttermilk mixture, margarine and egg to the flour mixture and mix just until moistened.

Pour the batter onto a hot waffle iron sprayed with nonstick cooking spray and bake using manufacturer's directions.

ELIZA PASCHALL PETZNICK

Photograph for this recipe on page 14.

MAPLE PECAN BACON

SERVES 4 TO 6

10 thick-cut slices smoked bacon
¹/₄ cup maple syrup
¹/₄ cup finely chopped pecans

Preheat the oven to 400 degrees. Line an 11×15-inch baking pan with foil and place a baking rack over the foil. Arrange the bacon in a single layer on the rack. Brush with the syrup and sprinkle with the pecans. Bake for 20 minutes or until brown and crisp.

ROBIN LEIGH BEARDSLEY

CHEESE GRITS SOUFFLÉ

SERVES 8

2 cups milk
1 cup water
1 teaspoon salt
1 cup quick-cooking grits
3 egg whites
1/4 cup (1/2 stick) butter

3 tablespoons all-purpose flour
1 tablespoon dry mustard
1/4 teaspoon cayenne pepper
2 cups (8 ounces) shredded Swiss or
    Gruyère cheese
3 egg yolks, lightly beaten

Preheat the oven to 350 degrees. Bring the milk, water and salt to a boil in a saucepan over medium-high heat. Gradually add the grits to the boiling milk mixture, whisking constantly. Cook over medium heat for 10 minutes, stirring occasionally. Beat the egg whites in a mixing bowl until stiff peaks form.

Melt the butter in a small saucepan over medium-low heat. Add the flour, dry mustard and cayenne pepper and stir until blended. Add the flour mixture, 1 1/2 cups of the cheese and the egg yolks to the grits and mix well. Fold in the egg whites and spoon into a buttered 2-quart baking dish. Sprinkle with the remaining 1/2 cup cheese and bake for 30 minutes. Serve immediately.

SUSAN MEADOWS LEACH

SWEET POTATO HASH BROWNS

This dish is great for brunch as well as a fresh side with grilled steak or pork tenderloin.

SERVES 4

3 large sweet potatoes, peeled
    (about 2 pounds)
8 slices bacon
1 large onion, chopped

1/4 cup chopped fresh flat-leaf parsley
1/2 teaspoon salt
1/4 teaspoon pepper

Combine the sweet potatoes with enough water to cover in a saucepan and bring to a boil. Cook for 20 to 25 minutes or just until tender; the potatoes should be slightly undercooked. Cool and cut into 1-inch pieces. Cook the bacon in a large skillet until brown and crisp. Drain, reserving 1 tablespoon of the bacon drippings. Crumble the bacon. Sauté the onion in the reserved bacon drippings for 8 minutes or until tender. Fold in the sweet potatoes, parsley, salt and pepper; do not overmix. Cook over medium-high heat until heated through. Spoon the potatoes into a serving bowl and sprinkle with the bacon.

DENISE CALDERARO MODLING

Photograph for this recipe on page 43.

ANGEL BISCUITS

This is a great biscuit for those, "I need something extra special," moments.
When you make these, your family will know they are in for a treat.

MAKES 38 (1½-INCH) BISCUITS

1 envelope fast-rising yeast
2 tablespoons lukewarm water (110 degrees)
5 cups all-purpose flour
4 teaspoons baking powder
¼ cup sugar
1 teaspoon salt
1 teaspoon baking soda
1 cup shortening
2 cups buttermilk

Preheat the oven to 400 degrees. Dissolve the yeast in the lukewarm water in a bowl and let stand for 5 minutes or until bubbly. Sift the flour, baking powder, sugar, salt and baking soda into a bowl and mix well. Cut in the shortening until crumbly. Add the yeast mixture and buttermilk and stir just until combined.

Remove the dough to a lightly floured surface and gently fold the dough over several times. Roll ¼ to ½ inch thick and cut into rounds with an 1½-inch cutter. Arrange the rounds on a lightly greased baking sheet and bake for 12 minutes. You may substitute a mixture of ½ cup shortening and ½ cup butter for 1 cup shortening.

AMY HANSFORD UNDERWOOD

Each year local nonprofit organizations request funding and volunteer hours from the JLB. In 2005–2006 JLB supported thirty-seven community projects.

The Junior League is unique in that it provides both monetary support and highly trained volunteers.

BASIC SOUTHERN BISCUITS

MAKES 22 BISCUITS

2 cups all-purpose flour
2¹/2 teaspoons baking powder
1 teaspoon salt
¹/4 cup (¹/2 stick) butter, chilled and cut into
    small pieces
2 tablespoons shortening
1 cup milk
2 tablespoons all-purpose flour
2 tablespoons butter, melted

Preheat the oven to 425 degrees. Whisk 2 cups flour, the baking powder and salt in a bowl until combined. Cut in the chilled butter and shortening with a pastry blender or 2 knives until the mixture resembles coarse meal. Add the milk and stir just until moistened.

Sprinkle the work surface with 2 tablespoons flour and knead the dough on the floured surface 10 times or until smooth. Pat or roll the dough into a 9-inch circle and cut into rounds using a 2-inch cutter. Reroll the scraps and repeat the procedure.

Arrange the rounds 2 inches apart on a lightly greased baking sheet and brush the tops with the melted butter. Bake for 12 to 15 minutes or until golden brown. Served topped with poached eggs and Tomato Gravy on page 40.

Photograph for this recipe on page 43.

A pastry blender is an essential item when making flakey biscuits because it cuts the butter into tiny pieces into the flour mixture without warming the butter. It can be found at most kitchen supply stores.

RED-HOT BISCUITS

SERVES 6 TO 8

2³/4 cups all-purpose baking mix
1/2 teaspoon crushed red pepper
1/4 teaspoon garlic powder
1 cup milk

1 cup (4 ounces) shredded
 Cheddar cheese
2 tablespoons butter, melted
1/4 teaspoon garlic powder

Preheat the oven to 425 degrees. Combine the baking mix, red pepper and 1/4 teaspoon garlic powder in a bowl and mix well. Add the milk and cheese and stir with a fork until a soft dough forms.

Drop the dough by spoonfuls onto a greased baking sheet and brush with a mixture of the butter and 1/4 teaspoon garlic powder. Bake for 10 to 12 minutes or until light brown and serve immediately.

JEANNIE TATUM PATE

ALMOND SKILLET COFFEE CAKE

SERVES 12

1¹/2 cups sugar
3/4 cup (1¹/2 sticks) butter, softened
2 eggs
1¹/2 cups all-purpose flour

2 teaspoons almond flavoring
1/16 teaspoon salt
1/2 cup sliced almonds
2 teaspoons sugar

Preheat the oven to 350 degrees and line a 12-inch cast-iron skillet with foil shiny side up. Using a spoon, mix 1¹/2 cups sugar and the butter in a bowl. Add the eggs and stir until blended; do not use an electric mixer. Stir in the flour, flavoring and salt.

Spread the batter in the prepared skillet and sprinkle with the almonds and 2 teaspoons sugar. Bake for 30 to 40 minutes or until light brown.

SHERRI STAMP PLEDGER

BUTTERMILK CRUMB COFFEE CAKE

I started making these coffee cakes when I was in elementary school.
So simple—it makes one to keep and one to give away.

MAKES 2 (8-INCH) COFFEE CAKES

3 cups all-purpose flour
2 cups sugar
1 cup (2 sticks) butter, softened
1¹/2 teaspoons ground cinnamon
1 teaspoon baking soda
¹/4 teaspoon ground nutmeg
¹/4 teaspoon ground cloves
1 cup buttermilk
3 eggs

Preheat the oven to 375 degrees. Combine the flour, sugar and butter in a mixing bowl and beat at low speed until coarse crumbs form. Reserve 1 cup of the crumb mixture for the topping. Add the cinnamon, baking soda, nutmeg and cloves to the remaining crumb mixture and beat until combined. Add the buttermilk and eggs and beat just until moistened; do not overbeat.

Spoon the batter evenly into 2 greased and floured 8-inch baking pans and sprinkle with the reserved crumb mixture. If desired, lightly press the crumb mixture together to form larger crumbs. Bake for 30 to 40 minutes or until the edges pull from the sides of the pans.

LEIGH HARDIN HANCOCK

FAVORITE BANANA BREAD

The wheat flour gives the bread a nutty, rich flavor even without the
pecans. I omit the pecans for my child—he eats this up!

MAKES 2 (9-INCH) LOAVES

1 1/2 cups whole wheat flour
1 teaspoon baking soda
1/2 teaspoon salt
1 cup sugar
1/2 cup (1 stick) butter, softened
1 cup mashed very ripe bananas
    (about 3 or 4 bananas)
1/2 cup sour cream
2 eggs
1 teaspoon vanilla extract
1 teaspoon ground cinnamon
1/2 cup chopped pecans (optional)

Preheat the oven to 350 degrees. Mix the whole wheat flour, baking soda and salt together. Beat the sugar and butter in a mixing bowl at medium speed until blended, scraping the bowl occasionally. Stir in the bananas, sour cream, eggs, vanilla and cinnamon. Add the flour mixture gradually, beating constantly just until blended. Stir in the pecans.

Spoon the batter into 2 greased and floured 5×9-inch loaf pans and bake for 50 to 60 minutes or until the tops are brown and the loaves test done. Cool in the pans on a wire rack for 10 minutes. Remove the loaves from the pans and cool completely on the wire rack.

LYNN COMPTON CHAPMAN

JLB volunteers give approximately 50,000 hours of service each year, however, the value goes far beyond the time spent. The annual economic impact on the city of Birmingham in 2004– 2005 was almost $2 million.

Each provisional class is given a budget of $10,000 to develop and implement mini projects in our community— a powerful component of each new member's first- year experience.

BLUEBERRY LEMON BREAD

Use a microplane zester for the lemon zest to make this recipe even faster.

MAKES 2 (9-INCH) LOAVES

3 cups all-purpose flour
1 teaspoon baking powder
1/2 teaspoon salt
8 ounces cream cheese, softened
1 cup (2 sticks) butter or margarine, softened
3 cups sugar
8 eggs, at room temperature
3 tablespoons lemon juice
1 tablespoon finely grated lemon zest
2 teaspoons vanilla extract
2 cups fresh or frozen blueberries
1 tablespoon all-purpose flour

Preheat the oven to 325 degrees. Mix 3 cups flour, the baking powder and salt together. Beat the cream cheese and butter in a mixing bowl at medium speed until creamy, scraping the bowl occasionally. Add the sugar gradually, beating constantly until blended. Add the eggs 1 at a time, beating until combined after each addition. Add the flour mixture gradually and beat at low speed just until combined. Stir in the lemon juice, lemon zest and vanilla.

Toss the blueberries and 1 tablespoon flour in a bowl until coated. Fold the coated berries into the batter and spoon the batter into 2 greased and floured 5×9-inch loaf pans. Bake for 1 hour or until wooden picks inserted in the centers come out clean. Add 10 to 15 minutes to the baking time if using frozen blueberries. Cool in the pans on a wire rack for 10 to 15 minutes. Remove the loaves from the pans and let cool completely on the wire rack.

LEIGH HARDIN HANCOCK

Try these variations of Blueberry Lemon Bread. Substitute lime zest and lime juice for the lemon zest and lemon juice for **Blueberry Lime Bread.** *For* **Raspberry Lemon Bread** *or* **Raspberry Lime Bread** *substitute fresh or frozen raspberries for the blueberries.*

CHOCOLATE-FILLED MAPLE PECAN STICKY BUNS

*This divine recipe is based on a bread dough made in the brioche tradition.
It is enriched with eggs and butter and beaten with an electric mixer to develop a satiny dough
and thus a light airy bread. However, if pressed for time, substitute with frozen bread dough
and proceed with the recipe. The chocolate filling is an optional flavor element that balances the syrupy
sweetness. Feel free to substitute a more traditional filling of butter, sugar, and ground cinnamon.*

MAKES 16 BUNS

Buns
1 cup warm milk (100 to 110 degrees)
1/2 cup sugar
1 envelope dry yeast
2 eggs
1/2 teaspoon salt
4 1/2 cups all-purpose flour
1/2 cup (1 stick) unsalted butter, chilled and
    cut into tablespoons

Chocolate Filling
3 ounces semisweet chocolate, coarsely chopped
1/4 cup heavy cream or whipping cream
1 tablespoon unsalted butter

Sticky Topping and Assembly
3/4 cup (1 1/2 sticks) unsalted butter, softened
1 cup packed dark brown sugar
2/3 cup maple syrup
48 pecan halves
3 tablespoons unsalted butter, melted

For the buns, mix the warm milk, sugar and yeast in a mixing bowl and let stand for 5 minutes or until bubbly. Add the eggs and salt to the yeast mixture and beat gently until combined. Using a dough hook, gradually add the flour to the milk mixture and beat at medium speed until the flour is incorporated. Increase the mixer speed and add the butter 1 tablespoon at a time, beating until blended after each addition. Beat at medium-high speed for 5 minutes longer or until the dough is springy and elastic. The mixer may jump a little on the counter.

Place the dough in a lightly greased bowl, turning to coat the surface. Let rise, covered with plastic wrap, in a warm place for 1 hour or until doubled in bulk. Punch the dough down and cover. Chill for 4 to 10 hours, punching down as needed during the first couple hours. Remove from the refrigerator and let stand for 20 minutes or until room temperature. Roll the dough into a 14×18-inch rectangle on a lightly floured surface.

For the filling, combine the chocolate, cream and butter in a microwave-safe dish. Microwave on High for 45 seconds or until the chocolate melts and stir until smooth. Spread the filling evenly all the way to the edge on 3 sides of the dough rectangle, leaving a 1/2-inch border on one of the long sides of the rectangle. Roll jelly-roll fashion, starting with the long side coated in chocolate to the edge to form an 18-inch log. Cover with plastic wrap and freeze for 20 minutes or until firm.

For the topping, coat the bottoms of two 9-inch baking pans with tall sides equally with 3/4 cup butter. Sprinkle each pan with 1/2 cup brown sugar and drizzle each with 1/3 cup syrup. Remove the log from the freezer and discard the plastic wrap. Cut the log into halves and cut each half into 8 equal slices. Arrange 3 pecan halves in a spoke like pattern in the bottom of one the pans and center 1 dough slice over the pecans. Repeat the procedure with the remaining pecans and remaining dough slices until both pans are filled. Brush the buns lightly with 3 tablespoons melted butter. Let stand, loosely covered with plastic wrap, in a warm place for 1 hour or until doubled in bulk.

Preheat the oven to 350 degrees. Bake the buns for 35 to 40 minutes or until golden brown. Cool in the pans on a wire rack for 5 minutes. Run a sharp knife around the edge of each pan and invert the buns onto serving plates. Carefully spoon the sticky topping remaining in the pans over the buns. Serve warm or carefully transfer the buns to a cooling rack to cool completely. For an added treat, drizzle with a mixture of 2 cups confectioners' sugar and 2 tablespoons milk. You may freeze the buns in an airtight container for up to 2 months.

J ULIE G RIMES B OTTCHER

Photograph for this recipe on page 42.

QUICK CINNAMON ROLLS

MAKES 2 DOZEN MINIATURE ROLLS

2 (8-count) cans crescent rolls
1/4 cup (1/2 stick) butter, melted
3 to 4 tablespoons sugar
    and cinnamon

1 cup confectioners' sugar
2 tablespoons milk

Preheat the oven to 375 degrees. Unroll the crescent roll dough and separate into 8 rectangles, pressing the diagonal perforations together to seal. Brush the rectangles with the butter and sprinkle with the sugar and cinnamon.

Roll each rectangle from the long side into a log and cut each roll into 3 small slices. Arrange the slices cut side down in a lightly greased 9×13-inch baking pan. Bake for 12 to 15 minutes or until light brown. Drizzle with a mixture of the confectioners' sugar and milk and serve immediately. For testing purposes, Domino Sugar 'N Cinnamon was used.

JULIE MATHIS FREELAND

ICEBOX GINGER MUFFINS

MAKES 16 MUFFINS

2 cups all-purpose flour
2 teaspoons ground ginger
1/4 teaspoon ground cinnamon
1/4 teaspoon ground allspice
1/4 cup raisins
1/4 cup chopped toasted pecans

1/2 cup (1 stick) butter, softened
1/2 cup sugar
2 eggs
1/2 cup molasses
1/2 cup buttermilk
1 teaspoon baking soda

Preheat the oven to 400 degrees. Mix the flour, ginger, cinnamon and allspice in a bowl. Stir in the raisins and pecans. Beat the butter and sugar in a mixing bowl until creamy. Add the eggs 1 at a time, beating just until blended after each addition. Add the molasses and beat until smooth.

Mix the buttermilk and baking soda in a bowl and let stand until the mixture begins to foam. Stir the buttermilk mixture into the molasses mixture. Add the flour mixture and stir just until moistened. Fill lightly greased muffin cups 2/3 full and bake for 12 to 15 minutes or until the muffins test done.

LENA CLARK BLAKENEY

SCONES

MAKES 8 SCONES

2 cups all-purpose flour, sifted

1/3 cup sugar

1 tablespoon baking powder

2 teaspoons dried lavender

1/4 teaspoon salt

6 tablespoons unsalted butter,
    cut into small pieces

1/2 cup heavy cream or
    whipping cream

1 egg, beaten

1 tablespoon heavy cream or
    whipping cream

Sugar to taste

Preheat the oven to 400 degrees. Combine the flour, 1/3 cup sugar, the baking powder, lavender and salt in a bowl and mix well. Cut in the butter with a pastry blender until the mixture resembles small pebbles. Stir in 1/2 cup cream and the egg. Turn the dough onto a lightly floured surface and knead gently until smooth. Place the dough on a lightly greased baking sheet and shape into an 8-inch round. Cut the round into 8 triangles; do not separate the triangles on the baking sheet. Brush the tops with 1 tablespoon cream and sprinkle with sugar to taste. Bake for 18 to 20 minutes or until light brown. Serve warm with lemon curd or clotted cream.

For **Cherry Almond Scones**, add 1/2 teaspoon almond extract and substitute 1/3 cup dried cherries for the lavender. For **Cranberry Orange Scones**, add 1/2 teaspoon grated orange zest and substitute 1/3 cup dried cranberries for the lavender. Proceed as directed in the original recipe.

MARGARET REYNOLDS OPOLKA

PEACH BLUEBERRY SMOOTHIE

MAKES 4 (1-CUP) SERVINGS

1 cup frozen sliced peaches

1 cup ice cubes

3/4 cup plain yogurt

1/2 banana, sliced

1/2 cup frozen blueberries or
    raspberries

1/4 cup orange juice

2 tablespoons honey

Combine the peaches, ice cubes, yogurt, banana, blueberries, orange juice and honey in a blender and process until smooth. Pour into 4 glasses or goblets and serve immediately.

KATHERINE ADAMS MCKNIGHT

Nutritional Profile for this recipe on page 327.

BERRIES WITH CHAMPAGNE SYRUP

The perfect brunch dish. This fruit captures the essence of a glass of Champagne with fresh berries floated in it. You may prepare the syrup in advance, and although you will lose the fizz, the flavor of the Champagne remains.

MAKES 6 (1-CUP) SERVINGS

1/2 cup sugar	2 cups quartered fresh strawberries
1/4 cup water	1 pint fresh blueberries
1/4 cup Champagne or other sparkling wine	1 pint fresh blackberries
	3 tablespoons chopped fresh mint

Combine the sugar and water in a microwave-safe dish and microwave on High for 3 minutes or until the sugar dissolves. Stir the syrup and cool to room temperature. Stir in the Champagne. Toss the strawberries, blueberries, blackberries and mint in a bowl. Drizzle the syrup over the berry mixture and toss gently to coat. Serve immediately in Champagne flutes.

CATHERINE NORVILLE BEDINGFIELD

Photograph for this recipe on page 43.
Nutritional Profile for this recipe on page 327.

WINTER FRUIT COMPOTE

MAKES 6 (3/4-CUP) SERVINGS

1 (6-ounce) package dried apricots	2 tablespoons fig preserves
2 pears, peeled and sliced	1 teaspoon ground ginger
2 McIntosh apples, peeled and sliced	1/16 teaspoon salt
1/2 cup packed light brown sugar	3 tablespoons butter, cut into
3 tablespoons orange juice	small pieces

Preheat the oven to 400 degrees. Chop the apricots. Combine the apricots, pears, apples, brown sugar, orange juice, preserves, ginger and salt in a bowl and mix gently. Spoon the apricot mixture into a lightly greased 8-inch baking dish and dot with the butter. Bake for 25 minutes or until the mixture is slightly thickened and the fruit is tender. Serve with yogurt and granola or baked ham.

LYDA HELEN JONES

Nutritional Profile for this recipe on page 327.

CRANBERRY CHUTNEY

*This versatile dish is delicious around the clock. Serve with baked
ham for an elegant brunch, over cream cheese for a quick appetizer, or with
grilled pork tenderloin for a simple supper.*

MAKES 6 CUPS

1 (20-ounce) can juice-pack crushed pineapple
2 cups sugar
1 pound fresh cranberries
1 cup each golden raisins and chopped pecans
1/2 teaspoon ground cinnamon
1/4 teaspoon each ground ginger, ground
        allspice, ground nutmeg and
        cayenne pepper
1/4 teaspoon almond extract

Drain the pineapple, reserving the juice. Combine the reserved juice with enough
water to measure 1 cup and pour into a saucepan. Stir in the pineapple, sugar,
cranberries, raisins, pecans, cinnamon, ginger, allspice, nutmeg, cayenne pepper
and flavoring. Bring to a boil and reduce the heat. Simmer for 30 minutes or until
thickened, stirring occasionally.

JENNIFER RUBY MCCAIN

ORANGE BUTTER SPREAD

MAKES 1 CUP

1/2 cup (1 stick) unsalted butter
3 ounces cream cheese, softened
1/4 cup confectioners' sugar
2 tablespoons orange juice
1 tablespoon grated orange zest

Combine the butter, cream cheese, confectioners' sugar, orange juice and orange
zest in a food processor and process until blended. Serve as a spread with bagels,
croissants, toast or plain muffins.

BARCLEY ROEDDER HARDWICK

*A few examples of provisional
mini projects include turning
an ordinary teacher's lounge
at Glenn Middle School into
a cheery refuge, building a
house for Habitat for
Humanity, and collecting
basic baby necessities for a
homeless child care center
at the YWCA.*

TOMATO GRAVY

Ladle over hot biscuits or grits for breakfast. Or, serve this gravy at your next brunch as a substitute for hollandaise sauce: eggs Benedict-style over English muffins stacked with poached eggs and topped off with crisp-cooked bacon. Add a dash of Tabasco sauce to the gravy and serve over pan-fried catfish for supper.

MAKES 1 1/2 CUPS

1 tablespoon butter
1 tablespoon bacon drippings or butter
2 tablespoons all-purpose flour
1 (14-ounce) can petite diced tomatoes
3 tablespoons chicken broth
1 1/2 teaspoons red wine vinegar
3 tablespoons half-and-half
Salt and pepper to taste

Heat the butter and bacon drippings in a small saucepan over medium heat. Gradually whisk in the flour and cook over medium heat for 5 minutes or until the mixture is the color of peanuts, whisking constantly. Whisk in the undrained tomatoes, broth and vinegar.

Cook for 7 minutes or until slightly thickened, stirring occasionally. Reduce the heat to low and stir in the half-and-half. Cook just until heated through and season to taste with salt and pepper. Serve immediately.

KATHERINE ADAMS MCKNIGHT

Photograph for this recipe on page 43.

The JLB's cookbook Magic *launched in 1982. In 2004 the membership voted to reprint the book for the eighth time.*

Over the past twenty-four years more than 66,000 copies of Magic *have been sold to fund community projects. Several recipes are featured in* The Best of the Best from Alabama, *a collection of Alabama's most beloved recipes.*

40

VANILLA-SCENTED GRANOLA

*A wonderful staple for breakfast and brunch. Keep this granola sealed
in an airtight container and it will stay fresh for weeks. It is great on top of yogurt,
paired with fresh fruit, or in a bowl with milk. Customize the recipe to
your taste by using your favorite nuts and dried fruit.*

MAKES 5 CUPS

2 cups rolled oats
1 cup whole almonds
1/2 cup walnut halves
1/2 cup whole hazelnuts
1/2 cup packed light brown sugar
1/4 cup sunflower seeds
1/4 teaspoon salt
1/2 cup (1 stick) butter, melted
1/4 cup honey
1 tablespoon vanilla extract
1/3 cup dried sour cherries
1/3 cup chopped dried peaches

Preheat the oven to 300 degrees. Combine the oats, almonds, walnuts, hazelnuts,
brown sugar, sunflower seeds and salt in a bowl and mix well. Whisk the butter,
honey and vanilla in a bowl until blended and drizzle over the oats mixture,
tossing to coat.

Spread the oats mixture in an even layer on a baking sheet and bake for 40 minutes,
stirring once. Remove from the oven and stir in the cherries and peaches. Bake
for 15 minutes longer or until golden brown. Let stand until cool and store in an
airtight container.

BEATY EVANS COLEMAN

Photograph for this recipe on page 43.

The JLB's second cookbook,
Food for Thought, *debuted
in 1995. It is in its third
printing, and more than
58,000 copies have been sold.*

Food for Thought *was
named "The Official
Cookbook of Birmingham"
by* Birmingham Magazine.

Chocolate-Filled Maple Pecan Sticky Buns

Farmer's Frittata

Rise and Shine

BREAKFAST AND BRUNCH TIPS

- When taking food gifts to a friend with a new baby, consider breakfast foods as a great alternative to dinner.

- Hosting a brunch is a creative way to throw a luncheon.

- If you feel like you cannot get it all done before Christmas, prepare sweet rolls and deliver them to your friends to enjoy on New Year's morning.

- Treat your children to breakfast in bed as a reward for a big accomplishment, a treat following a hard week, or just to say, "I love you."

- Start a small garden or collection of containers with herbs, vegetables, and fruits and invite your children to help with the maintenance. Make a morning activity of checking the progress of the garden, allowing your children to harvest the produce.

SUNDAY BRUNCH
MENU

SUGGESTED WINES:
- *Zardetto Prosecco Brut*
- *Roederer Estate Brut Rosé*

Basic Southern Biscuits with Tomato Gravy
Vanilla-Scented Granola
Berries with Champagne Syrup

Great Beginnings

Widgets. Hmmm…although they are often small, most industrial engineers would agree they are critical to the big picture. And you will find lots of colorful widgets, gadgets, and doodads among the giant dormant furnaces dominating Birmingham's northeastern skyline.

In 1882, North Alabama planter and investor James Withers Sloss built what became known as the "City Furnaces." By 1883 at the Louisville Exposition, the sixty-foot furnaces had earned the company the distinction of a bronze medal for the best "pig iron." And at full production, the steel-jacketed furnace employed an estimated five hundred workers and produced four hundred tons daily.

Although a leading foundry iron producer until 1971, Sloss is currently the only twentieth-century blast furnace in the United States being preserved and interpreted as a historic industrial site. Now recognized as a National Historic Landmark, Sloss Furnaces are open to the public as a museum of industry that speaks to the contributions of the working men who labored there. With its massive furnaces, web of pipes, and tall smokestacks, it offers us a glimpse into the great industrial past of the South and our nation.

Think of the appetizers in this chapter as food widgets and doodads. Cooking "engineers" would agree that while they may be small, they are a colorful and important addition to the big picture. Try Baked Chile Lime Chips on page 68. Add Hotz Crawfish Dip on page 56. Enjoy a glass of White Sangria on page 77, or maybe a Mango Daiquiri on page 76. And remember, a plate full of creatively arranged food widgets may just make a complete meal.

Visit Sloss Furnaces at www.slossfurnaces.com.

Sloss Furnaces

Best Margarita
Roasted Cashews with Rosemary

Appetizers and Beverages

CONTENTS

ROASTED CASHEWS WITH ROSEMARY

*These nuts will stay fresh for several weeks in an airtight
container making them the perfect gift.*

MAKES 5 CUPS

2¹/2 (9-ounce) cans roasted whole cashews
    (1¹/2 pounds)
2 tablespoons unsalted butter
1¹/2 tablespoons brown sugar
3 tablespoons chopped fresh rosemary
1 teaspoon kosher salt
¹/2 teaspoon cayenne pepper

Preheat the oven to 375 degrees. Spread the cashews in a single layer on a lightly greased baking sheet and heat for 5 minutes. Maintain the oven temperature. Melt the butter and brown sugar in a large stockpot over medium heat, stirring frequently. Remove from the heat and stir in the rosemary, salt and cayenne pepper.

Add the cashews to the stockpot and toss to coat. Spread the cashews in a single layer on the baking sheet and roast for 5 to 10 minutes or until light brown, stirring occasionally. Serve alone or sprinkled over salads.

JEANIE PARKER CENTENO

Photograph for this recipe on page 80.

HOT AND HOT BOILED PEANUTS

SERVES 100

1 (30-pound) case green peanuts in shells
1¹/2 pounds kosher salt

Combine the peanuts and salt with enough water to cover in a large stockpot and bring to a boil. Reduce the heat and simmer for 7 to 10 hours or until the peanuts are tender. Let stand until cool and store undrained in the refrigerator. Drain before serving. To serve 8 guests, use 2 pounds raw peanuts and 6 tablespoons kosher salt and proceed as directed above.

IDIE AND CHRIS HASTINGS, HOT AND HOT FISH CLUB IN SOUTHSIDE

SPICY PICKLED BEANS

These beans make great little munchies. Keep them on hand for a snack, or serve at a summer cocktail party.

SERVES 16

8 ounces fresh green beans, trimmed
8 ounces fresh wax beans, trimmed
1/4 cup kosher salt
1/2 cup sugar
1 1/4 cups red wine vinegar
1/2 cup sherry vinegar
1/2 cup vodka (optional)

2 tablespoons mustard seeds
1 tablespoon black peppercorns
2 teaspoons crushed red pepper
2 teaspoons fennel seeds
4 garlic cloves
4 sprigs of dill weed
2 bay leaves

Bring enough water to cover the beans to a boil in a medium saucepan and add the beans and salt. Cook for 2 to 4 minutes or until tender-crisp; drain. Combine the remaining ingredients in a saucepan and bring to a boil. Boil for 1 minute. Pour the vinegar mixture over the beans in a nonreactive heatproof bowl and toss to coat. Marinate, covered, in the refrigerator for 24 hours, stirring occasionally. Discard the dill weed and bay leaves and drain, if desired, before serving.

CATHERINE NORVILLE BEDINGFIELD

SMOKED TROUT AND
HERB CREAM CHEESE WITH ENDIVE

The cream cheese mixture may be prepared up to two days in advance and stored, covered, in the refrigerator. Bring to room temperature before spreading on the endive.

SERVES 34

8 ounces cream cheese, softened
1/2 cup minced fresh dill weed
2 green onions, finely chopped
1 teaspoon (heaping) grated
    lemon zest
Freshly ground pepper to taste

4 heads Belgian endive, separated
    into spears
8 ounces smoked trout, torn into
    1-inch pieces
Sprigs of dill weed for garnish

Combine the cream cheese, 1/2 cup dill weed, the green onions and lemon zest in a bowl and mix well. Season to taste with pepper. Spoon a small amount of the cream cheese mixture onto the stem end of each endive spear and top with 1 piece of smoked trout. Garnish with sprigs of dill weed.

CHRISTIANA DUNN ROUSSEL

BACON AND HERB-STUFFED EGGS

MAKES 2 DOZEN HALVES

1 dozen eggs
3 ounces cream cheese, softened
3 tablespoons milk
1/4 teaspoon salt
4 slices bacon, crisp-cooked and crumbled
2 tablespoons finely chopped fresh chives
2 tablespoons finely chopped fresh dill weed

Hard-boil the eggs using 1 of the methods in the sidebar. Cut the eggs lengthwise into halves and carefully remove the yolks. Process the yolks, cream cheese, milk and salt in a food processor until smooth, scraping the side of the bowl once.

Reserve 1 tablespoon of the bacon. Stir the remaining bacon, chives and dill weed into the yolk mixture. Spoon or pipe the yolk mixture into the egg white halves and sprinkle with the reserved bacon. Serve immediately or store, covered, in the refrigerator.

HOLLEY CONTRI JOHNSON

DEVILED EGGS

Simply delicious! A must at tailgate parties or picnics.

MAKES 4 DOZEN HALVES

2 dozen fresh eggs
2/3 cup mayonnaise (no substitution)
1 tablespoon drained sweet pickle relish
1 teaspoon prepared mustard
3/4 teaspoon fine sea salt, or to taste
1/2 teaspoon freshly ground pepper

Hard-boil the eggs using 1 of the methods in the sidebar. Slice the eggs lengthwise using a serrated knife and place the yolks in a small bowl. Add the mayonnaise, pickle relish, prepared mustard, salt and pepper to the yolks and mash gently but thoroughly with a fork until combined. Mound the yolk mixture in the egg whites. Store, covered, in the refrigerator until serving time. Garnish, if desired, with additional freshly ground pepper; do not use paprika.

ELLEN MacELVAIN RHETT

HARD-BOILED EGGS

The following are two methods of preparing hard-boiled eggs:

1. Combine cold eggs with enough cold water to cover in a saucepan and bring to a rolling boil. Reduce the heat and simmer for fifteen minutes; drain. Immediately peel the eggs under cold running water.

2. Bring six inches of water to a boil in a saucepan. Pierce the tips of each egg with a clean sewing needle or pin. Using a slotted spoon, place the eggs gently in the boiling water and boil for fifteen minutes; drain. Immediately peel the eggs under cold running water.

Cooked and peeled eggs may be chilled overnight. When ready to prepare, blot off the excess moisture with clean paper towels and then slice lengthwise with a sharp serrated knife. Proceed with your favorite recipe.

MINI BLTs

Miniature "sinful" BLTs with applewood-smoked bacon, Roma tomatoes, arugula, and rémoulade sauce.

SERVES 12

Rémoulade Sauce
3 cups mayonnaise
1 cup Creole mustard or spicy mustard
1/4 cup fresh lemon juice
1/3 cup chopped fresh parsley
1/4 cup rinsed drained capers, chopped
Salt and pepper to taste

BLTs
8 slices white or wheat sandwich bread,
   crusts trimmed
3 or 4 thick slices applewood-smoked bacon
1/4 cup packed light brown sugar
1/2 cup fresh basil, julienned
1/4 cup extra-virgin olive oil
Salt and pepper to taste
4 Roma tomatoes, cut into 3/4-inch slices
8 ounces arugula or spinach, trimmed
Sprigs of fresh basil for garnish

For the sauce, combine the mayonnaise, Creole mustard, lemon juice, parsley and capers in a bowl and mix well. Season to taste with salt and pepper.

For the BLTs, preheat the oven to 325 degrees. Cut the bread slices into rounds or squares and arrange on a baking sheet. Toast for 5 to 8 minutes or until light brown on both sides. Maintain the oven temperature. Arrange the bacon in a single layer on a baking sheet and sprinkle lightly with the brown sugar. Bake until brown and crisp. Break the bacon into pieces the size of the toast points.

Whisk 1/2 cup basil, the olive oil, salt and pepper in a bowl. Add the tomatoes and turn gently to coat. Arrange the toast points on a platter. Layer each with 1 tomato slice, 1 teaspoon of the sauce, arugula and bacon. Garnish the platter with sprigs of basil.

JASON MEZRANO, KATHY MEZRANO, KATHY G & COMPANY

Arising out of a need for affordable home health care, the Visiting Nursing Association was founded in 1938 by the JLB and provided professional home care as an alternative to hospitalization, serving thousands of patients in a three-county area.

MARINATED SHRIMP

SERVES 6 TO 8

2 pounds medium shrimp
1 cup canola, corn or vegetable oil
1/2 cup each cider vinegar and ketchup
1/4 cup tarragon vinegar
1 small jar capers, drained and rinsed
6 to 8 bay leaves

2 tablespoons fresh lemon juice
1 tablespoon Worcestershire sauce
2 teaspoons sugar
1 teaspoon salt
1/2 teaspoon dry mustard
2 small white onions, thickly sliced

Bring enough water to generously cover the shrimp to a boil in a stockpot and add the shrimp. Boil for 3 minutes or until the shrimp turn pink; drain. Peel and devein the shrimp, leaving the tails intact. Whisk the remaining ingredients in a bowl. Layer the shrimp and onions in a large shallow dish and pour the canola oil mixture over the layers. Marinate, covered, in the refrigerator for 1 to 2 days, stirring occasionally. Discard the bay leaves before serving. For a spicer taste add crushed red pepper or Tabasco sauce. Leaving the tails on the shrimp makes them easy to pick up and avoids the use of wooden picks.

STEPHANIE STEVENS CAROTHERS

SHRIMP AND GRITS TARTLETS

MAKES 3 DOZEN TARTLETS

36 small shrimp
   (about 8 ounces)
2 cups chicken broth
1 cup milk
1/2 teaspoon salt
1/2 teaspoon pepper
1 cup grits

1 cup (4 ounces) shredded
   Parmesan cheese
2/3 cup finely chopped
   Virginia-baked ham
1/4 cup (1/2 stick) butter
2 tablespoons chopped fresh parsley
Sprigs of parsley for garnish

Bring enough water to generously cover the shrimp to a boil in a stockpot and add the shrimp. Boil for 3 minutes or until the shrimp turn pink. Drain and peel. Bring the broth, milk, salt and pepper to a light boil in a saucepan; do not bring to a full boil. Stir in the grits and reduce the heat. Simmer, covered, for 10 to 15 minutes or until the creaminess has disappeared and the grits start to pull from the side of the pan. Stir in the cheese, ham, butter and chopped parsley. Preheat the oven to 350 degrees. Fill greased tartlet pans 3/4 full with the grits mixture. Bake for 15 to 20 minutes or just until the tops begin to brown. Insert 1 shrimp tail up into the top of each tartlet and bake for 8 to 10 minutes longer or until the grits are light brown. Garnish with sprigs of parsley.

JEANNE REID SHEARER

MINI TOMATO TARTS

This is a colorful summer appetizer when prepared in two-inch tartlet pans. If you cannot find these pans, use miniature brioche molds, or four-inch tart pans.

MAKES 3 DOZEN TARTS

Pastry
1 1/2 cups all-purpose flour
1/4 cup yellow cornmeal
1 1/2 teaspoons kosher salt
1/4 cup sour cream
6 tablespoons butter, chilled and
    cut into small pieces
3 tablespoons ice water

Tomato Filling and Assembly
1 quart red cherry tomatoes, cut into
    1/4-inch slices
1 quart yellow pear tomatoes, cut into
    1/4-inch slices
1/2 cup extra-virgin olive oil
1 1/2 teaspoons kosher salt
3/4 teaspoon freshly ground pepper
1 cup (4 ounces) shredded
    fontina cheese
1/2 cup (2 ounces) freshly grated
    Parmigiano-Reggiano
3 tablespoons all-purpose flour
2 garlic cloves, minced
1/2 cup julienned fresh basil

For the pastry, mix the flour, cornmeal and salt in a bowl with a whisk. Stir in the sour cream. Cut in the butter with a pastry blender or 2 knives until the mixture resemble coarse meal. Mix in the ice water and knead until a soft dough forms. Shape the dough into a 4-inch round on a sheet of plastic wrap. Wrap tightly with the plastic wrap and chill for 1 hour.

For the filling, preheat the oven to 425 degrees. Combine the tomatoes, olive oil, salt and pepper in a bowl and toss gently to coat. Combine the fontina cheese, Parmigiano-Reggiano, flour, garlic and basil in a bowl and mix well.

Discard the plastic wrap from the dough and roll 1/4 inch thick on a lightly floured surface. Cut the dough into 36 rounds using tartlet pans as a pattern. Working in batches, lightly coat the pans with nonstick cooking spray and press the rounds into the prepared pans. Spoon about 2 1/2 teaspoons of the cheese mixture over the bottom of each pastry-lined pan and top with 2 to 3 tomato slices. Drizzle each with enough of the remaining olive oil mixture to prevent the tomatoes from drying out, approximately 1/2 teaspoon. Arrange the pans in a single layer on a baking sheet and bake for 20 minutes or until golden brown. Serve warm or at room temperature.

LYDIA DEGARIS PURSELL

Photograph for this recipe on page 80.

BLACK-EYED PEA ARTICHOKE DIP

SERVES 8

2 slices hickory-smoked bacon
2 tablespoons butter
1 onion, chopped
1/2 cup sour cream
1/2 cup mayonnaise
2 1/2 tablespoons chopped fresh chives
1 teaspoon onion powder
1 teaspoon garlic powder

1/2 teaspoon salt
1 (15-ounce) can black-eyed peas, drained and rinsed
1 (14-ounce) can quartered artichoke hearts, drained and rinsed
2 ounces mozzarella cheese, shredded
1/4 cup chopped green onions

Preheat the oven to 350 degrees. Heat a skillet over medium-high heat and add the bacon. Cook until crisp. Remove the bacon to a paper towel to drain, reserving the pan drippings. Crumble the bacon. Heat the butter with the reserved pan drippings and sauté 1 chopped onion in the butter mixture for 5 minutes.

Mix the sour cream and mayonnaise in a bowl. Stir in the bacon, chives, onion powder, garlic powder and salt. Add the sautéed onion, black-eyed peas and artichokes and mix well. Spoon the black-eyed pea mixture into an 8×11-inch or 2-quart baking dish and sprinkle with the cheese and green onions. Bake for 20 to 25 minutes or until brown and bubbly. Let stand for 10 minutes before serving. Serve with assorted party crackers and/or chips.

KELLY PRIDE HARGROVE

HOT FETA CHEESE AND ARTICHOKE DIP

Double the recipe for a large crowd as it will go quickly.

SERVES 8

4 ounces oil-pack sun-dried tomatoes, drained and rinsed
1 (14-ounce) can artichoke hearts, drained and chopped

8 ounces feta cheese, crumbled
1 cup mayonnaise
2 garlic cloves, minced

Preheat the oven to 375 degrees. Pat the sun-dried tomatoes dry with a paper towel and chop. Combine the tomatoes, artichokes, cheese, mayonnaise and garlic in a bowl and mix well. Spoon the artichoke mixture into a shallow 1 1/2-quart baking dish and bake for 15 to 20 minutes or until bubbly; do not overbake. Serve with bagel chips and/or thin plain crackers.

MELANIE REMMERT KOHN

HILARY'S CRAB DIP

This is a nice cool summer time appetizer that can be prepared in advance.

SERVES 6

6 ounces fresh lump
   crab meat, drained
8 ounces cream cheese, softened
1/2 small onion, minced (1/4 cup)
1/4 cup mayonnaise

1 1/2 teaspoons lemon juice
1 1/2 teaspoons Worcestershire sauce
1/2 teaspoon garlic salt
Cocktail sauce to taste
Parsley flakes for garnish

Discard the shells and cartilage from the crab meat. Combine the crab meat and cream cheese in a bowl and mix well. Fold in the onion and mayonnaise and stir in the lemon juice, Worcestershire sauce and garlic salt.

Line a small bowl with plastic wrap allowing enough overhang for complete coverage. Spoon the dip into the prepared bowl and cover with the plastic wrap. Chill for 8 to 10 hours. Pull the edges of the plastic wrap back and invert the dip onto a serving platter, removing the bowl and plastic wrap. Smooth the top of the dip with a flexible spatula to form a smooth dome. Spoon cocktail sauce in lines over the dip and garnish with parsley flakes. Serve with assorted party crackers.

HILARY HOWARD ROSS

MARGARITA DIP

Serve at a party or for brunch. This dip can also be used to ice your favorite chocolate cake or pound cake.

SERVES 10

3 ounces cream cheese, softened
1/2 cup sour cream
1/2 cup sifted confectioners' sugar
2 tablespoons frozen orange
   juice concentrate

2 tablespoons lime juice
2 tablespoons tequila (optional)
1/2 cup heavy cream or
   whipping cream

Beat the cream cheese in a bowl until smooth. Combine the sour cream, confectioners' sugar, orange juice concentrate, lime juice and tequila in a bowl and mix well. Add the cream cheese and heavy cream to the sour cream mixture and blend with a whisk until fluffy. Serve immediately with gingersnaps and/or assorted sliced fruits and berries, or chill, covered, for up to 24 hours.

MICHELLE MARIE MATHEWS

HOTZ CRAWFISH DIP

I am from Lafayette, Louisiana, and I throw a Mardi Gras party every year. This dip is always a favorite, and guests even call ahead to make sure it is being served. I have seen people wipe down the serving dish with bread. Pour any leftovers over grits for breakfast.

SERVES 30 TO 40

1/2 cup (1 stick) butter
1 cup minced onion (about 1 onion)
1/2 cup minced bell pepper
        (about 1/2 bell pepper)
1/4 cup minced celery (about 2 ribs celery)
2 tablespoons minced garlic
2 tablespoons chopped fresh basil
2 tablespoons parsley flakes
2 teaspoons Cajun seasoning
2 teaspoons Tabasco sauce
1 teaspoon salt
1 teaspoon pepper
3 tablespoons all-purpose flour
3 cups half-and-half
8 ounces cream cheese, cut into 8 pieces
2 teaspoons Worcestershire sauce
1 pound fresh crawfish tails, steamed
        and peeled

Melt the butter in a 2-quart saucepan over high heat. Sauté the onion, bell pepper, celery and garlic in the butter for 10 minutes. Add the basil, parsley flakes, Cajun seasoning, Tabasco sauce, salt and pepper and sauté for 3 minutes.

Mix the flour into the sautéed mixture until combined and cook over high heat for 1 minute, stirring constantly. Stir in the half-and-half and cook for 7 minutes or until the mixture begins to thicken, whisking constantly. Reduce the heat to low and simmer, covered, for 5 minutes. Add the cream cheese and cook until melted, stirring constantly. Whisk in the Worcestershire sauce and stir in the crawfish, including the fat and juices.

Simmer, covered, over low heat for 20 minutes or until a meat thermometer registers 160 degrees. Spoon the hot dip into a chafing dish and serve with sliced French bread.

CHRISTY HOTZ

Children Can Soar began in 1982 by a JLB member who wanted to turn the drab waiting room of the Crippled Children's Service into a learning place. Each year, more than 25,000 families of physically challenged children learn to provide for children's special needs while getting emotional support. The project is now part of Gateway, a United Way agency.

BAKED MEXICAN DIP

SERVES 10 TO 12

1 (10-ounce) package frozen chopped
    spinach, thawed and drained
2 tablespoons vegetable oil
1 cup chopped onion
1 cup chopped seeded peeled tomato
3 tablespoons chopped jalapeño chiles
2 cups (8 ounces) shredded Monterey
    Jack cheese
1 cup half-and-half
3 ounces cream cheese, cut into
    1/2-inch cubes
1/3 cup sliced canned black olives
1 tablespoon red wine vinegar
1/8 teaspoon ground cumin
Salt and pepper to taste
1/2 cup (2 ounces) shredded Monterey
    Jack cheese
1/2 cup chopped seeded peeled tomato
2 tablespoons chopped fresh cilantro

Preheat the oven to 400 degrees Press the excess moisture from the spinach. Heat the oil in a large skillet and add the onion. Sauté until tender. Stir in 1 cup tomato and the jalapeño chiles and cook for 2 minutes, stirring frequently. Drain and spoon the tomato mixture into a bowl. Stir in the spinach, 2 cups Monterey Jack cheese, the half-and-half, cream cheese, olives, vinegar, cumin, salt and pepper.

Spoon the spinach mixture into a 1 1/2-quart baking dish and bake for 35 minutes or until hot and bubbly. Sprinkle with 1/2 cup Monterey Jack cheese, 1/2 cup tomato and the cilantro. Serve with tortilla chips.

ANN LOWE MOORE

In 1985, the JLB started Magic Moments, a statewide program that fulfills dreams of terminally ill children.

ALABAMA ONION DIP

An updated version of the standard soup-mix onion dip.

SERVES 10

2 tablespoons vegetable oil
1 tablespoon butter
2 pounds yellow onions, cut into halves and
    coarsely chopped
1/2 teaspoon kosher salt
2 garlic cloves, chopped
1 tablespoon balsamic vinegar
1/2 teaspoon kosher salt
1/2 teaspoon freshly ground black pepper
1/4 teaspoon cayenne pepper
1/4 teaspoon Tabasco sauce
8 ounces cream cheese, cubed
11/2 cups sour cream
1 to 2 tablespoons minced fresh chives
Minced fresh chives or chopped green onions
    for garnish

Heat the oil and butter in a large nonstick skillet until the butter melts and stir in the yellow onions and 1/2 teaspoon salt. Cook over medium-low heat for 15 minutes, stirring occasionally. Stir in the garlic and cook for 5 minutes longer or until the onions are very tender and light brown, stirring occasionally. Mix in the vinegar. Let stand until cool. Reserve 1 cup of the onion mixture.

Combine the remaining onion mixture, 1/2 teaspoon salt, the black pepper, cayenne pepper and Tabasco sauce in a food processor and process briefly. Add the cream cheese, sour cream and 1 to 2 tablespoons chives and process until smooth. Stir in the reserved onion mixture. Chill, covered, for 2 hours or longer. Spoon into a serving bowl and garnish with additional minced chives. Serve with thick potato chips coated with sea salt.

LEIGH HARDIN HANCOCK

CARIBBEAN SALSA

This salsa will stay fresh for four to five days in the refrigerator. Serve as an accompaniment to fish or chicken, as a side salad, or as a dip with chips. Serve over Fried Green Tomatoes on page 275 and sprinkle with feta cheese.

MAKES 18 (¼-CUP) SERVINGS

1 (15-ounce) can black beans, drained and rinsed

1 each ripe papaya and mango, peeled and finely chopped (½ cup each)

1 cup finely chopped pineapple

¾ cup pineapple juice

½ cup fresh lime juice (about 4 limes)

½ cup each finely chopped red and green bell pepper

½ cup finely chopped red onion

½ cup cilantro, chopped

1½ teaspoons ground cumin

¼ teaspoon kosher salt

¼ teaspoon pepper

Combine the beans, papaya, mango, pineapple, pineapple juice, lime juice, bell peppers, onion and cilantro in a bowl and mix well. Stir in the cumin, salt and pepper. Chill, covered, in the refrigerator.

NANCY BEDSOLE BYNON

Nutritional Profile for this recipe on page 327.

GREEK SALSA

This salsa is something different to take to gatherings. It is light and packed with flavor.

MAKES 4 CUPS

8 ounces feta cheese, crumbled, or water-pack block feta cheese

1 large ripe tomato, seeded and chopped

1 cucumber, peeled, seeded and chopped

½ cup sliced canned black olives

¼ cup minced fresh parsley

3 green onions, chopped

⅓ cup olive oil

2 tablespoons minced fresh oregano, or 1½ teaspoons dried oregano

2 tablespoons minced fresh dill weed, or 1½ teaspoons dried dill weed

Juice of ½ lemon

Freshly ground pepper to taste

Mix the first 6 ingredients in a bowl. Add the olive oil, oregano, dill weed, lemon juice and pepper and toss to coat. Chill, covered, for 2 to 24 hours. Serve with pita chips and/or crostini, or as a side dish to grilled chicken. If you use the block feta cheese, cut it into small pieces rather than crumbling it.

TOOKIE DAUGHERTY HAZELRIG

SWEET APPLE SPREAD

This is a very quick, kid-friendly, and low-fat spread that can be prepared
in advance. My guests are always asking for this recipe.

MAKES 1¹/₂ CUPS

1 cup packed brown sugar
8 ounces cream cheese, softened
¹/₂ cup granulated sugar

1 teaspoon vanilla extract
1 (8-ounce) package toffee bits
6 to 8 Granny Smith apples, sliced

Beat the brown sugar and cream cheese in a mixing bowl until blended. Let stand for 15 minutes to thicken and stir in the granulated sugar and vanilla. Chill, covered, for 2 hours and stir in the toffee bits. Serve with the apple slices. To prevent the apples slices from browning, drizzle with any citrus juice such as lemon or pineapple juice. For testing purposes, Heath Bits O' Brickle were used.

LEIGH RUMBLEY CREEKBAUM

SMOKED SALMON SPREAD

The flavor is enhanced if prepared one day in advance. Chopped toasted
pecans may be added to the spread for extra flavor and texture.

SERVES 10

8 ounces cream cheese, softened
¹/₂ cup sour cream
Juice of 1 lemon
1 tablespoon chopped fresh dill weed

1 teaspoon prepared horseradish
Salt to taste
4 ounces smoked salmon, chopped

Stir the cream cheese in a bowl with a spatula until smooth. Add the sour cream, lemon juice, dill weed, horseradish and salt and mix well. Fold in the salmon. Chill, covered, for 2 hours or longer. Serve with assorted party crackers and/or spread on cucumber slices.

CHRISTINE MCGRATH VELEZIS

SOUTHWEST PIMENTO CHEESE

MAKES 3 CUPS

8 ounces mild Cheddar and white Cheddar
   cheese, shredded
8 ounces Pepper Jack cheese, shredded
1 (7-ounce) jar diced pimentos, drained
3/4 cup plus 3 tablespoons mayonnaise
1 tablespoon adobo seasoning
1/2 teaspoon salt
1/4 teaspoon Worcestershire sauce
1/8 teaspoon ground cumin
1/8 teaspoon ground coriander

Combine the Cheddar cheese, Pepper Jack cheese, pimentos, mayonnaise, adobo seasoning, salt, Worcestershire sauce, cumin and coriander in a bowl and mix well. Or, process in a food processor to the desired consistency. Chill, covered, in the refrigerator until serving time. For a creamier texture, grate one block of cheese on the large side of a box grater and grate the other block of cheese on the small side of the box grater.

LYDA HELEN JONES

PAULA'S PIMENTO CHEESE

This was my mother-in-law's recipe. It is great all year around and stores well in the refrigerator.

MAKES 3 CUPS

1 cup mayonnaise
1 (4-ounce) jar sliced pimentos, drained
1/2 teaspoon garlic salt
16 ounces Cheddar cheese, shredded
8 ounces cream cheese, softened

Combine the mayonnaise, pimentos and garlic salt in a bowl and mix well. Add the Cheddar cheese and cream cheese and mix until combined. Chill, covered, in the refrigerator until serving time. Serve as a spread on crackers or tea sandwiches, or use as a stuffing for celery sticks.

SHERYL WILLIAMS KIMERLING

BASIL AND SUN-DRIED TOMATO BRIE

Toasting nuts releases the natural oils. These released oils give the best potential flavor to the nut and is a must for this appetizer.

SERVES 4 TO 6

1 (5-inch) round Brie cheese
4 ounces oil-pack sun-dried tomatoes, drained
4 garlic cloves
1 tablespoon grated Parmesan cheese
1 1/2 tablespoons chopped pine nuts, toasted
   (see sidebar)
1 1/2 tablespoons chopped fresh basil

Cut off the top rind of the Brie and discard. Arrange the round on a platter. Process the sun-dried tomatoes, garlic and Parmesan cheese in a food processor until finely chopped. Spread the sun-dried tomato mixture over the top of the Brie. Sprinkle with the pine nuts and basil just before serving. Serve at room temperature with bagel chips.

LUDIE SEARCY'S CRANBERRY BRIE

SERVES 4 TO 6

1 (8-ounce) round Brie cheese
1/2 cup canned whole cranberry sauce
2 tablespoons brown sugar
1/4 teaspoon rum extract
1/8 teaspoon freshly grated nutmeg
2 tablespoons chopped pecans, toasted
1 teaspoon grated orange zest

Preheat the oven to 500 degrees. Cut off the top rind of the Brie, leaving a 1/4-inch rim. Arrange the Brie on a baking sheet.

Mix the cranberry sauce, brown sugar, flavoring and nutmeg in a bowl and spread over the top of the Brie. Sprinkle with the pecans and orange zest and bake for 4 minutes. Serve with assorted party crackers.

ELIZA PASCHALL PETZNICK

TOASTING TIPS

To toast nuts or whole seeds, place them in a small skillet and cook over medium-high heat for about 4 to 5 minutes or until fragrant and light brown, stirring constantly. Remove from skillet to cool.

WALNUT STILTON TORTA

This is a tasty and colorful make-ahead appetizer. You may prepare the torta several days in advance and store, wrapped tightly, in the refrigerator. If time is of the essence, you can prepare the torta and freeze it until set.

SERVES 10

2 1/2 tablespoons butter
1/2 cup chopped walnuts
1/4 cup packed light brown sugar
1/8 teaspoon salt
16 ounces cream cheese, softened
1/2 cup (1 stick) butter, softened
1/4 cup port (sweet, white wine)
1 1/2 cups (6 ounces) crumbled Stilton cheese
1 cup seedless raspberry jam,
    at room temperature
1 bunch seedless red grapes for garnish
1/4 cup thinly sliced green onions for garnish

Melt 2 1/2 tablespoons butter in a small skillet over medium heat. Stir in the walnuts, brown sugar and salt and cook for 5 minutes or until the brown sugar dissolves and the mixture is bubbly, stirring frequently. Spread the walnut mixture in an even layer on a sheet of baking parchment. Let stand until cool and break into pieces.

Combine the cream cheese and 1/2 cup butter in a mixing bowl and beat at medium speed until blended. Add the wine and beat until smooth. Line a small ring mold or small round bowl with plastic wrap.

Spread 1 cup of the cream cheese mixture in the prepared mold and sprinkle with 3/4 cup of the Stilton cheese. Spread with 1/2 cup of the jam and sprinkle with 1/3 of the candied walnuts. Layer with 1 cup of the remaining cream cheese mixture, the remaining Stilton cheese, the remaining jam and 1/2 of the remaining candied walnuts. Spread with the remaining cream cheese mixture.

Chill, tightly covered with plastic wrap, for 8 hours or until set. Invert the torta onto a serving platter and sprinkle with the remaining candied walnuts. Garnish with the grapes and green onions and serve with toasted French bread slices.

SUSAN SMITH ELLARD

Photograph for this recipe on page 81.

Teacher Take Wing is a mini-grant program started by the JLB in 2000. Teachers submit requests to a JLB committee for up to $500 in grants for specific classroom needs. In the first five years of the program, the JLB gave $100,000 to teachers in Birmingham City Schools.

OLIVE TAPENADE

MAKES 2 CUPS

1 cup kalamata olives, pitted
3 garlic cloves, chopped
1 tablespoon rinsed drained capers
1 tablespoon anchovy paste
Zest of 1/2 lemon, chopped (about 1 tablespoon)
Juice of 1/2 lemon (about 2 tablespoons)
1 1/2 tablespoons extra-virgin olive oil
1 tablespoon chopped flat-leaf parsley
1 1/2 teaspoons Dijon mustard
1/2 teaspoon freshly ground pepper

Combine the olives, garlic, capers, anchovy paste and lemon zest in a food processor and pulse several times until coarsely chopped; do not purée. Spoon into a bowl and stir in the olive oil, parsley, Dijon mustard and pepper. Serve with baguette slices.

LEIGH HARDIN HANCOCK

BLACK OLIVE PÂTÉ

This was my grandmother's recipe. She always made the pâté for parties, but I love it anytime.

MAKES 4 CUPS

3 cups (12 ounces) shredded American cheese
1 cup mayonnaise
2 (4-ounce) cans black olives, drained and chopped
1/2 cup thinly sliced green onions
1 teaspoon curry powder
1/4 teaspoon salt

Line a pâté mold or small loaf pan with plastic wrap. Combine the cheese, mayonnaise, olives, green onions, curry powder and salt in a food processor fitted with a plastic blade and process until blended.

Press the cheese mixture into the prepared mold and chill, covered, until firm. Invert onto a serving platter and serve with assorted party crackers or toasted melba rounds.

AMY LYN TOOTHAKER

CHEESY ARTICHOKE BITES

MAKES 32 BITES

32 (3×3-inch) won ton wrappers
8 ounces light cream cheese
1 cup (4 ounces) shredded
    Cheddar cheese
1 tablespoon Dijon mustard

1/4 teaspoon cayenne pepper
1 (14-ounce) can artichoke hearts,
    drained and chopped
1/4 cup chopped red bell pepper

Preheat the oven to 350 degrees. Coat 32 miniature muffin cups with nonstick cooking spray and gently press 1 won ton wrapper into each prepared cup, allowing the edges to extend above the cups. Spray the edges of the wrappers with nonstick cooking spray and bake for 2 to 3 minutes. Maintain the oven temperature.

Combine the cream cheese, Cheddar cheese, Dijon mustard and cayenne pepper in a bowl and mix well. Stir in the artichokes and bell pepper. Spoon 1 tablespoon of the cheese mixture into each cup and bake for 18 to 20 minutes or until the edges begin to brown. Serve warm.

SUSAN DEAL GUILSHER

JUNE BUGS

MAKES 50 APPETIZERS

1 cup (4 ounces) shredded
    Cheddar cheese
1/2 cup (1 stick) butter, softened
1 1/2 cups all-purpose flour

1/8 teaspoon red pepper
1/8 teaspoon paprika
25 pitted dates
1/2 cup confectioners' sugar

Preheat the oven to 400 degrees. Beat the cheese and butter in a mixing bowl until combined. Mix the flour, red pepper and paprika and add to the cheese mixture, beating until combined.

Cut the dates lengthwise into halves and wrap each half with enough of the dough to enclose. Arrange in a single layer on an ungreased baking sheet and bake for 15 to 18 minutes or until light brown. Remove to a wire rack to cool. Sprinkle lightly with the confectioners' sugar before serving.

NANCY LeBEY BAXLEY

CRAB AU GRATIN

SERVES 10

1/2 cup (1 stick) butter
1/2 cup finely chopped onion
1 rib celery, finely chopped
1/3 cup all-purpose flour
1 (12-ounce) can evaporated milk
1/2 cup milk
2 egg yolks, lightly beaten

1 teaspoon salt
1/2 teaspoon ground red pepper
1/4 teaspoon black pepper
1 pound crab meat, shells and
    cartilage removed
8 ounces Cheddar cheese, shredded

Preheat the oven to 375 degrees. Melt the butter in a large nonstick skillet and add the onion and celery. Sauté until the vegetables are tender. Remove from the heat and stir in the flour. Mix the evaporated milk and milk in a bowl and stir in the egg yolks. Stir the milk mixture into the onion mixture and mix in the salt, red pepper and black pepper. Cook over medium heat for 5 minutes or until thickened and of a sauce consistency, stirring constantly. Combine the sauce and crab meat in a bowl and mix gently. Spoon the crab meat mixture into a greased 9×13-inch baking dish and sprinkle with the cheese. Bake for 10 to 15 minutes or until the cheese melts and the top is light brown. Great as an entrée too.

CINDY BISHOP DOODY

SCALLOPED OYSTER CHABLIS

My mom would always prepare this on New Year's Eve because the oysters were supposed to bring good luck. It is delicious and different.

SERVES 3 TO 4

1 1/2 cups cracker crumbs
1/3 cup butter, melted
1 pint oysters, drained
Salt and pepper to taste

1/3 cup Chablis or other white wine
1/2 cup half-and-half
1 cup (4 ounces) shredded sharp
    Cheddar cheese

Preheat the oven to 425 degrees. Toss the cracker crumbs with the butter in a bowl until coated. Spread 1/3 of the crumb mixture over the bottom of a 6×10-inch baking dish. Layer with 1/2 of the oysters and sprinkle with salt and pepper. Top with 1/2 of the remaining crumb mixture, the remaining oysters, salt, pepper and remaining crumb mixture. Pour the wine and then the half-and-half over the prepared layers. Sprinkle with the cheese and bake for 20 minutes. Serve immediately.

ADRIANA WAHL MORROS

BLUE CHEESE AND STEAK QUESADILLAS

MAKES 16 WEDGES

2 teaspoons olive oil
12 ounces flank steak, thinly sliced
   across the grain
1 cup chopped red onion
1 garlic clove, minced

4 (10-inch) flour tortillas
2 cups torn fresh spinach
4 ounces blue cheese, crumbled
2 tablespoons butter

Heat the olive oil in a large skillet over medium-high heat. Sauté the steak, onion and garlic in the hot oil for 4 to 5 minutes or until the steak is the desired degree of doneness. Remove the steak mixture to a plate using a slotted spoon and cover to keep warm. Spread 1/2 of each tortilla evenly with the steak mixture, spinach and blue cheese and fold over to enclose the filling. Melt 1 tablespoon of the butter in a skillet over medium-high heat. Add 2 quesadillas to the hot butter and cook for 2 minutes on each side or until golden brown. Remove to a heated platter and repeat the process with the remaining 1 tablespoon butter and remaining 2 quesadillas. Cut each quesadilla into 4 wedges.

HOLLEY CONTRI JOHNSON

GREEK CHICKEN BITES WITH HERB CREAM DIP

MAKES 15 (2-SKEWER) SERVINGS

1 cup plain yogurt, drained
1 small cucumber, peeled, seeded,
   grated and drained (about 1/3 cup)
1 tablespoon chopped fresh parsley
1 garlic clove, minced
1 teaspoon salt
1 teaspoon grated lemon zest

1 teaspoon fresh lemon juice
1 pound boneless skinless chicken
   breasts, cut into 30 pieces
1 teaspoon Greek seasoning
1/8 teaspoon black pepper
1/4 teaspoon ground red pepper
2 tablespoons olive oil

Combine the yogurt, cucumber, parsley, garlic, salt, lemon zest and lemon juice in a bowl and mix well. Chill, covered, in the refrigerator. Toss the chicken with the Greek seasoning, black pepper and red pepper in a sealable plastic bag. Heat the olive oil in a large skillet over medium-high heat and add the chicken. Sauté for 8 to 10 minutes or until cooked through. Thread the chicken pieces individually on wooden picks and serve warm or chilled with the dip.

RAMI MARIE PERRY

Nutritional Profile for this recipe on page 327.

BAKED CHILE LIME CHIPS

MAKES 6 DOZEN CHIPS

2$^1/2$ tablespoons olive oil
2 garlic cloves, minced
1 chipotle chile, minced
1 tablespoon kosher salt
2 teaspoons brown sugar

1 teaspoon finely grated lime zest
$^1/2$ teaspoon baking cocoa
$^1/4$ teaspoon ground cumin
6 (12-inch) flour tortillas

Preheat the oven to 500 degrees. Combine the olive oil, garlic, chipotle chile, salt, brown sugar, lime zest, baking cocoa and cumin in a bowl and mix well. Brush 1 side of each tortilla with the olive oil mixture and cut into long strips or triangles.

Arrange the strips in batches in a single layer on a baking sheet and bake for 5$^1/2$ minutes or until brown and crisp. Remove to a wire rack to cool. Store in an airtight container.

ABBY CURRY FINNEY

PLANTAIN CHIPS

SERVES 8 TO 10

1 tablespoon kosher salt
1 teaspoon chipotle chile powder
1 teaspoon sugar
$^1/4$ teaspoon ground cumin

$^1/4$ teaspoon garlic powder
5 green plantains
Canola oil or peanut oil for frying

Mix the salt, chipotle chile powder, sugar, cumin and garlic powder in a bowl. Cut the plantains lengthwise into paper-thin slices with a sharp knife or use a mandoline to speed up the process.

Heat canola oil in a deep skillet to 350 to 375 degrees. Fry the plantain slices in batches in the hot oil for 2 to 3 minutes per side or until golden brown and crisp. Drain on paper towels and immediately sprinkle with the spice mixture.

MARIA ADLERCREUTZ ALEXANDER

BLACK AND WHITE SESAME WON TON CRISPS

Won ton wrappers or won ton skins can be found in the produce section of your supermarket.

MAKES 4 DOZEN CRISPS

1 egg
1 tablespoon water
1/16 teaspoon salt
12 won ton wrappers or won ton skins
Black sesame seeds to taste
White sesame seeds to taste

Preheat the oven to 325 degrees. Whisk the egg, water and salt in a bowl until blended. Cut the won ton wrappers diagonally into quarters and arrange on a lightly greased baking sheet. Brush with the egg wash and sprinkle with black and white sesame seeds.

Bake for 8 minutes or until golden brown. Immediately remove to a wire rack to cool completely. Serve alone or with dip.

MARY SPOTSWOOD BOX

PARMESAN PITA ROUNDS

SERVES 32

1 (7-ounce) package miniature pita rounds
1/3 cup finely grated Parmesan cheese
3 tablespoons finely chopped fresh chives
1/4 teaspoon salt

Preheat the oven to 400 degrees. Cut the pita rounds crosswise into halves and coat with nonstick cooking spray. Combine the cheese, chives and salt in a bowl and mix well. Spread the cheese mixture over 1 side of each pita half and arrange cheese side up in a single layer on a baking sheet. Bake for 8 to 10 minutes or until brown and crisp. Serve as a side to soup, salad or chili.

KIMBERLY WOOD GEISLER

Grants from Teacher Take Wing enable at-risk children to have a more fulfilling learning environment while rewarding exceptional teachers.

Teen Court was established in 1997 by the JLB in partnership with the Alabama Center for Law and Civic Education. The program helps first-time juvenile offenders of misdemeanor crimes avoid a permanent criminal record by agreeing to be held accountable before a jury of their peers.

CHEESE STRAWS

*I have provided these Cheese Straws for countless school bake sales,
football tailgates, Christmas gifts, cooking parties, casual supper clubs, and formal
dinner parties. It took me two years to perfect this recipe, and I have
learned there are no shortcuts in making this family favorite.*

MAKES 2 POUNDS

16 ounces block-style extra-sharp Cheddar cheese,
    coarsely grated
1/2 cup (1 stick) unsalted butter
2 cups all-purpose flour
1 teaspoon kosher salt
11/2 to 2 teaspoons crushed red pepper flakes
    (not cayenne pepper)
1/2 teaspoon Tabasco sauce

Let the cheese and butter stand at room temperature for 8 to 10 hours. Preheat the oven to 350 degrees. Sift the flour into a mixing bowl and stir in the salt. Add the cheese, butter, red pepper flakes and Tabasco sauce. Beat using a mixer fitted with a paddle attachment at low speed for 1 minute or until the mixture adheres to the paddle.

Spoon about 3/4 cup of the dough into a cookie press fitted with a small star attachment. Pipe out straws 5 inches long onto a baking sheet lined with a silicone baking sheet and bake for 15 minutes, checking after 10 minutes for doneness. The straws should feel slightly crisp to the touch, but do not allow to brown. Let stand for 1 minute on the baking sheet and remove to a wire rack to cool completely. Repeat the process with the remaining dough. Store in airtight tins for up to 1 week. Do not store in plastic containers or bags. For testing purposes, Land O' Lakes Extra-Sharp Cheddar Cheese was used.

ELLEN MACELVAIN RHETT

PARMESAN CRISPS

Good as an appetizer or to garnish savory dishes such as risotto, soups, or salads.

MAKES 3 DOZEN CRISPS

6 ounces Parmigiano-Reggiano,
   shredded
1/2 cup shelled pistachios,
   finely chopped

1 tablespoon cornmeal
1/2 teaspoon freshly grated
   black pepper
1/8 teaspoon ground red pepper

Preheat the oven to 350 degrees. Line 2 large baking sheets with foil and coat with nonstick cooking spray. Combine the cheese and pistachios in a food processor and pulse until finely ground. Add the cornmeal, black pepper and red pepper and process until combined. Mound a level 1 1/2 teaspoons per crisp of the cheese mixture 2 inches apart on the prepared baking sheets. Flatten each mound lightly to form a 2-inch round. Bake for 8 to 10 minutes or until light brown. Remove the crisps to a wire rack to cool using a metal spatula.

PAT McCABE FORMAN

Photograph for this recipe on page 81.

SPICY CHEESE CRISPIES

Similar in taste and texture to cheese straws, but easy! As with cheese straws, the secret is to let the cheese and butter stand at room temperature for eight to ten hours to soften.

MAKES 4 DOZEN CRISPIES

8 ounces block-style extra-sharp
   Cheddar cheese, coarsely shredded
   (do not use preshredded cheese)
1 cup (2 sticks) unsalted
   butter, softened
2 1/2 cups all-purpose flour

1 1/2 to 2 teaspoons crushed red pepper
   flakes (not cayenne pepper)
1 teaspoon fine sea salt
1 teaspoon Tabasco sauce
1 1/2 cups crisp rice cereal

Preheat the oven to 350 degrees. Combine the cheese, butter, flour, red pepper flakes, salt and Tabasco sauce in a mixing bowl and beat at low speed for 1 minute or until combined. Fold in the cereal. Shape the cereal mixture into 1-inch balls and arrange on a baking sheet. Flatten each ball into a round, using a fork or hand if necessary. Bake for 12 minutes or until light brown. Cool on the baking sheet for 1 minute and remove to a wire rack to cool completely. Store in an airtight tin for up to 1 week.

ELLEN MacELVAIN RHETT

PECAN CORNMEAL ROUNDS

Use seasonal cookie cutters to give these rounds a special touch.

MAKES 30 ROUNDS

1½ cups all-purpose flour
½ cup self-rising yellow cornmeal
3 tablespoons sugar
¾ teaspoon salt

¾ cup (1½ sticks) plus 2 tablespoons
   butter, softened
1 egg, lightly beaten
¾ cup pecans, toasted and chopped

Mix the flour, cornmeal, sugar and salt in a bowl. Beat the butter in a mixing bowl until creamy. Add the flour mixture and mix well. Blend in the egg and stir in the pecans. Chill, covered, in the refrigerator until the dough is easily handled.

Preheat the oven to 350 degrees. Roll the dough ½ inch thick on a lightly floured surface. Cut into rounds using a 2½-inch cutter and arrange the rounds on a lightly greased baking sheet. Bake for 25 minutes or until light brown and crisp. Top with a slice of ham or preserves.

KATHLEEN SPROUSE DOSS

AMARETTO

*Amaretto is an almond liqueur that is perfect over ice cream,
pound cake, or in coffee. Tastes great as a cordial.*

MAKES 3½ CUPS

1 cup water
1 cup granulated sugar
½ cup packed brown sugar

2 cups vodka
2 tablespoons almond extract
2 teaspoons vanilla extract

Bring the water, granulated sugar and brown sugar to a boil in a medium saucepan over medium heat. Boil until the sugar dissolves, stirring occasionally. Remove from the heat and let stand for 10 minutes. Stir in the vodka and flavorings. Pour the amaretto into a bottle and seal tightly. Let stand for 2 to 4 weeks before serving, preferably 4 weeks. Store for up to 6 months.

AMBER LYNNE MCKINSTRY

Photograph for this recipe on page 80.

AMARETTO SLUSH

This recipe has been served at every special occasion in my husband's family for the past twenty years. Now we are serving this slush at every special occasion in my family, even small get-togethers, because everyone keeps requesting the drink. Both sides of our families get upset if we don't make it.

SERVES 8 TO 10

1 (16-ounce) can juice-pack
   pineapple slices
1 (6-ounce) jar maraschino cherries
1 (2-liter) bottle lemon-lime soda

1 (32-ounce) can pineapple juice
1 (6-ounce) can frozen orange
   juice concentrate
2 cups amaretto, or to taste

Drain the pineapple and cut the slices into quarters, reserving the juice. Drain the cherries and cut the cherries into halves, reserving the juice. Combine the reserved pineapple juice, reserved cherry juice, lemon-lime soda, canned pineapple juice, orange juice concentrate and liqueur in a large freezer container and mix well. Stir in the pineapple and cherries. Freeze for 24 hours or longer, stirring every few hours until slushy.

For a nonalcoholic slush, omit the amaretto and add an additional 4 ounces frozen orange juice concentrate and an additional 1 cup canned pineapple juice.

POWELL ANDERSON OWENS

THE BEACH TODDY

MAKES 17 CUPS

1 (46-ounce) can pineapple or
   pineapple mango juice
1 (6-ounce) can frozen
   lemonade concentrate
1 (6-ounce) can frozen
   limeade concentrate

1 (3-ounce) can frozen orange
   juice concentrate
1 pint rum
1 (2-liter) bottle Fresca or ginger ale
Lime slices

Combine the pineapple juice, lemonade concentrate, limeade concentrate, orange juice concentrate and rum in a large freezer container and mix well. Freeze until slushy. Spoon enough of the slushy mixture into glasses to fill 3/4 full. Top off with the soda and garnish with lime slices or other citrus fruit slices. Serve immediately.

VIRGINIA BAXLEY WINN

BOURBON SLUSH

A Thanksgiving tradition established by my father is now continued each year at our large family gathering with a toast in his memory.

MAKES 11 CUPS

1 cup sugar
6 cups hot tea
1 (12-ounce) can frozen
    lemonade concentrate

1 (6-ounce) can frozen orange
    juice concentrate
2 cups bourbon

Dissolve the sugar in the hot tea in a heatproof bowl. Add the lemonade concentrate and orange juice concentrate and stir until blended. Let stand until cool and stir in the bourbon. Pour the bourbon mixture into a 1-gallon freezer container and freeze until slushy. Let stand at room temperature until partially thawed and spoon into glasses. Serve immediately.

JAN PHILLIPPI SHANNON

SOUTHERN EGGNOG

My grandmother made this, and now my mother makes it, every Christmas night. We always laugh about these sweet Southern Baptist ladies making the eggnog with bourbon!

MAKES 30 TO 35 CUPS

12 egg yolks
1 cup sugar
1/2 to 1 cup bourbon
12 egg whites

1/2 teaspoon salt
3 pints heavy cream or
    whipping cream
Freshly grated nutmeg

Beat the egg yolks and sugar in a mixing bowl until thick and pale yellow in color. Gradually add the bourbon, beating constantly at low speed until blended. Chill, covered, for 2 to 3 hours. Beat the egg whites and salt in a mixing bowl until peaks form. Beat the cream in a mixing bowl until stiff peaks form. Fold the whipped cream into the chilled egg yolk mixture and then fold the egg whites into the whipped cream mixture. Chill, covered, for 1 to 2 hours.

Serve in cups with freshly grated nutmeg and spoons. If you are concerned about using raw eggs, use eggs pasteurized in their shells, which are sold at some specialty food stores, or use an equivalent amount of pasteurized egg substitute.

PRATT AUSTIN-TRUCKS

HOMEMADE KAHLÚA

A college friend gave me this recipe in 1976 after spring break at Ft. Walton. She served it "on the rocks" and "on the beach!" This is a perfect after-dinner drink and makes a nice gift.

MAKES 5¹/₂ CUPS

4 cups sugar
2 cups strong coffee
¹/₄ teaspoon salt
2¹/₂ cups vodka
3 tablespoons vanilla extract

Bring the sugar, coffee and salt to a boil in a 3- or 4-quart saucepan over high heat. Boil until the sugar dissolves, stirring occasionally. Reduce the heat to low and simmer for 1 hour, stirring occasionally. Stir in the vodka and vanilla. Let stand until cool. Pour into clean glass bottles and seal tightly.

REBECCA BRADBERRY MOODY

Photograph for this recipe on page 80.

FROZEN LEMON DROP MARTINI

SERVES 4

1 cup water
³/₄ cup sugar
¹/₂ cup fresh lemon juice
1 large sprig of mint, finely chopped
1 cup lemon-flavored vodka
¹/₄ cup sparkling water
Sprigs of mint for garnish
1 tablespoon grated lemon zest for garnish

Bring the water and sugar to a boil in a small saucepan and boil for 3 minutes to make a simple syrup, stirring occasionally. Let stand until cool. Combine the simple syrup, lemon juice and chopped mint in a bowl and mix well. Pour the lemon mixture into sealable freezer bags and freeze for 1 hour or longer.

Process the frozen mixture, vodka and sparkling water in a blender until blended and pour evenly into 4 sugar-rimmed martini or margarita glasses. Garnish with additional sprigs of mint and the lemon zest.

KATE GILMER PHILLIPS

MANGO DAIQUIRI

MAKES 5 CUPS

Crushed ice
2/3 to 1 large ripe mango, peeled
    and sliced
1 cup spiced rum

1 (6-ounce) can frozen
    limeade concentrate
1/8 teaspoon salt

Fill a blender 2/3 full with crushed ice. Add the mango, rum, limeade concentrate and salt and process until blended, adding additional ice and additional mango for the desired consistency. Pour into glasses and serve immediately.

PAT SANDLIN JOHNSON

BEST MARGARITA

*It is worth investing in a juicer for making these margaritas. You will not regret the purchase.
When the weather begins to turn warm, you will find yourself looking for the juicer.*

SERVES 4

Simple Syrup
1 cup water
3/4 cup sugar

Margaritas
3/4 cup fresh lime juice (about 6 limes)
2/3 cup tequila
1/3 cup Grand Marnier, or other
    orange liqueur
Lime slices for garnish

For the syrup, mix the water and sugar in a microwave-safe bowl. Microwave on High for 3 minutes or until the sugar dissolves and stir. Let stand until cool. Store any extra syrup in the refrigerator and use to sweeten tea.

For the margaritas, combine 1 cup of the syrup, the lime juice, tequila and liqueur in a pitcher and mix well. Pour over ice in salt-rimmed margarita glasses and garnish with lime slices. For testing purposes, Blue Agave tequila was used. Microwave the limes for 30 seconds to make them juicier and easier to squeeze.

CARMEN LaGRANGE MORROW

Photograph for this recipe on page 46.

WHITE SANGRIA

Easy and refreshing!

SERVES 8

1/2 cup sugar
1/2 cup lemon juice
1 (750-milliliter) bottle dry
   white wine
1 1/2 cups orange juice

1 (10-ounce) bottle club soda
1 lemon, sliced
Ice cubes
Orange twists, strawberries and mint
   leaves for garnish

Dissolve the sugar in the lemon juice in a large pitcher. Add the wine, orange juice, club soda, lemon slices and ice cubes and mix well. Pour into glasses and garnish with orange twists, strawberries and/or mint leaves.

LAIDE LONG KARPELES

HEITMEYER CHAMPAGNE PUNCH

I loved to take sips of this from my mom's silver punch cup at her parties. My mom tells me that when you drink this to, "Be careful, it goes down so smoothly that you do not realize it and all of a sudden you are tipsy." Enjoy and "be careful."

SERVES 30

1 (750-milliliter) bottle Champagne or pink Champagne,
   chilled (need not be expensive)
1 (750-milliliter) bottle white wine, chilled
   (need not be expensive)
1 (2-liter) bottle lemon-lime soda or soda water, chilled
3 ounces brandy
3 ounces orange liqueur
3 ounces frozen lemonade concentrate

Combine the Champagne, wine, soda, brandy, liqueur and lemonade concentrate in a punch bowl and mix well. Ladle into punch cups. If desired, keep the punch chilled by adding an ice ring. Simply freeze water, maraschino cherries and/or a drop or two of food coloring in a ring mold.

ADRIANA WAHL MORROS

LIMEADE

*This is good if it is hot outside and you are a kid or just a kid at
heart! If you are ten or under, it tastes best if you squeeze the limes yourself.
This is when that investment in a juicer really pays off.*

SERVES 1

Simple Syrup
1 cup sugar
1 cup water

Limeade
1 large lime
Ice cubes
Water

For the syrup, bring the sugar and water to a boil in a saucepan. Reduce the heat to low and simmer for 5 minutes, stirring occasionally. Store, covered, in the refrigerator.

For the limeade, pour 1/4 cup of the chilled syrup into a glass. Microwave the lime for 30 seconds to make it juicier and easier to squeeze. Squeeze the lime directly over the glass to release the juice. Add enough ice to reach the top of the glass and then fill with water. Stir and serve immediately.

CARMEN LaGRANGE MORROW

In Teen Court, JLB volunteers serve as judges while teen volunteers act as attorneys, bailiffs, clerks, and jurors in order to create "constructive sentences." Statistics show that eighty percent of Teen Court participants do not become repeat offenders.

COOL COFFEE PUNCH

Good for brunches and showers.

MAKES 1¹/₃ GALLONS

1 cup sugar
¹/₂ cup instant coffee granules
³/₄ cup hot water
¹/₂ gallon vanilla ice cream, softened
   (not thawed)
3 quarts milk
12 ounces whipped topping
Chocolate shavings for garnish

Mix the sugar and coffee granules in a heatproof bowl. Add the hot water and stir until dissolved. Chill, covered, for 8 to 10 hours. The mixture should be slightly thickened. Spoon the ice cream into a punch bowl. Pour the coffee mixture and milk over the ice cream and stir. Top with the whipped topping. Ladle into punch cups and garnish with chocolate shavings.

CHRISTINE MCGRATH VELEZIS

HOLIDAY PARTY PUNCH

My mother served this punch at parties when I was a young child.

SERVES 35

2 (46-ounce) cans pineapple juice, chilled
1 (64-ounce) bottle cranberry juice, chilled
1 (12-ounce) can frozen pink
   lemonade concentrate
3 lemonade cans cold water
1 (2-liter) bottle ginger ale, chilled

Mix the pineapple juice, cranberry juice, lemonade concentrate and cold water in a large punch bowl. Stir in the ginger ale just before serving and ladle into punch cups. Make an ice ring for the punch bowl by freezing water with cranberries or any other fruit in a ring mold. For a slushy version, freeze the punch mixture for 8 to 10 hours. Let stand at room temperature for 1 hour before serving.

MOLLY CAMERON MARTIN

In 1948 the JLB established the Junior League Speech and Hearing Center, which in 1957 became the Alabama Foundation for Speech and Hearing.

Today the Alabama Foundation for Speech and Hearing is part of Children's Hospital and averages more than 1,200 patients treated per month.

Great Beginnings

CHEESE, PLEASE

Cheese makes an elegant yet simple no-cook appetizer. Cooking with cheese adds flavor and texture to any dish. Here are a few tips on selecting and storing cheese, as well as a rundown of widely available favorites.

• Taste is the best test. Most cheese counters will cut you a sample.

• Wrap cheese in waxed paper or foil and store in the refrigerator drawer. Storing cheese in the door exposes it to temperature swings and can have an adverse effect on the cheese.

• The texture of the cheese clues you in to the flavor. Soft cheeses tend to be mild, and hard cheeses often have a more pronounced nutty and salty flavor.

• Save the rind of Parmesan cheese. Use it as you might use a ham bone to flavor soups, stews, or beans. Discard the rind after cooking.

• Cheese is one of the most interchangeable ingredients. The most important guideline is to substitute similar textures. Use personal flavor preferences and the information below as a guide.

Mini Tomato Tarts

Amaretto and Homemade Kahlúa

Roasted Cashews with Rosemary

SOFT FRESH CHEESES: Despite the category name, the texture of different varieties can vary from crumbly to silky smooth, and their culinary uses are just as broad. Cream cheese, goat cheese, mascarpone cheese, fresh mozzarella, ricotta and feta are examples of soft fresh cheeses.

SOFT-RIPENED CHEESES: Soft-ripened cheeses are good eating cheeses because of their creamy texture, but because they are ripened or aged most of these cheeses pack a pungent flavor. They are also well-suited for cooking and melt smoothly. Brie, Camembert, Explorateur, St. André, and Teleme are all examples of soft-ripened cheeses.

SEMISOFT CHEESES: Semisoft cheeses are good table cheeses, and they make tasty accents baked in breads, tossed with salads, and stirred into salad dressings. Taleggio, Reblochon, Brillat-Savarin, and Roquefort cheese are all examples.

SEMIHARD CHEESES: Semihard cheeses are excellent for cooking, and they melt easily. Shred these cheeses to scatter atop pizzas or casseroles. Fontina, Gouda, Monterey Jack, provolone, sharp Cheddar, and domestic mozzarella are examples of semihard cheeses.

HARD CHEESES: Often used as grating cheeses, these are good to sprinkle on top of baked dishes, such as gratins, because they brown nicely. These are also good shaving cheeses because of their low moisture content. Use shavings over hot pasta dishes or salads. Remember, these cheeses are usually full-flavored and slightly salty, so just a bit goes a long way. Asiago, Gruyère, manchego, Parmigiano-Reggiano, and Swiss are all examples of hard cheeses.

SPECIAL OCCASION

75	Frozen Lemon Drop Martini
63	Walnut Stilton Torta
101	Roquefort Salad
182	Pepper Chutney Beef Tenderloin
149	Wild Mushroom Risotto
293	Apricot and Almond Torte

SUGGESTED WINES:
- *Zaca Mesa Syrah*
- *Joseph Phelps Pastiche Red*
- *Errazuriz Late Harvest
  Sauvignon Blanc 2004*

Parmesan Crisps

Walnut Stilton Torta

From the Garden

SALADS

In-the-know Birmingham gardeners run, not walk, to the Annual Plant Sale fund-raiser at the Birmingham Botanical Gardens. They know that once a year, local growers lovingly share specialty plants as well as a variety of old favorites. Add to that event periodic Shakespeare plays, weddings, picnics, children's photographers, educational programs, a library and herbarium, and symphonies on the grass, and you will find that most Birmingham residents go for the green at the beautiful Botanical Gardens.

In 1960, Birmingham mayor James W. Morgan established the sixty-seven-acre Birmingham Botanical Gardens and commissioned the first master plan. It included not only the Japanese Gardens, Garden Center, and the first garden and plant collections, but

also the largest clear-span conservatory in the Southeast. Today it features, among other things, a Native American area, a wildflower garden, a vegetable garden, an orchard, and a special needs garden.

That proves not all gardens are green, and neither are all salads. In this chapter, unusual lettuces and fruit combinations add color to salads. Vegetables are combined in interesting ways, bites of fish or meat may be added, but if it's light and refreshing, let's call it a salad. Try our Sun-Dried Tomato Basil Pasta Salad on page 97, or the Coral Shrimp with Rice Salad on page 94. When you go for the green, we know what you mean.

Visit the Birmingham Botanical Gardens on line at www.bbgardens.org.

Birmingham Botanical Gardens

Tomato Salad with Basil
Oil Dressing

Salads

CONTENTS

WATERMELON, TOMATO, FETA CHEESE SALAD WITH FRESH MINT

SERVES 8

4 cups medium-chopped seedless
   watermelon, chilled
4 cups medium-chopped tomatoes
1/3 cup balsamic vinegar

1/4 cup honey
1/4 cup chopped fresh mint
1/8 teaspoon salt
1/2 cup crumbled feta cheese

Mix the watermelon and tomatoes in a salad bowl. Whisk the balsamic vinegar and honey in a small bowl and add to the watermelon mixture, tossing to coat. Stir in the mint and salt. Sprinkle with the cheese and serve immediately. Or, serve over a bed of baby spinach leaves tossed with a mixture of 1/4 cup balsamic vinegar, 1/4 cup olive oil, salt and cracked pepper.

JASON MEZRANO, KATHY MEZRANO, KATHY G & COMPANY

Photograph for this recipe on page 113.

SWEET TART SALAD

SERVES 8

Poppy Seed Dressing
1/2 cup sugar
1/2 cup vegetable oil
1/4 cup apple cider vinegar
1 tablespoon poppy seeds
1/4 teaspoon paprika
1/4 teaspoon Worcestershire sauce

Salad
10 ounces salad greens, or 16 cups
   torn lettuce
4 cups chopped Granny Smith apples
2 cups garlic bagel chips, crushed
4 ounces blue cheese, crumbled
1/4 cup chopped pecans
1 tablespoon pepper

For the dressing, combine the sugar, oil, vinegar, poppy seeds, paprika and Worcestershire sauce in a jar with a tight-fitting lid and seal tightly. Shake to mix. Chill, covered, in the refrigerator until serving time. The flavor is enhanced if made in advance and chilled.

For the salad, mix the salad greens, apples, bagel chips, cheese, pecans and pepper in a salad bowl. Add the dressing and toss to coat. Serve immediately.

ALICE CAREY

MOST REQUESTED CRANBERRY SALAD

Our family serves this at Thanksgiving and Christmas as well as throughout the year.

SERVES 8 TO 10

1 (15-ounce) can pitted dark cherries
1 (3-ounce) package dark cherry gelatin
1 (3-ounce) package raspberry gelatin
1 (16-ounce) can jellied cranberry sauce
1 cup sour cream
1 (8-ounce) can crushed pineapple, drained
Mayonnaise

Drain the juice from the cherries into a measuring cup and add enough water to measure 2 cups, reserving the cherries. Bring the juice mixture to a boil in a saucepan. Add the gelatin and stir until dissolved. Let stand until cool. Add the cranberry sauce to the gelatin mixture and mash to combine. Freeze for 25 minutes.

Stir the sour cream into the cranberry mixture and mix in the pineapple. Pour into a large mold sprayed with nonstick cooking spray. Arrange the reserved cherries evenly over the top and chill, covered, for 4 hours or until set. Top each serving with a dollop of mayonnaise.

NATALIE TORTORICI GILLESPIE

PINEAPPLE SALAD

MAKES 9 (1/2-CUP) SERVINGS

3/4 cup sweetened flaked coconut
1 pineapple, peeled, cored and chopped (4 cups)
6 tablespoons brown sugar
2 tablespoons fresh lime juice
1/4 teaspoon salt

Preheat the oven to 350 degrees. Spread the coconut in an even layer on a baking sheet and toast for 10 minutes or until light brown, stirring once. Let stand until cool. Combine the pineapple, brown sugar, lime juice, salt and coconut in a bowl and toss to mix. Serve immediately or chill if desired before serving.

ROBIN LEIGH BEARDSLEY

Nutritional Profile for this recipe on page 327.

FROZEN FRUIT SALAD

A great recipe to prepare in advance and store in the refrigerator for those unexpected guests. This salad was served years ago at Christine's Tea Room, a gift shop in Mountain Brook Village.

SERVES 24

1 cup sugar
1/4 cup fresh lemon juice
6 cups sour cream
1 (12-ounce) can crushed pineapple, drained
2 cups quartered sliced bananas (about 3 bananas)

1 cup maraschino cherries, cut into halves
1 cup chopped pecans, toasted
1/4 cup reserved maraschino cherry juice

Whisk the sugar and lemon juice in a bowl until most of the sugar dissolves. Add the sour cream and stir until smooth. Stir in the pineapple, bananas, cherries and pecans. Add the cherry juice and stir until streaks disappear and the mixture turns pink. Spoon the cherry mixture into paper-lined muffin cups or into a 3-quart dish. Freeze for 4 hours or longer.

CHRISTINE'S TEA ROOM, MOUNTAIN BROOK VILLAGE

MEXICAN LAYERED SALAD

SERVES 6 TO 8

1 pound ground beef
1 (15-ounce) can kidney beans, drained and rinsed
1/4 teaspoon salt
1 1/2 cups chopped onions
1 cup chopped green bell pepper
1 (8-ounce) bottle Catalina salad dressing

Tabasco sauce to taste
Tortilla chips
10 ounces shredded lettuce
4 tomatoes, chopped
4 ounces Cheddar cheese or Mexican blend cheese, shredded
1 tablespoon sour cream (optional)

Brown the ground beef in a skillet, stirring until crumbly; drain. Return the ground beef to the skillet and stir in the beans and salt. Simmer for 10 minutes, stirring occasionally. Mix the onions, bell pepper, salad dressing and Tabasco sauce in a bowl. Layer the tortilla chips, ground beef mixture, lettuce, tomatoes, onion mixture and cheese in a shallow dish. Top with the sour cream.

CHRISTINE MCGRATH VELEZIS

GILCHRIST'S EGG SALAD SANDWICHES

Gilchrist is a popular place for a quick lunch in Mountain Brook. Their egg salad is among the best in the South and one of their best selling items on the menu.

MAKES 4 SANDWICHES

8 eggs
3 tablespoons salt
2 tablespoons heavy mayonnaise

Salt to taste
8 slices whole wheat bread, toasted
Lettuce and sliced tomatoes to taste

Combine the eggs and 3 tablespoons salt with enough water to generously cover in a saucepan. Bring to a boil and boil for 12 to 15 minutes. Drain and place the eggs in a bowl of cold water. Let stand for 5 minutes. Drain and then peel the eggs.

Process the eggs in a food processor for 15 to 30 seconds or until chopped. Combine the eggs and mayonnaise in a bowl and mix well. Season with salt to taste. Serve on whole wheat bread dressed with lettuce and sliced tomatoes. Or, serve warm with crackers.

GILCHRIST OF MOUNTAIN BROOK

CHÉZ ZEE CHICKEN SALAD

Jicama root resembles a rutabaga and adds a nice crunch to salads. It is in season through August and September.

MAKES 8 CUPS

4 boneless skinless chicken breasts
2 tablespoons Southwest seasoning
1 cup chopped celery (about 3 ribs)
1 cup chopped jicama

1 cup pecans, toasted and chopped
1/2 cup chopped dates
1/4 cup chopped onion
1/2 cup mayonnaise

Season the chicken with the Southwest seasoning and panfry in a large nonstick skillet until cooked through, turning once or twice. Let stand until cool and finely chop. Combine the chicken, celery, jicama, pecans, dates and onion in a bowl and mix well. Fold in the mayonnaise. You may add an additional 1 teaspoon Southwest seasoning for added flavor. Use as a spread on sandwiches or spoon over a bed of lettuce and serve as a salad.

ELLIE SMOTHERMAN TAYLOR

GINGERED CHICKEN SALAD

SERVES 2 TO 4

2 tablespoons butter
2 tablespoons olive oil
2 to 4 boneless skinless chicken breasts,
    coarsely chopped
1/4 cup chopped crystallized ginger
8 ounces mixed salad greens

Heat the butter and olive oil in a wok over high heat until bubbly. Add the chicken and stir-fry until brown on all sides and the juices run clear. Add the ginger and stir-fry until the ginger is slightly soft and sugar is no longer evident. Turn off the heat and add the salad greens, tossing to mix. The greens will wilt slightly. Serve immediately.

REBECCA BRADBERRY MOODY

INGRAM'S CHICKEN SALAD

SERVES 10

3 pounds boneless skinless chicken breasts
    (about 8)
1 1/2 cups mayonnaise
1 tablespoon dill weed
1 teaspoon onion powder
1 teaspoon garlic salt
1 teaspoon celery seeds
Salt and pepper to taste
3/4 cup red grape halves
1/2 cup chopped pecans, toasted

Combine the chicken with enough water to cover in a stockpot and cover. Bring to a boil and reduce the heat to low. Simmer for 8 minutes. Remove from the heat and let stand, covered, for 15 to 20 minutes. Remove the chicken to a platter and let stand until cool. Process in a food processor until ground.

Combine the ground chicken, mayonnaise, dill weed, onion powder, garlic salt, celery seeds, salt and pepper in a bowl and mix well. Stir in the grapes and pecans. Chill, covered, until serving time.

The JLB hosted the Antiques and Garden Show for twenty-three consecutive years. In 2004 more than seventy dealers from the U.S. and abroad exhibited in the final show.

NINA HAAS DANIELS

GRILLED LEMON CHICKEN SALAD

SERVES 10

Chicken
1 cup fresh lemon juice (4 large lemons)
3/4 cup olive oil
2 teaspoons kosher salt
1 1/2 tablespoons minced fresh thyme, or
    3/4 teaspoon dried thyme
1 1/2 teaspoons freshly ground pepper
3 pounds boneless skinless chicken breasts

Lemon Dressing
1/2 cup fresh lemon juice (2 large lemons)
1/2 cup olive oil
1 tablespoon Dijon mustard
1 teaspoon minced fresh thyme
1/4 teaspoon each kosher salt and freshly ground pepper

Salad
8 ounces mixed salad greens
1 bunch asparagus, trimmed, blanched and
    cooled (refer to sidebar)
1 red and 1 yellow bell pepper, cut into thin strips
1/2 teaspoon kosher salt
1 lemon, thinly sliced for garnish

To blanch asparagus, bring water to a boil in a large skillet. Add the asparagus and boil for 3 to 5 minutes or until bright green. Remove the asparagus to a colander to drain and rinse with cold water to stop the cooking process.

For the chicken, whisk the lemon juice, olive oil, salt, thyme and pepper in a bowl. Pour over the chicken in a shallow dish, turning to coat. Marinate, covered, in the refrigerator for 6 to 8 hours, turning occasionally. Preheat the grill. Drain the chicken, discarding the marinade. Grill the chicken over hot coals for 5 to 6 minutes per side or until cooked through. Let stand until cool and cut into 1-inch strips.

For the dressing, combine the lemon juice, olive oil, Dijon mustard, thyme, salt and pepper in a jar with a tight-fitting lid and seal tightly. Shake to combine.

For the salad, arrange the salad greens evenly on 10 salad plates. Toss 1/2 of the dressing, the chicken, asparagus, bell peppers and salt in a bowl and arrange evenly on the salad greens. Garnish with the lemon slices and drizzle with the remaining dressing.

SHANNON BARNHILL LISENBY

Photograph for this recipe on page 112.

Marinated Chicken Raspberry Salad

SERVES 4 TO 6

Chicken
1/4 cup Dijon mustard
3 tablespoons water
2 tablespoons brown sugar
1 tablespoon raspberry wine vinegar
1 teaspoon olive oil
2 garlic cloves, minced
1/4 teaspoon pepper
4 (6-ounce) boneless skinless chicken breasts

Maple Raspberry Vinaigrette
2/3 cup vegetable oil
1/4 cup raspberry vinegar
2 tablespoons maple syrup

Salad
Butterhead lettuce
Mesclun or red leaf lettuce
1/2 cup (2 ounces) crumbled blue cheese or Gorgonzola cheese
1/2 cup fresh raspberries
1/2 cup pine nuts or almonds, toasted

For the chicken, whisk the Dijon mustard, water, brown sugar, vinegar, olive oil, garlic and pepper in a bowl until combined. Pour over the chicken in a shallow dish, turning to coat. Marinate, covered, in the refrigerator for 2 hours or longer, turning occasionally. Preheat the grill. Drain the chicken, discarding the marinade. Grill the chicken over hot coals until cooked through, turning occasionally. Cool slightly and slice into thin strips. You may cook in a skillet if desired.

For the vinaigrette, combine the oil, vinegar and syrup in a jar with a tight-fitting lid and seal tightly. Shake to combine.

For the salad, arrange a mixture of butter lettuce and mesclun on salad plates and top with the chicken. Sprinkle evenly with the cheese, raspberries and pine nuts and drizzle with the vinaigrette.

MARTHA ROONEY WALDRUM

COCONUT CRAB AND SHRIMP SALAD

MAKES 4 (1-CUP) SERVINGS

8 ounces medium shrimp, peeled
and deveined
1/4 teaspoon salt
8 ounces lump crab meat, shells and
cartilage removed
1 cup fresh or thawed frozen
corn kernels
1/2 cup minced fresh cilantro
1/3 cup finely chopped onion

1/2 cup flaked sweetened coconut,
toasted (see procedure on page 87
for toasting coconut)
1/3 cup chopped avocado
1 jalapeño chile, seeded and minced
1/4 teaspoon salt
5 tablespoons fresh lemon juice
2 teaspoons extra-virgin olive oil
6 cups torn Boston lettuce

Heat a medium nonstick skillet over medium-high heat and coat with nonstick cooking spray. Add the shrimp and 1/4 teaspoon salt to the hot skillet and sauté for 4 minutes or until the shrimp turn pink, turning once. Let stand until cool and coarsely chop. Combine the crab meat, corn, cilantro, onion, coconut, avocado, jalapeño chile and 1/4 teaspoon salt in a bowl and mix well. Stir in the shrimp. Whisk the lemon juice and olive oil in a bowl until blended and add to the shrimp mixture, tossing to coat. Spoon the salad onto lettuce-lined plates. The coconut may be omitted and additional avocado may be added according to taste.

JOANNE MCCRARY BRASSEAL

Nutritional Profile for this recipe on page 327.

COOKED SHRIMP SALAD

MAKES 6 TO 8 CUPS

1/4 cup mayonnaise
Juice of 1 lemon
Cayenne pepper to taste
2 pounds cooked shrimp, peeled
and deveined

1 cup chopped celery
1 small onion, finely chopped
3 tablespoons rinsed drained capers
8 teaspoons caper juice
Lettuce leaves

Combine the mayonnaise, lemon juice and cayenne pepper in a bowl. Coarsely chop the shrimp and mix with the celery, onion, capers and caper juice in a bowl. Add the mayonnaise mixture and stir until coated. Chill, covered, until serving time. Serve on a bed of lettuce, or with crackers and/or French bread.

KIMBERLY ARMBRUSTER TEW

Coral Shrimp with Rice Salad

This is a beautiful summertime dish that may be prepared in advance.

SERVES 6

Creamy Chili Dressing
1/3 cup mayonnaise
1/4 cup sour cream
1 tablespoon chili sauce
1 1/2 teaspoons apple cider vinegar
1/4 teaspoon onion salt
1/8 teaspoon pepper

Salad
2 pounds medium shrimp, cooked
1 1/2 cups cooked converted rice
1/2 cup chopped cucumber
1/2 cup chopped celery
1/4 cup chopped green onions or chives
Lettuce leaves

For the dressing, combine the mayonnaise, sour cream, chili sauce, vinegar, onion salt and pepper in a bowl and mix well. Chill, covered, in the refrigerator.

For the salad, peel and devein the shrimp. Combine the shrimp, rice, cucumber, celery and green onions in a bowl and mix well. Add the dressing and mix until coated. Chill, covered, for 2 hours or longer. Serve on a bed of lettuce. For testing purposes, Uncle Ben's Converted Rice was used.

Elizabeth Little Allen

PRAWNS WITH MANGO, PAPAYA AND GRAPEFRUIT

This salad takes some time to make, but it is worth it!

SERVES 6

Shrimp
1/2 cup apple juice
1/3 cup fresh lime juice
1/4 cup minced fresh ginger
3 tablespoons soy sauce
4 garlic cloves, crushed
1 tablespoon sesame oil
1 teaspoon honey
24 large shrimp, peeled and deveined

Sesame Dressing
1 cup mirin (found in Asian section
　of grocery store)
1/4 cup rice vinegar
1 tablespoon sesame oil
1 tablespoon chopped fresh parsley
1 tablespoon chopped fresh basil
1 tablespoon chopped fresh chives

Vinegar Dressing
2 tablespoons balsamic vinegar
2 tablespoons chopped fresh parsley
2 tablespoons chopped fresh basil
2 tablespoons chopped fresh chives
2 tablespoons olive oil
Salt and pepper to taste

Salad
4 cups mixed salad greens
1 mango, peeled and sliced (1 cup)
1 papaya, peeled and sliced (1 cup)
1 cup pink grapefruit sections
Thinly sliced avocado (optional)
1 cup chopped tomato

For the shrimp, mix the apple juice, lime juice, ginger, soy sauce, garlic, sesame oil and honey in a shallow dish. Add the shrimp to the apple juice mixture and turn to coat. Marinate at room temperature for 30 minutes, turning occasionally. Sauté the undrained shrimp in a skillet for 5 to 7 minutes or until the shrimp turn pink. Chill, covered, in the refrigerator.

For the sesame dressing, combine the mirin, vinegar, sesame oil, parsley, basil and chives in a jar with a tight-fitting lid and seal tightly. Shake to mix.

For the vinegar dressing, combine the vinegar, parsley, basil, chives, olive oil, salt and pepper in a jar with a tight-fitting lid and seal tightly. Shake to mix.

For the salad, toss the shrimp with the sesame dressing in a bowl. Arrange the salad greens evenly on 6 plates and top each with 4 shrimp in a swirling pattern. Arrange the mango, papaya, grapefruit and avocado around the shrimp and place the tomato in the center. Drizzle with the vinegar dressing and serve immediately.

KATE GILMER PHILLIPS

CHICKEN PASTA SALAD

Great for picnics.

SERVES 6 TO 8

6 boneless skinless chicken breasts,
    cooked and finely chopped (6 cups)
1/4 cup balsamic vinegar
1 1/2 teaspoons salt
8 ounces linguini or rotini
1 tablespoon olive oil
1 (8-ounce) can whole kernel yellow
    corn, drained
1 cup finely chopped celery
1/2 cup chopped red bell pepper
1/2 cup chopped yellow bell pepper
1/2 cup chopped fresh parsley
3/4 cup mayonnaise
2 teaspoons lemon juice
1/2 teaspoon dill weed
1/2 teaspoon celery seeds
1/4 teaspoon Creole seasoning
1/8 teaspoon pepper

Toss the chicken with the vinegar and salt in a bowl. Chill, covered, for 8 to 10 hours. Cook the pasta using package directions and drain. Toss the pasta with the olive oil in a bowl. Combine the chicken, corn, celery, bell peppers and parsley in a bowl and mix well.

Mix the mayonnaise, lemon juice, dill weed, celery seeds, Creole seasoning and pepper in a bowl and add to the chicken mixture. Add the pasta and toss until combined. Chill, covered, in the refrigerator. Taste and adjust the seasonings before serving.

LEE HARCROW TAPSCOTT

Between 1982 and 2004 over $3.7 million was raised through proceeds from the Antiques and Garden Show to fund JLB community projects.

The League's "Can You Dig It?" program showcases the Birmingham Botanical Gardens to inner-city school children through hands-on learning in an authentic environment surrounded by nature.

SUN-DRIED TOMATO BASIL PASTA SALAD

Prepare this in the morning and it will be ready at supper time.

MAKES 10 CUPS

4 (6-ounce) boneless skinless chicken breasts
Greek seasoning to taste
16 ounces penne
4 ounces tomato-basil feta cheese, crumbled
1¹/2 cups fresh basil, finely chopped
1¹/2 cups fresh parsley, finely chopped
1 bunch green onions, chopped
1 (3-ounce) jar oil-pack sun-dried tomatoes,
    drained and julienned
1 yellow bell pepper, chopped
1 (8-ounce) bottle light Caesar Dressing
Mixed greens or baby spinach
Pine nuts for garnish

Preheat the grill. Season the chicken with Greek seasoning and grill over hot coals until cooked through. Cool slightly and chop. Cook the pasta using the package directions until al dente and drain. Combine the chicken, pasta, cheese, basil, parsley, green onions, sun-dried tomatoes and bell pepper in a bowl and mix well. Add ³/4 of the dressing to the chicken mixture and toss to coat.

Chill, covered, for 8 hours. Add the remaining dressing to the pasta salad just before serving and mix well. Serve on a bed of mixed greens and garnish with pine nuts. For testing purposes, Ken's Lite Caesar Dressing was used.

MARGARET REYNOLDS OPOLKA

GLOSSARY

Coarsely chop: *This term implies that the cut shapes and sizes do not have to be uniform, and it generally intends that pieces will be rather chunky.*

Chop: *This term implies a bit more uniformity in the shapes and sizes of the end product, and it usually intends that pieces will be cut into* 1/2- *to* 3/4-*inch square pieces.*

Dice: *This term implies precision in the cutting, and it intends that the end product will be uniform and about* 1/4-*inch square.*

Mince: *This term means to chop food (usually garlic and herbs) into tiny uniform pieces.*

Julienne: *This term directs you to cut (usually vegetables or fruit) into matchsticks, about* 1/8 *inch wide,* 1/8 *inch thick, and 1 to 2 inches long.*

Chiffonade: *This term usually refers to herbs and it means to cut into thin ribbons.*

Broccoli Slaw with Blue Cheese and Bacon

MAKES 10 CUPS

1 (12-ounce) package broccoli florets	1/2 to 1 cup dried cranberries
1 (12-ounce) package broccoli slaw	1/2 cup finely chopped red onion
4 ounces blue cheese, crumbled	1 (12-ounce) bottle coleslaw dressing
1/2 cup crumbled crisp-cooked bacon	Salt and pepper to taste

Combine the broccoli florets, broccoli slaw, cheese, bacon, cranberries and onion in a bowl and mix well. Add the dressing and toss to coat. Season to taste with salt and pepper.

Chill, covered, for 2 hours or longer before serving. You may substitute Homemade Slaw Dressing on page 109 for the commercially prepared coleslaw dressing.

JENNIFER BOLEN ROGERS

Mom's Favorite Slaw

This is a GREAT slaw and a wonderful crowd pleaser.

SERVES 8

Blue Cheese Dressing	Slaw
1/2 cup mayonnaise	4 cups shredded green cabbage
1/2 cup crumbled blue cheese	2 cups shredded purple cabbage
1/4 cup buttermilk	1/4 cup chopped onion
2 teaspoons minced garlic	2 teaspoons chives
1 teaspoon kosher salt	1/2 cup crumbled blue cheese
1 teaspoon pepper	1/4 cup crumbled crisp-cooked bacon
1/16 teaspoon sugar	1/4 cup chopped green bell pepper

For the dressing, combine the mayonnaise, cheese, buttermilk, garlic, salt, pepper and sugar in a food processor and process to the desired consistency.

For the slaw, toss the cabbage, onion and chives in a large bowl. Add the dressing and mix until coated. Stir in the cheese, bacon and bell pepper and chill, covered, for 3 to 4 hours.

MELANIE REMMERT KOHN

COPPER PENNIES

This is an old but familiar salad that can be prepared in advance and served as a side dish.

SERVES 8 TO 10

2 pounds carrots, peeled
Salt to taste
1 green bell pepper, sliced
2 small onions, sliced and separated
   into rings
1 (10-ounce) can tomato soup

1 cup sugar
3/4 cup apple cider vinegar
1/2 cup vegetable oil
1 teaspoon Worcestershire sauce
Pepper to taste

Slice the carrots into rounds to resemble pennies. Combine the carrots and salt with enough water to cover in a saucepan and bring to a boil. Boil for 12 to 15 minutes or until the carrots are tender. Drain and cool. Alternate layers of the carrots, bell pepper and onions in a large bowl until all of the ingredients are used. Whisk the soup, sugar, vinegar, oil, Worcestershire sauce, salt and pepper in a bowl until blended and pour over the layers. Marinate, covered, in the refrigerator for several hours. Drain most of the marinade before serving.

LEANN HOLIFIELD COX

SUMMER CORN AND TOMATO SALAD

SERVES 4

2 ears Silver Queen or Silver King
   corn, shucked
4 ripe tomatoes, peeled and cut into
   1/4-inch slices
3 green onions, chopped
2 tablespoons extra-virgin olive oil

2 tablespoons balsamic vinegar
Salt and freshly ground pepper to taste
2 ounces (or more) feta cheese,
   crumbled
1 tablespoon fresh thyme

Cook the corn in boiling water in a saucepan for 3 minutes. Immediately plunge the corn into a bowl of ice water to stop the cooking process. Let stand until cool and drain. Cut the kernels off the cob into a bowl using a sharp knife.

Arrange the tomato slices overlapping on a large platter. Sprinkle with the corn and green onions. Whisk the olive oil and vinegar in a bowl until blended and season to taste with salt and pepper. Drizzle the olive oil mixture over the prepared layers and sprinkle with the cheese and thyme. Serve at room temperature. For a different flavor, sprinkle with 2 teaspoons chopped fresh rosemary and garlic salt.

PAT McCABE FORMAN

EDAMAME SALAD

Edamame is a sophisticated name for soybeans and is considered to be an acquired taste. This salad is healthy and best eaten the day of preparation. Soybeans can be found in the organic section of most grocery stores.

SERVES 8 TO 10

1 (16-ounce) package frozen
    edamame, shelled
4 to 6 ounces grape
    tomatoes, chopped
1/2 small red onion, chopped
2 tablespoons balsamic vinegar

1 tablespoon olive oil
1/2 teaspoon salt
Pepper to taste
4 ounces Parmesan cheese, freshly
    grated (no substitutions)

Cook the soybeans using the package directions. Drain and rinse. Combine the soybeans, tomatoes and onion in a bowl and mix well. Whisk the vinegar, olive oil, salt and pepper in a bowl until blended and stir into the soybean mixture. Chill, covered, until serving time. Stir in the cheese just before serving.

ELIZABETH LASSITER FITZPATRICK

CRUNCHY SPRING SALAD

SERVES 10

Red Wine Vinaigrette
1/2 cup vegetable oil
1/2 cup sugar
3 tablespoons red wine vinegar
1/4 teaspoon salt
1/4 teaspoon pepper

Salad
1 (20-ounce) can mandarin
    oranges, drained
1 package ramen noodles, broken and
    toasted (discard seasoning packet)
10 ounces spring salad mix
4 ounces feta cheese, crumbled
1 cup pecan halves, toasted
1/2 cup dried cranberries

For the vinaigrette, combine the oil, sugar, vinegar, salt and pepper in a jar with a tight-fitting lid and seal tightly. Shake to blend. Chill in the freezer for 10 minutes or in the refrigerator for 30 minutes.

For the salad, toss the oranges, noodles, salad mix, cheese, pecans and cranberries in a salad bowl. Add the vinaigrette and mix well. Serve immediately.

LORI JOHNSON GOODSON

ROQUEFORT SALAD

SERVES 4 TO 6

Roquefort Vinaigrette
4 ounces Roquefort cheese, coarsely crumbled
2 tablespoons white wine vinegar
1 tablespoon chopped fresh parsley
1 shallot, finely chopped
Salt and pepper to taste
1 tablespoon Dijon mustard
1/2 cup olive oil
3 tablespoons buttermilk

Salad
1 head Boston lettuce, separated into leaves
1 small cucumber, peeled and sliced
2 tomatoes, sliced
1/4 red onion, sliced
1 cup chopped fresh parsley
Salt and pepper to taste
1 tablespoon pine nuts for garnish
Crumbled Roquefort cheese for garnish

For the vinaigrette, place the cheese in a bowl and add the vinegar, parsley and shallot. Season to taste with salt and pepper and mix well. Stir in the Dijon mustard. Add the olive oil in a steady stream, whisking constantly until blended. Stir in the buttermilk. Taste and adjust the seasonings.

For the salad, mix the lettuce, cucumber, tomatoes and onion in a large salad bowl. Add the parsley and season to taste with salt and pepper. Add the vinaigrette and toss to coat. Sprinkle with the pine nuts and cheese and serve immediately.

CAROLYN RITCHEY KING

DINNER SALAD WITH CRANBERRIES AND PECANS

SERVES 6 TO 8

1 cup pecan halves
1/2 cup extra-virgin olive oil
1/4 cup red wine vinegar
3 garlic cloves, crushed
3 tablespoons lemon juice
1 teaspoon salt

1/2 teaspoon pepper
1/4 teaspoon dry mustard
8 ounces spring salad mix
1/2 cup dried cranberries
1 cup crumbled feta cheese

Spread the pecans in a single layer on a microwave-safe plate lined with waxed paper. Microwave on High for 1 minute and stir. Microwave for 20 seconds longer if needed to toast the pecans.

Combine the olive oil, vinegar, garlic, lemon juice, salt, pepper and dry mustard in a jar with a tight-fitting lid and seal tightly. Shake to combine. Toss the pecans, salad mix, cranberries and cheese in a salad bowl. Add 1/4 cup of the vinaigrette and toss to coat. Taste and add additional vinaigrette if desired. Serve immediately. Store the remaining vinaigrette in the refrigerator.

AIMEE SISK PRUITT

HEARTS OF PALM AND ARTICHOKE SALAD

SERVES 6

1 (14-ounce) can artichoke hearts,
    drained and chopped
1 (14-ounce) can hearts of palm,
    drained and chopped
4 ounces blue cheese, crumbled
1/4 cup crumbled crisp-cooked bacon
    (about 6 slices)
1/4 cup chopped green onions

2 tablespoons finely chopped
    fresh parsley
2 garlic cloves, crushed
6 tablespoons olive oil
2 tablespoons lemon juice
Salt and cracked pepper to taste
1 1/2 heads romaine

Mix the artichokes and hearts of palm in a bowl. Stir in the cheese, bacon, green onions, parsley and garlic. Whisk the olive oil and lemon juice in a bowl until blended and add to the artichoke mixture, tossing to coat. Season to taste with salt and pepper. Chill, covered, in the refrigerator. Tear the romaine into bite-size pieces and place in a sealable plastic bag. Chill in the refrigerator. To serve, toss the lettuce with the artichoke mixture in a bowl and spoon onto chilled salad plates.

KIMBERLY ARMBRUSTER TEW

OLIVE SALAD

*This is a very popular salad any time of the year. Great served on crackers with
cream cheese, added to pasta, or used on a sandwich like a muffuletta.*

MAKES 7 CUPS

4 cups pimento-stuffed green olives
1 cup black olives
1 cup kalamata olives
1 cup carrots
2 ribs celery
1/2 red bell pepper

1/2 yellow bell pepper
1 teaspoon minced garlic
2 tablespoons olive oil
1 tablespoon balsamic vinegar
Salt and pepper to taste

Process the green olives, black olives, kalamata olives, carrots, celery, red bell pepper and yellow bell
pepper separately in a food processor until finely chopped, adding each ingredient to a large bowl after
processing. Add the garlic to the olive mixture and mix well. Whisk the olive oil and vinegar in a bowl
until emulsified and add to the olive mixture, tossing to coat. Store, covered, in the refrigerator.

HOME GROWN SPECIAL FOODS, HOMEWOOD, ALABAMA

PEPPER PLACE VEGETABLE SALAD

*During the summer months, Pepper Place Saturday Market is a favorite spot to socialize with friends,
take in a cooking demonstration, or buy the freshest produce in the state of Alabama.*

SERVES 4 TO 6

Red Wine Vinaigrette
1/3 cup canola oil
3 tablespoons red wine vinegar
2 tablespoons sugar
2 or 3 drops of Tabasco sauce
    (optional)
Salt and pepper to taste

Salad
2 large cucumbers, peeled,
    seeded and chopped
1 large tomato, peeled, seeded
    and chopped
1 small green bell pepper, chopped
1 small purple onion, chopped

For the vinaigrette, combine the canola oil, vinegar, sugar, Tabasco sauce, salt and pepper in a jar with
a tight-fitting lid and seal tightly. Shake to mix.

For the salad, combine the cucumbers, tomato, bell pepper and onion in a salad bowl and mix well.
Add the vinaigrette and toss to coat. Chill, covered, for 3 hours or longer before serving.

LISA BELL LEWIS

SOUTHERN POTATO SALAD

MAKES 6 CUPS

2 pounds Idaho or russet potatoes, peeled
Salt to taste
1/3 cup vegetable oil
2 tablespoons apple cider vinegar
1 teaspoon salt
1 teaspoon freshly ground pepper
1/4 teaspoon dry mustard
1/4 teaspoon paprika
2/3 cup chopped celery
1 onion, minced
3 hard-boiled eggs, chopped
1/2 cup mayonnaise
1 tablespoon prepared mustard
1 teaspoon celery salt
1 tablespoon finely chopped fresh flat-leaf
    parsley for garnish
Paprika for garnish

Combine the potatoes and salt to taste with enough water to cover in a saucepan and bring to a boil. Boil for 10 to 12 minutes or until tender but not mushy. Drain the potatoes and cut into bite-size pieces and place in a large bowl. Whisk the oil, vinegar, 1 teaspoon salt, pepper, dry mustard and 1/4 teaspoon paprika in a bowl until combined. Pour over the warm potatoes and mix gently. Chill, covered, in the refrigerator.

Add the celery, onion, eggs, mayonnaise, prepared mustard and celery salt to the potato mixture several hours before serving and return to the refrigerator. Garnish with the parsley and additional paprika just before serving.

PAIGE DOWDY ALBRIGHT

The "Can You Dig It?" program at the Botanical Gardens is critical to continuing education outside the classroom. JLB volunteers continue to lead field trips for more than 3,000 Birmingham city school students each year.

MEDITERRANEAN POTATO SALAD

SERVES 6

Olive Oil Vinaigrette
1/4 cup olive oil
1/4 cup red wine vinegar
Kosher salt and pepper to taste

Potato Salad
1 pound unpeeled small white creamer
    potatoes
1 pound unpeeled small red creamer potatoes
3/4 cup chopped tomato
1/2 cup chopped fresh parsley
1/2 green bell pepper, chopped
1 shallot, finely chopped
3/4 teaspoon salt

For the vinaigrette, combine the olive oil, vinegar, salt and pepper in a jar with a tight fitting lid and seal tightly. Shake to blend.

For the salad, combine the potatoes with enough water to cover in a saucepan and bring to a boil. Boil for 10 minutes or until tender and drain. Mix the potatoes, tomato, parsley, bell pepper, shallot and salt in a bowl. Add the vinaigrette to the potato mixture and toss to coat. Serve at room temperature. For a variation, cut the potatoes into bite-size pieces.

RHANYA LYNN MALKI

Photograph for this recipe on page 112.

THINK LIKE A CHEF

Always read through the entire recipe before you begin. Take out all of the ingredients that you'll need, and do all of your chopping, slicing, measuring, toasting, and other prep in advance. This will make the recipe much quicker and easier to assemble and cook.

Many ingredients can be prepared in advance. You can even peel potatoes or sweet potatoes hours before they are needed. Simply peel, cut to the desired size and shape, and store them in water to maintain crispness and color.

PAINTED SOUTHWESTERN SALAD

*Great with barbecue or as a summer side salad. May be prepared in advance
and stored, covered, in the refrigerator. Be sure to use gloves when seeding chiles and
onions to prevent hands from smelling.*

MAKES 12 CUPS

White Wine Vinaigrette
3/4 cup olive oil
1/4 cup white wine vinegar
1 teaspoon salt
1/4 teaspoon tarragon
1/4 teaspoon pepper

Salad
2 (16-ounce) cans chick-peas, drained and rinsed
2 (11-ounce) cans white Shoe Peg corn, drained and rinsed
1 (16-ounce) can black beans, drained and rinsed
1 (2-ounce) can sliced black olives, drained
8 ounces feta cheese, crumbled
1 large purple onion, chopped (1 1/2 to 2 cups)
1 red bell pepper, chopped
1/2 bunch cilantro, chopped (1/2 cup)
1 jalapeño chile, seeded and finely chopped
    (1 1/2 tablespoons)

For the vinaigrette, combine the olive oil, vinegar, salt, tarragon and pepper in a jar with a tight-fitting lid and seal tightly. Shake to combine.

For the salad, combine the chick-peas, corn, beans, olives, cheese, onion, bell pepper, cilantro and jalapeño chile in a bowl and mix well. Add the vinaigrette and toss to coat. Spoon into a glass serving bowl and chill, covered, until serving time.

KELLY ELIZABETH STRAUGHN

FRESH TOMATOES WITH CHAMPAGNE VINAIGRETTE

SERVES 6

Champagne Vinaigrette
2 tablespoons Champagne vinegar
2 shallots, minced
Salt and freshly ground pepper to taste
2 tablespoons plus 1 teaspoon
    extra-virgin olive oil

Salad
5 ripe tomatoes of assorted sizes,
    colors and varieties
10 to 12 cherry tomatoes and/or
    yellow pear tomatoes
3 cups assorted lettuce
2 tablespoons chopped fresh thyme
    for garnish

For the vinaigrette, mix the vinegar, shallots, salt and pepper in a bowl. Add the olive oil gradually, whisking constantly until combined.

For the salad, cut the assorted tomatoes into slices and wedges. Leave the cherry tomatoes and pear tomatoes whole. Toss the tomatoes with some of the vinaigrette in a bowl. Line 6 salad plates with the lettuce and arrange the tomatoes over the lettuce. Drizzle with the desired amount of vinaigrette and garnish with the thyme.

ANNA BICKLEY COOPER

SEVEN VEGETABLE SALAD

MAKES 12 CUPS

1 (15-ounce) can white Shoe Peg
    corn, drained
1 (15-ounce) can French-style green
    beans, drained
1 (15-ounce) can green peas, drained
1 (2-ounce) jar pimento, drained

1 cup chopped celery
1 onion, chopped
1 red or yellow bell pepper, chopped
2/3 cup sugar
1/3 cup white vinegar
1/3 cup olive oil

Combine the corn, beans, peas, pimento, celery, onion and bell pepper in a bowl and mix well. Bring the sugar, vinegar and olive oil to a boil in a saucepan and boil until the sugar dissolves, stirring frequently. Remove from the heat and let stand until cool. Pour the vinegar mixture over the corn mixture and toss to coat. Chill, covered, until serving time.

HOLLY HOLMES WILLIAMS

TOMATO SALAD
WITH BASIL OIL DRESSING

This dressing can be used on pork, grilled chicken, and pasta.

SERVES 6

Basil Oil Dressing
3 cups loosely packed fresh basil leaves
    (3 ounces)
3/4 cup extra-virgin olive oil
1 tablespoon fresh lemon juice
1 teaspoon kosher salt
1 garlic clove

Tomato Salad
3 pounds fresh heirloom tomatoes of various
    assortments and sizes
3 ounces goat cheese
Salt and freshly ground pepper to taste
6 sprigs of basil for garnish

For the dressing, combine the basil, olive oil, lemon juice, salt and garlic in a blender or food processor and process until smooth.

For the salad, core each tomato and cut into halves. Cut each half into quarters. Arrange the tomatoes evenly on 6 salad plates. Crumble 1/2 ounce of the goat cheese over each serving and season to taste with salt and pepper. Drizzle about 2 tablespoons of the dressing over each salad and garnish with a sprig of basil. Serve immediately.

JULIE GRIMES BOTTCHER

Photograph for this recipe on page 84.

The Basil Oil Dressing is a snap to make and will keep in the refrigerator for up to one week. The oil will solidify in the refrigerator. Bring to room temperature before serving.

SWEET BALSAMIC DRESSING

MAKES 1¹/₂ CUPS

¹/₂ cup red or white balsamic vinegar
¹/₂ cup olive oil
¹/₂ cup vegetable oil
¹/₄ cup sugar
¹/₄ cup fresh parsley, chopped
2 teaspoons salt
¹/₄ teaspoon pepper
4 dashes of Tabasco sauce

Combine the vinegar, olive oil, vegetable oil, sugar, parsley, salt, pepper and Tabasco sauce in a jar with a tight-fitting lid and seal tightly. Shake to combine. Drizzle over chilled asparagus, tomatoes or hearts of palm. Store in the refrigerator for up to 1 month. Bring to room temperature before serving.

JILL DEWITT ACOSTA

BLACKBERRY PRESERVE SALAD DRESSING

MAKES 1¹/₂ CUPS

³/₄ cup vegetable oil
¹/₂ (10-ounce) jar seedless blackberry
   or raspberry preserves
¹/₄ cup red wine vinegar or raspberry
   wine vinegar
6 fresh basil leaves
1 garlic clove, chopped
¹/₂ teaspoon salt
¹/₂ teaspoon pepper

Combine the oil, preserves, vinegar, basil, garlic, salt and pepper in a blender or food processor and pulse until smooth. Store in the refrigerator.

MARY CARSON BAKER LARUSSA

HOMEMADE SLAW DRESSING

Whisk 1 cup white vinegar, 3/4 cup sugar, 1/3 cup vegetable oil, 1 teaspoon salt and 1/4 teaspoon freshly ground pepper in a bowl until blended or process in a blender until smooth.

HERB VINAIGRETTE

MAKES 1¹/₄ CUPS

¹/₄ cup red wine vinegar
3 tablespoons chopped fresh basil
3 tablespoons chopped fresh chives
3 tablespoons chopped fresh flat-leaf parsley
2 tablespoons finely chopped shallots
1 tablespoon Dijon mustard
1 tablespoon honey
¹/₄ teaspoon salt
¹/₄ teaspoon freshly ground pepper
³/₄ cup olive oil

Whisk the vinegar, basil, chives, parsley, shallots, Dijon mustard, honey, salt and pepper in a medium bowl until combined. Add the olive oil gradually, whisking constantly until the olive oil is incorporated.

SHARON HILYER JONES

HONEY DIJON DRESSING

MAKES 4 CUPS

2 cups mayonnaise
¹/₂ cup plus 1 tablespoon Dijon mustard
¹/₂ cup plus 1 tablespoon honey
¹/₂ cup vegetable oil
¹/₃ cup apple cider vinegar
¹/₄ teaspoon kosher salt
¹/₈ teaspoon garlic powder
¹/₈ teaspoon cayenne pepper

Combine the mayonnaise, Dijon mustard, honey, oil, vinegar, salt, garlic powder and cayenne pepper in a bowl and mix well. Store, covered, in the refrigerator for up to 21 days. Discard the dressing when the oil begins to separate.

SUSAN CARTER HANCOCK

CREAMY LEMON DRESSING

Light and very easy to prepare.

MAKES 1 CUP

1/4 cup lemon juice
1 1/2 teaspoons Dijon mustard
1 teaspoon grated lemon zest
1 teaspoon Worcestershire sauce

2 garlic cloves, finely chopped
1/2 teaspoon each salt and pepper
1/2 cup extra-virgin olive oil
1 1/2 tablespoons sour cream

Combine the lemon juice, Dijon mustard, lemon zest, Worcestershire sauce, garlic, salt and pepper in a bowl and mix well. Add the olive oil gradually, whisking constantly until the olive oil is incorporated and the mixture is smooth. Whisk in the sour cream until blended. Store, covered, in the refrigerator.

ANDREA GARRETT MCCASKEY

THAI PEANUT DRESSING

Serve this dressing over mixed salad greens or pair with chicken, pork, or an Asian-inspired pasta dish.

MAKES 1 1/4 CUPS

1 green onion, coarsely chopped
3 tablespoons crunchy peanut butter
3 tablespoons fresh lime juice
3 tablespoons rice vinegar
3 tablespoons soy sauce
3 tablespoons honey
3/4 teaspoon kosher salt

1 (2-inch) piece fresh ginger, peeled
    and finely chopped
1 garlic clove, minced
1/4 cup peanut oil or corn oil
1 tablespoon dark sesame oil
2 green onions, finely chopped
1 tablespoon crunchy peanut butter

Process 1 green onion, 3 tablespoons peanut butter, the lime juice, vinegar, soy sauce, honey, salt, ginger and garlic in a blender until combined, scraping the side as needed. Strain the peanut butter mixture through a sieve, discarding the solids. Return the strained mixture to the blender. Whisk the peanut oil and sesame oil in a bowl until blended and gradually add to the peanut butter mixture, processing constantly at low speed until the oil mixture is incorporated. Pour into a small bowl and whisk in 2 green onions and 1 tablespoon peanut butter. Serve immediately or chill, covered, in the refrigerator.

STEPHANIE GIBSON MIMS

From the Garden

SPECIALTY OILS

Just as Italians have long extolled the virtues of extra-virgin olive oil, the French have been using quality toasted nut oils, and Asian cuisine has relied on toasted sesame oil. These oils are gaining popularity in America because of their superior flavor, but many of them have gained an even wider following because of their health benefits. Much more than a mere cooking medium, these oils play a role as significant as any other ingredient in the dish—they are supreme examples of oil as a seasoning.

Grilled Lemon Chicken Salad

Mediterranean Potato Salad

EXTRA-VIRGIN OLIVE OIL comes from the first pressing of olives, and as the most prized unrefined oil it is rare and expensive. True extra-virgin or cold-pressed olive oil has a strong fruity aroma along with an amazing olive flavor and a peppery bite.

To select the best olive oil, buy the freshest. If you cannot tell when the oil was produced, it may not be worth the extra expense. Look on the bottle for the expiration date, which will usually be two years after the oil was made, since this is roughly the shelf life. Or better yet, look to see if the bottle tells you when the olives were harvested, as the oil will have been produced immediately afterward.

Specialty nut oils are more common and increasingly available. They are also delicious. A few drops of toasted walnut oil will breathe new life into ordinary pasta or rice. The secret to these nut and seed oils is the toasting. Think of the difference between raw and toasted nuts. It is the same concept with the oil. Below is a list of oils with a bit about the flavor and the characteristics of each.

WALNUT OIL: Imagine the essence of toasted walnuts in a bottle, complete with all of their healthy monounsaturated fats and Omega-3 fatty acids. This delicious oil is fabulous in most any vinaigrette. It works well in pasta dishes, paired with butternut squash, blue cheese, apples, or pears, and for a tasty snack drizzled over popcorn.

ALMOND OIL: This subtle, delicate oil has been the darling of the health-conscious crowd for years. It is low in saturated fats and high in vitamin E. Use this oil with fish, chicken, and summer stone fruits, such as peaches, plums, and apricots.

AVOCADO OIL: The oil is extracted from the flesh (not the seed) of the ripe fruit, so the oil tastes like liquid avocado. Obviously it works in vinaigrettes. Or pair with beef, pork, shrimp, and/or tomatoes, or brush on grilled corn instead of butter.

TRUFFLE OIL: The heady aroma of truffles captivates chefs and food lovers. These fungi are wild, difficult to find, and therefore highly prized. Olive oil or sometimes grapeseed oil is infused with truffles to form a flavorful and pricey oil. Use as a dipping oil, pair with mushrooms, or drizzle over pasta dishes or pizza as a finishing touch.

SESAME OIL: Toasted sesame oil is a secret ingredient in the Asian pantry. Just a bit goes a long way. Use this oil in dipping sauces, stir-fries, and noodle dishes.

HIGH NOON

SUGGESTED WINES:
- *Broglia Gavi Di Gavi 2004*
- *Esencia Valdemar Grenache Rosé 2004*
- *Saracco Moscato D'Asti 2004*

Assorted Dressings

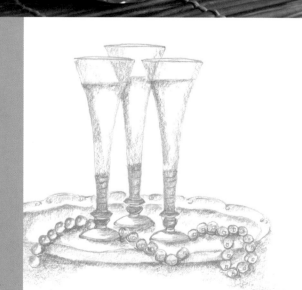

Watermelon, Tomato, Feta Cheese Salad with Fresh Mint

Grains of Knowledge

PASTA, BREADS AND GRAINS

Nurse a wounded bird to health or feed a llama by hand. Experience a butterfly landing on your finger, stroke a python, or adopt your favorite animal—all at Alabama's most popular nonprofit attraction, the Birmingham Zoo. For more than fifty years, the Birmingham Zoo has served as one of Alabama's favorite attractions and currently draws more than 450,000 visitors annually.

The Birmingham Zoo offers many opportunities for "grains of knowledge" about animals and their environments through such activities as camps, classes, educational programs, and volunteer opportunities. Approximately 750 animals of 250 species live in well-maintained environments that reflect their natural habitats. The Junior League of Birmingham-Hugh Kaul Children's Zoo is a fifteen-million-dollar anchor exhibit dedicated to educating children about their natural environment. Its focus is urban, rural, and wild animals and environs of Alabama. But it is great fun as well, with spurting fountains, a carousel, and a petting zoo mimicking a real working farm.

It is grains of cereal, wheat, and rice that form the foundation for many wonderful recipes found in this chapter. Try Rosemary Olive Bread on page 135, Cream Cheese and Chive Potato Bread on page 137, Sausage, Apple and Sage Stuffing on page 141, or Spoon Rolls on page 140. For where there are grains, there is a meal to feed and satisfy the mind, the body, and the soul.

Visit the Birmingham Zoo at www.birminghamzoo.com.

Birmingham Zoo

Rosemary Olive Bread

Pasta, Breads and Grains

CONTENTS

SEAFOOD PASTA PRIMAVERA

SERVES 6

9 ounces fresh angel hair pasta
1 tablespoon olive oil
1/2 cup (1 stick) margarine
1 onion, finely chopped
1 garlic clove, minced
1 carrot, thinly sliced
4 ounces broccoli florets
4 ounces snow peas (optional)
2 tablespoons Chef Paul Prudhomme's Magic
    Seasoning Blends Vegetable Magic
Salt and pepper to taste
1 tablespoon brandy
1 cup half-and-half
1 pound shrimp, peeled and deveined
8 ounces scallops

Cook the pasta using the package directions, adding the olive oil to the water. Drain the pasta and place in a heated bowl. Melt the margarine in a large sauté pan over medium-high heat and add the onion and garlic. Sauté until the onion is tender. Stir in the carrot, broccoli, snow peas, Chef Paul Prudhomme's seasoning, salt and pepper.

Sauté until the vegetables are tender-crisp. Add the brandy and cook until the alcohol evaporates. Stir in the half-and-half and cook over medium heat for 4 to 5 minutes or until thickened, stirring frequently. Add the shrimp and scallops and cook for 4 minutes, stirring occasionally. Add the seafood sauce to the pasta and toss to mix. Serve immediately.

EILEEN HALLMARK

CHICKEN TETRAZZINI

My neighbor, Jennifer Gentle, made this for me after I had a baby. Now I take this dish to all of my friends when they have babies, and we all love it.

SERVES 8

1/2 cup (1 stick) butter
1/2 cup all-purpose flour
2 cups heavy cream or whipping cream
1 1/2 cups chicken broth
6 tablespoons white wine
1 teaspoon salt
1 teaspoon white pepper
3 cups chopped cooked chicken breasts
8 ounces angel hair pasta, cooked
1/2 cup (2 ounces) shredded Parmesan cheese
2 tablespoons butter
1/2 cup fresh bread crumbs
1/4 teaspoon salt

Preheat the oven to 325 degrees. Melt 1/2 cup butter in a large stockpot over medium-high heat. Whisk in the flour until blended and cook for 1 minute, whisking constantly. Stir in the cream, broth, wine, 1 teaspoon salt and white pepper and bring to a boil.

Cook for 8 minutes or until thick and bubbly, whisking constantly. Remove from the heat and stir in the chicken, pasta and cheese. Spoon the pasta mixture into a greased 9×13-inch baking dish.

Melt 2 tablespoons butter in a skillet. Brown the bread crumbs in the butter and remove from the heat. Stir in 1/4 teaspoon salt and sprinkle the bread crumb mixture over the top of the chicken mixture. Bake for 20 minutes or until brown and bubbly.

ADRIANA WAHL MORROS

GRILLED MARINATED PORTOBELLO MUSHROOMS OVER ANGEL HAIR PASTA

*This is a quick and easy weeknight supper that I suggest serving with a side salad.
The grilled portobello mushrooms may also be served as an appetizer.*

SERVES 6

1/2 cup canola oil
1/3 cup red wine vinegar
1/3 cup light teriyaki sauce
1/4 cup sugar
3 tablespoons balsamic vinegar
2 dashes of Tabasco sauce
Salt and pepper to taste
6 portobello mushroom caps
16 ounces angel hair pasta
6 tablespoons butter, softened
Chopped fresh parsley for garnish
Freshly grated Parmesan cheese for garnish

Whisk the canola oil, red wine vinegar, teriyaki sauce, sugar, balsamic vinegar, Tabasco sauce, salt and pepper in a bowl until blended. Slice the mushroom caps into halves and place in a large sealable plastic bag. Pour the oil mixture over the mushrooms and seal the bag tightly. Turn to coat and marinate in the refrigerator for 15 minutes, turning occasionally.

Preheat the grill to medium. Cook the pasta using the package directions. Drain and toss with the butter until coated. Cover to keep warm. Drain the mushrooms, discarding the marinade. Grill the mushrooms for 6 minutes, turning once. Slice the mushrooms into spears and arrange over the hot buttered pasta on a serving platter. Sprinkle with parsley and cheese and serve immediately.

KATHRYN LAVALLET TORTORICI

For more than twenty-five years the JLB has participated in the Partners in Education program with Lincoln and Glenn Middle Schools. The JLB has been recognized as "Partner of the Year" multiple times.

120

ANGEL HAIR PASTA

SERVES 6

16 ounces angel hair pasta, cooked
    and chilled
5 Roma tomatoes, cut into halves
1 tablespoon extra-virgin olive oil
1 tablespoon chopped fresh basil
Salt and pepper to taste
3 tablespoons extra-virgin olive oil
2 garlic cloves, minced
2 teaspoons red pepper flakes
1 roasted red bell pepper, peeled, seeded
    and chopped
2 tablespoons red wine vinegar
7 tablespoons chopped fresh basil
1/4 cup chopped fresh parsley
4 ounces feta cheese, crumbled

Preheat the oven to 375 degrees. Place the chilled pasta in a bowl. Toss the
tomatoes, 1 tablespoon olive oil, 1 tablespoon basil, salt and pepper in a roasting
pan until coated. Roast for 12 to 15 minutes or until the tomatoes are blistered.
Remove the tomatoes to a bowl and crush.

Heat 3 tablespoons olive oil in a medium sauté pan over medium heat. Add the
garlic and red pepper flakes and sauté for 1 minute. Remove from the heat and
mix in the roasted red pepper and vinegar. Add to the crushed tomatoes and mix
well. Add the crushed tomato mixture to the pasta and stir in 7 tablespoons basil,
the parsley and cheese. Season to taste with salt and pepper. You may substitute
3 tablespoons chopped drained jarred roasted red pepper for 1 roasted red
bell pepper.

JASON MEZRANO, KATHY MEZRANO, KATHY G & COMPANY

*Partners in Education
projects have included
tutoring, clothes closets,
field trips, and honor roll
incentive programs.*

EASY CRAWFISH FETTUCCINI

My husband, who is one hundred percent Cajun, loves this recipe.
Double the recipe and freeze for future use.

SERVES 8 TO 10

1/2 cup (1 stick) butter
1 cup chopped yellow onion
5 garlic cloves, minced
1 pound crawfish tail meat
1 (10-ounce) can cream of mushroom soup
1 cup sour cream
8 ounces Velveeta cheese, chopped
1 tablespoon Cajun seasoning
2 teaspoons salt
8 ounces fresh fettuccini, cooked and drained
3/4 cup (3 ounces) grated Parmesan cheese

Preheat the oven to 350 degrees. Melt the butter in a stockpot and add the onion. Sauté for 4 minutes and add the garlic. Sauté for 1 minute longer. Stir in the crawfish, soup, sour cream, Velveeta cheese, Cajun seasoning and salt.

Bring to a simmer and simmer until the cheese melts, stirring constantly. Add the pasta and toss to combine. Spoon the crawfish mixture into a greased 2-quart baking dish and sprinkle with the Parmesan cheese. Bake for 25 minutes or until heated through.

LYNN ALLEN ORTIS

Frozen seafood can be found at seafood markets and grocery stores when seafood is out of season.

FETTUCCINI WITH CHICKEN AND PESTO

Rotisserie chicken works well for this dish. An average-size bird should yield about four cups of chicken. One seven-ounce jar of commercially prepared pesto will also work. For a tasty variation, substitute feta cheese for the Parmesan cheese and sausage for the chicken.

SERVES 4 TO 6

9 ounces fresh fettuccini
2/3 cup basil pesto
2/3 cup part-skim ricotta cheese
1/4 cup (1 ounce) grated Parmesan cheese
2 tablespoons olive oil
3 garlic cloves, minced
1/2 teaspoon (or more) red pepper flakes
2 cups fresh baby spinach
4 cups shredded cooked chicken
1 (7-ounce) jar roasted red peppers, drained
    and coarsely chopped
1/2 cup kalamata olives, coarsely chopped
1/4 cup (1 ounce) grated Parmesan cheese

Cook the pasta using the package directions. Drain, reserving 1/3 cup of the cooking liquid. Combine the pesto, ricotta cheese and 1/4 cup Parmesan cheese in a serving bowl and mix well. Add the pasta and reserved cooking liquid and mix well.

Heat the olive oil in a large sauté pan over medium-high heat. Sauté the garlic and red pepper flakes in the hot oil for 1 minute. Add the spinach and sauté until wilted. Remove from the heat. Add the spinach mixture, chicken, roasted peppers and olives to the pasta mixture and mix well. Sprinkle with 1/4 cup Parmesan cheese and serve immediately.

CLAIRE MAJOR TYNES

The JLB made a five-year commitment and a $1 million donation to establish our signature project, the Junior League of Birmingham-Hugh Kaul Children's Zoo at the Birmingham Zoo. It was the first major new project at the zoo in twenty-five years.

FETTUCCINI WITH PROSCIUTTO, ASPARAGUS AND MUSHROOMS

SERVES 6 TO 8

6 ounces asparagus (about 1 bunch)
12 ounces fettuccini
3 tablespoons unsalted butter
3 to 4 ounces prosciutto, thinly sliced and cut into 1/4-inch strips
4 to 6 ounces cremini mushrooms, sliced

1 cup frozen petite peas, thawed
1/2 cup plus 2 tablespoons heavy cream or whipping cream
12 cherry tomatoes, cut into halves
Salt and pepper to taste
2/3 cup grated Parmesan cheese

Snap off the thick woody ends of the asparagus spears. Cook the asparagus in boiling water in a saucepan for 3 minutes. Remove the asparagus to a platter and add the pasta to the boiling water. Boil for 10 minutes and drain. Cut the asparagus spears into 1-inch pieces. Melt the butter in a large skillet and add the prosciutto. Cook for 1 minute and stir in the mushrooms. Cook for 3 minutes and stir in the asparagus, peas and cream. Simmer for 2 minutes and add the pasta, tossing to coat. Remove from the heat and stir in the tomatoes. Season with salt and pepper and spoon into a serving bowl. Sprinkle with the cheese.

ANNA BICKLEY COOPER

BOW TIES WITH SAUSAGE, TOMATOES AND CREAM

SERVES 4 TO 6

2 tablespoons olive oil
1 1/2 pounds sweet Italian sausage
1 cup chopped onion
3 garlic cloves, minced
1/4 teaspoon red pepper flakes
1 (28-ounce) can Italian tomatoes, drained and coarsely chopped

1 1/2 cups heavy cream or whipping cream
1/2 teaspoon salt
12 ounces bow tie pasta, cooked and drained
3 tablespoons minced fresh parsley
Freshly grated Parmesan cheese

Heat the olive oil in a large skillet over medium heat. Brown the sausage in the hot oil, stirring until the sausage is crumbly and no longer pink. Drain, reserving 1 tablespoon of the pan drippings. Cook the onion, garlic and red pepper flakes in the reserved pan drippings until the onion is tender, stirring frequently. Stir in the tomatoes, cream and salt and simmer for 4 minutes or until slightly thickened. Toss the tomato sauce with the pasta in a bowl until combined and sprinkle with the parsley and cheese.

KELLI NELSON JETMUNDSEN

MACARONI AND CHEESE

SERVES 8

8 ounces elbow pasta
2 tablespoons butter
2 tablespoons all-purpose flour
1 cup milk
1/2 teaspoon salt
1/4 teaspoon white pepper

1 1/2 cups (6 ounces) shredded
  Cheddar cheese
1 egg
1 cup sour cream
1/2 cup (2 ounces) shredded
  Cheddar cheese

Preheat the oven to 350 degrees. Cook the pasta using the package directions and drain. Melt the butter in a saucepan over medium heat. Stir in the flour and cook until bubbly, stirring constantly. Add the milk and cook until thickened. Stir in the salt, white pepper and 1 1/2 cups cheese and cook until blended and of a sauce consistency, stirring constantly.

Whisk the egg in a large bowl and stir in the sour cream. Add the cheese sauce and pasta to the egg mixture and mix well. Spoon the pasta mixture into a greased 2-quart baking dish and sprinkle with 1/2 cup cheese. Bake for 35 minutes.

MICHELE BREWER HILL

MACARONI WITH TOMATOES AND FETA CHEESE

SERVES 6

8 ounces macaroni
2 tablespoons butter
2 garlic cloves, minced
3/4 cup milk
8 ounces cream cheese, softened

1 bunch green onions, trimmed and
  thinly sliced
1 pint cherry tomatoes, cut into halves
1/2 teaspoon salt
6 ounces feta cheese, crumbled

Preheat the oven to 400 degrees. Cook the pasta using the package directions. Drain and rinse with cold water. Melt the butter in a large saucepan over medium-high heat and add the garlic. Sauté for 1 minute and then stir in the milk and cream cheese.

Cook for 3 minutes longer or until the cream cheese melts, stirring constantly. Add the pasta and toss to coat. Stir in the green onions, tomatoes and salt. Mix in 1/2 of the feta cheese and spoon into a greased 2-quart baking dish. Sprinkle with the remaining feta cheese and bake for 20 minutes or until light brown.

ABBY CURRY FINNEY

Photograph for this recipe on page 150.

BAKED PENNE WITH THREE CHEESES

SERVES 6 TO 8

2 tomatoes, quartered and seeded
1 yellow onion, quartered
1/3 cup olive oil
16 ounces penne
2 tablespoons olive oil
8 ounces Italian sausage,
   casings removed
2 tablespoons olive oil
3 garlic cloves, chopped
2 shallots, chopped

8 ounces mushrooms, sliced
1 cup dry white wine
2 cups half-and-half
1 cup heavy cream or whipping cream
3 ounces Gorgonzola cheese, crumbled
2 ounces fontina cheese, shredded
2 ounces Parmesan cheese,
   freshly grated
Salt and freshly ground pepper to taste
2 ounces fontina cheese, shredded

Preheat the oven to 425 degrees. Toss the tomatoes, onion and 1/3 cup olive oil in a baking dish until coated. Roast for 25 minutes or until the tomatoes are blistered. Remove the tomatoes to a bowl and continue roasting the onion for 15 minutes longer or until tender. Add the onion to the tomatoes and reduce the oven temperature to 350 degrees.

Cook the pasta using the package directions. Drain and toss with 2 tablespoons olive oil. Sauté the sausage in a large saucepan over medium heat, crumbling the sausage with a spoon as it cooks. Remove the sausage to a bowl using a slotted spoon and discard the pan drippings.

Heat 2 tablespoons olive oil in the same skillet and add the garlic and shallots. Sauté for 2 to 3 minutes and stir in the mushrooms. Sauté for 3 minutes or until the mushrooms are tender. Add the wine and cook until the liquid is reduced by 1/2, stirring frequently. Stir in the half-and-half and cream and cook for 5 minutes or until the mixture coats the back of a wooden spoon, stirring constantly. Whisk in the Gorgonzola cheese, 2 ounces fontina cheese and the Parmesan cheese and cook until the cheeses melt. Season to taste with salt and pepper. Remove from the heat and let stand until cool.

Coarsely chop the roasted onion and roasted tomatoes and toss with the pasta in a bowl. Stir in the sausage. Spoon the pasta mixture into a greased 9×13-inch baking dish and pour the cooled cheese sauce over the prepared layer, stirring gently to distribute the mushrooms. Sprinkle with 2 ounces fontina cheese and bake for 25 to 30 minutes or until golden brown. Let stand for 5 minutes before serving.

PENNEY PARKER HARTLINE

PENNE WITH PROSCIUTTO AND CHEESE

SERVES 8

16 ounces penne
1/4 cup (1/2 stick) butter
2 tablespoons all-purpose flour
2 cups half-and-half
3 cups (12 ounces) shredded white
   Cheddar cheese
1/2 cup (2 ounces) freshly grated
   Parmesan cheese

1 1/2 ounces prosciutto, cut into
   small pieces
1 teaspoon salt
1/2 teaspoon black pepper
1/8 teaspoon cayenne pepper
2 tablespoons freshly grated
   Parmesan cheese

Preheat the oven to 350 degrees. Cook the pasta using the package directions and drain. Rinse the pasta with cold water and spoon into a greased 9×13-inch baking dish.

Melt the butter in a saucepan over low heat and stir in the flour. Cook until bubbly and stir in the half-and-half. Cook for 10 minutes or until thickened, stirring constantly. Remove from the heat and stir in the white Cheddar cheese, 1/2 cup Parmesan cheese, the prosciutto, salt, black pepper and cayenne pepper. Spoon the cheese mixture over the pasta and sprinkle with 2 tablespoons Parmesan cheese. Bake for 30 minutes.

ELIZABETH LASSITER FITZPATRICK

BAKED RIGATONI

SERVES 8 TO 10

12 ounces rigatoni
1 1/2 cups chopped cooked ham
5 large plum tomatoes, chopped
1 cup (4 ounces) crumbled feta cheese
1/4 cup (1 ounce) shredded
   Swiss cheese
1 1/2 teaspoons thyme

1 teaspoon parsley flakes
1/2 teaspoon salt
1/2 teaspoon pepper
1 cup heavy cream or whipping cream
1/4 cup (1 ounce) shredded
   mozzarella cheese

Preheat the oven to 375 degrees. Cook the pasta using the package directions and drain. Combine the pasta, ham, tomatoes, feta cheese, Swiss cheese, thyme, parsley flakes, salt and pepper in a bowl and mix well. Stir in the cream. Spoon the pasta mixture into a lightly greased 9×13-inch baking dish and bake, covered, for 15 minutes. Stir and then sprinkle with the mozzarella cheese. Bake, covered, for 30 minutes longer.

NANCY BEDSOLE BYNON

SPAGHETTI À LA PUTTANESCA

SERVES 6

3 tablespoons olive oil

2 cups chopped onions

8 garlic cloves, minced

1 (28-ounce) can whole peeled
    tomatoes, drained

3 tablespoons tomato paste

2 teaspoons anchovy paste

1/2 teaspoon crushed red pepper flakes

1 cup reduced-sodium chicken broth

1 cup kalamata olives,
    coarsely chopped

2 tablespoons drained capers

16 ounces spaghetti, cooked
    and drained

1/2 cup (2 ounces) grated
    Parmesan cheese

Heat the olive oil in a large skillet over medium heat. Add the onions and cook for 4 minutes or until tender, stirring frequently. Reduce the heat to medium-low and add the garlic. Cook for 10 minutes, stirring occasionally; do not allow the garlic to brown. Stir in the tomatoes, tomato paste, anchovy paste and red pepper flakes. Cook for 10 minutes, stirring occasionally. Stir in the broth, olives and capers and bring to a boil. Reduce the heat to low and simmer for 15 minutes or until thickened, stirring occasionally. Divide the pasta evenly among 6 shallow pasta bowls and top each serving with about 1/2 cup of the sauce. Sprinkle evenly with the cheese and serve immediately.

LYDIA DeGARIS PURSELL

SOUTHWESTERN COUSCOUS

MAKES 6 (1-CUP) SERVINGS

2 cups chicken broth

1 (10-ounce) package plain couscous

1 (15-ounce) can black beans, drained
    and rinsed

1 large avocado, chopped

2 cups grape or cherry tomato halves

2 tablespoons chopped fresh cilantro

2 tablespoons chopped green onions

1 tablespoon fresh lemon juice

2 teaspoons olive oil

1/4 teaspoon salt

1/4 teaspoon freshly ground pepper

Bring the broth to a boil in a medium saucepan and gradually stir in the couscous. Remove from the heat and let stand, covered, for 5 minutes. Fluff with a fork and cool. Add the beans, avocado, tomatoes, cilantro and green onions and mix gently. Stir in the lemon juice, olive oil, salt and pepper. Serve immediately or chill in the refrigerator, adding the avocado to the chilled pasta just before serving.

RAMI MARIE PERRY

Nutritional Profile for this recipe on page 327.

MEXICAN CORN BREAD

Remove the seeds from the jalapeño chiles for a mild corn bread, or leave them in for a spicier version!

SERVES 9

1³/4 cups self-rising
   white cornmeal
1 cup milk
¹/3 cup vegetable oil
2 eggs, lightly beaten

1 cup (4 ounces) shredded sharp
   Cheddar cheese
1 cup cream-style corn
2 small jalapeño chiles, finely chopped
1 (2-ounce) jar diced pimento, drained

Preheat the oven to 400 degrees. Mix the cornmeal, milk, oil and eggs in a bowl and stir in the cheese, corn, jalapeño chiles and pimento. Spoon the batter into a 9×9-inch baking pan sprayed with nonstick cooking spray and bake for 30 minutes.

LeAnn Holifield Cox

SOUR CREAM CORN BREAD

MAKES 16 SQUARES

1 cup all-purpose flour
³/4 cup yellow cornmeal
¹/4 cup sugar
2 teaspoons baking powder
³/4 teaspoon salt

¹/2 teaspoon baking soda
1 cup sour cream
¹/4 cup milk
1 egg, beaten
2 tablespoons vegetable oil

Preheat the oven to 375 degrees. Combine the flour, cornmeal, sugar, baking powder, salt and baking soda in a bowl and mix well. Mix the sour cream, milk, egg and oil in a bowl and stir in the flour mixture. Spoon the batter into a greased 9×9-inch baking pan and bake for 30 to 40 minutes or until the corn bread tests done.

Mitzi Munger Ireland

CORN BREAD MUFFINS

MAKES 1 DOZEN MUFFINS

1³/4 cups cornmeal	2 cups buttermilk
³/4 cup all-purpose flour	2 eggs, lightly beaten
¹/4 cup sugar	¹/4 cup vegetable oil
4 teaspoons baking powder	2 ears fresh corn, cooked and
1 teaspoon salt	kernels removed
¹/4 teaspoon baking soda	3 green onion bulbs, minced

Preheat the oven to 450 degrees. Combine the cornmeal, flour, sugar, baking powder, salt and baking soda in a bowl and mix well. Whisk the buttermilk, eggs and oil in a bowl until blended and stir in the corn kernels and green onion bulbs. Add the buttermilk mixture to the cornmeal mixture and mix well.

Spoon the batter into lightly greased or paper-lined muffin cups and bake for 15 minutes or until a wooden pick inserted in the centers comes out clean.

BECKY SATTERFIELD, CHEF AND OWNER OF SATTERFIELD'S

CHEESY BEER BREAD

Great with soups and salads. Easy to prepare at the last minute.

MAKES 1 LOAF OR 18 MUFFINS

4 cups baking mix	3 tablespoons sugar
1 cup (4 ounces) shredded sharp	1 (12-ounce) can beer
Cheddar cheese	¹/4 cup (¹/2 stick) butter, melted
¹/2 cup (2 ounces) grated	1 egg, beaten
Parmesan cheese	

Preheat the oven to 400 degrees. Combine the baking mix, Cheddar cheese, Parmesan cheese and sugar in a bowl and mix well. Add the beer and butter and stir until combined.

Spoon the batter into a greased and floured 5×9-inch loaf pan or muffin cups and brush with the egg. Bake for 30 to 45 minutes or until golden brown if using a loaf pan. Bake for 10 to 15 minutes for muffins.

For **Vidalia Onion Bread**, omit the beer and add ¹/2 cup sweet Vidalia onion salad dressing.

NATALIE TORTORICI GILLESPIE

LEMON AND BLACK PEPPER SODA BREAD

SERVES 10 TO 12

2¹/₂ cups all-purpose flour
1 tablespoon sugar
2 teaspoons baking powder
1 teaspoon baking soda
³/₄ teaspoon salt
6 tablespoons butter, chilled and cut into small pieces
¹/₂ cup buttermilk
¹/₂ cup plain yogurt
2 tablespoons fresh lemon juice
2 tablespoons grated onion
1 tablespoon julienned lemon zest
2¹/₂ teaspoons freshly ground black pepper
1 egg
1 tablespoon milk

Preheat the oven to 350 degrees. Combine the flour, sugar, baking powder, baking soda and salt in a bowl and mix well. Cut in the butter with a pastry blender or 2 forks until the mixture resembles coarse meal. Whisk the buttermilk, yogurt, lemon juice, onion, lemon zest and black pepper in a bowl until combined. Add the buttermilk mixture to the flour mixture and stir just until moistened.

Knead the dough on a lightly floured surface for 3 minutes or until smooth. Shape the dough into an 8-inch round and place on a baking sheet lined with baking parchment. Whisk the egg and milk in a bowl until blended and brush over the round. Cut a large ¹/₄-inch-deep "X" in the top of the dough using a sharp knife and bake for 45 minutes or until golden brown. Remove to a wire rack to cool.

ELIZABETH LASSITER FITZPATRICK

GRILLED PARMESAN HERB BREADSTICKS

MAKES 1 DOZEN BREADSTICKS

Herb Spice Blend
2 teaspoons basil
2 teaspoons parsley flakes
1 teaspoon rosemary
$1^1/2$ teaspoons kosher salt
$1^1/2$ teaspoons oregano
1 teaspoon minced dried onion
$3/4$ teaspoon garlic powder
$1/2$ teaspoon paprika
$1/2$ teaspoon crushed red pepper flakes

Breadsticks
3 tablespoons freshly grated Parmesan cheese
2 tablespoons olive oil
1 (11-ounce) can refrigerator breadsticks

For the spice blend, combine the basil, parsley flakes, rosemary, salt, oregano, dried onion, garlic powder, paprika and red pepper flakes in a bowl and mix well. Store in an airtight container for up to 1 month. This makes $1/4$ cup.

For the breadsticks, lightly grease the grill rack and preheat the grill on low. Combine 2 tablespoons of the spice blend, the cheese and olive oil in a bowl and mix well. Brush the cheese mixture evenly on 1 side of each breadstick. Twist each breadstick and arrange on the prepared grill rack. Grill, covered, for 5 minutes or until light brown.

LYDA HELEN JONES

ITALIAN BREAD

SERVES 12 TO 15

1/2 cup (1 stick) butter, softened
1/4 cup (1 ounce) freshly grated
    Parmesan cheese
2 or 3 garlic cloves, minced
3/4 teaspoon chopped fresh marjoram,
    or 1/4 teaspoon dried marjoram
3/4 teaspoon chopped fresh oregano,
    or 1/4 teaspoon dried oregano
1 (16-ounce) loaf Italian bread,
    split lengthwise into halves

Preheat the oven to 350 degrees. Combine the butter, cheese, garlic, marjoram
and oregano in a bowl and mix well. Spread the butter mixture on the cut sides
of the bread halves and arrange cut side up on a baking sheet. Bake for 25 to
30 minutes or until crisp and brown. Slice and serve immediately.

CHRISTIANA DUNN ROUSSEL

HUSH PUPPIES

MAKES 3 DOZEN HUSH PUPPIES

Vegetable oil for frying
2 cups self-rising white cornmeal
1 cup all-purpose flour
4 teaspoons baking powder
1 teaspoon salt
1 small onion, chopped
1 egg, lightly beaten
1 (14-ounce) can chopped tomatoes, drained

Heat oil in a large deep skillet over medium-high heat. Combine the cornmeal,
flour, baking powder and salt in a bowl and mix well. Stir in the onion and egg.
Add the tomatoes and mix well. Drop the batter by teaspoonfuls into the hot oil
and fry until golden brown on all sides, turning as needed. Drain on a wire rack
lined with paper towels. Serve warm.

LEANN HOLIFIELD COX

*Since the opening of
the Junior League of
Birmingham-Hugh Kaul
Children's Zoo in September
2002, attendance at the zoo
has increased by 50 percent
and zoo memberships have
increased by 240 percent.*

CHOCOLATE CHERRY BREAD

This bread is more savory than sweet.

MAKES 1 LOAF

2¹/₂ cups bread flour
¹/₂ cup baking cocoa
1¹/₂ teaspoons salt
1 cup warm milk (100 to 110 degrees)
¹/₂ cup packed light brown sugar
1 envelope dry yeast (2¹/₄ teaspoons)
¹/₃ cup plus 3 tablespoons toasted almond oil or
   walnut oil
¹/₂ cup dried tart cherries
¹/₃ cup sliced almonds or walnuts, toasted
1 tablespoon milk
1 egg, lightly beaten

Combine the bread flour, baking cocoa and salt in a bowl and mix well. Mix the warm milk, brown sugar and yeast in a large bowl and let stand for 5 minutes. Add ¹/₃ cup of the almond oil to the yeast mixture and stir until combined. Add the flour mixture and stir until a soft dough forms. Knead the dough on a lightly floured surface for 8 minutes or until smooth and elastic. Knead in the cherries and almonds.

Coat a large bowl with 1 tablespoon of the remaining almond oil. Place the dough in the oiled bowl and turn to coat the surface. Let rise, covered with a lightly oiled sheet of plastic wrap, in a warm place (85 degrees) free from drafts for 1 hour or until doubled in bulk. Gently press 2 fingers into the dough and if the indentation remains, the dough has risen enough. Punch the dough down and let rest, covered, for 5 minutes.

Shape the dough into a 9-inch round and arrange on a baking sheet lined with baking parchment. Lightly brush with the remaining 2 tablespoons almond oil. Let rise, covered, for 1 hour or until doubled in bulk.

Preheat the oven to 350 degrees. Uncover the dough. Whisk 1 tablespoon milk and the egg in a bowl until blended and brush over the round. Make a ¹/₄-inch-deep cut down the center of the round using a sharp knife. Bake for 30 minutes or until the bread is brown on the bottom. Remove to a wire rack to cool.

ROSEMARY OLIVE BREAD

SERVES 4 TO 6

3/4 cup warm milk (100 to 110 degrees)
1 tablespoon sugar
1 envelope dry yeast (2 1/4 teaspoons)
1/2 cup extra-virgin olive oil
2 1/2 cups all-purpose flour
1 1/4 teaspoons salt
1/2 cup coarsely chopped kalamata olives
1/3 cup coarsely chopped green olives
3 tablespoons finely chopped shallots
2 tablespoons chopped fresh rosemary
1 teaspoon grated lemon zest
2 garlic cloves, crushed
1/2 teaspoon herbes de Provence
1 tablespoon yellow cornmeal
1 egg
1 tablespoon milk
1/2 teaspoon coarse sea salt

Mix the warm milk, sugar and yeast in a large bowl and let stand for 5 minutes. Stir in 3 tablespoons of the olive oil. Add 2 1/4 cups of the flour and 1 1/4 teaspoons salt and stir until a soft dough forms. Knead the dough on a lightly floured surface for 5 minutes or until smooth and elastic. Add enough of the remaining 1/4 cup flour, 1 tablespoon at a time, to prevent the dough from sticking to your hands. The dough will feel tacky.

Coat a large bowl with 1 tablespoon of the remaining olive oil. Place the dough in the oiled bowl, turning to coat the surface. Let rise, covered, in a warm place (85 degrees) free from drafts for 1 hour or until doubled in bulk. Gently press 2 fingers into the dough. If the indentation remains, the dough has risen enough. Punch the dough down and let rest, covered, for 5 minutes.

Combine the remaining 1/4 cup olive oil, the olives, shallots, rosemary, lemon zest, garlic and herbes de Provence in a food processor and pulse until coarsely chopped and combined. Punch the dough down. Sprinkle a sheet of baking parchment with the cornmeal. Roll the dough into a 9×13-inch rectangle on the baking parchment and spread the olive mixture evenly over the dough, leaving a 1/2-inch border on all sides. Starting with a long side, roll jelly roll fashion, pressing the edge to seal and tucking the ends under. Place the baking parchment and bread loaf seam side down on a baking sheet. Let rise, covered, for 1 hour or until doubled in bulk.

Preheat the oven to 425 degrees. Whisk the egg and milk in a bowl until blended and brush over the loaf. Sprinkle with 1/2 teaspoon coarse salt. Make three 1/4-inch-deep diagonal cuts across the top of the loaf using a sharp knife. Bake for 25 minutes or until golden brown and the loaf sounds hollow when lightly tapped. Remove to a wire rack to cool.

JULIE GRIMES BOTTCHER

Photograph for this recipe on page 116.

OLIVE BREAD

This recipe was given to me by my father, Dr. Harold Cannon, who collects bread recipes from all over the world.

MAKES 12 (1-SLICE) SERVINGS

1½ cups warm water (100 to 110 degrees)
1 envelope dry yeast
3 cups bread flour
2 tablespoons olive oil
1½ teaspoons salt
1 cup whole wheat flour
10 ounces kalamata olives, coarsely chopped

Mix the warm water and yeast in a large bowl and let stand for 5 minutes. Stir in 2 cups of the bread flour, the olive oil and salt. Add the whole wheat flour and olives and mix well. Gradually add the remaining 1 cup bread flour until the dough is too stiff to mix. Knead in enough additional bread flour until a soft dough forms.

Place the dough in a lightly oiled bowl and turn to coat. Let rise, covered with a piece of lightly oiled plastic wrap, in a warm place (85 degrees) free from drafts until doubled in bulk and punch the dough down. Shape the dough into an oval loaf and arrange on a lightly oiled baking sheet. Let rise, covered with plastic wrap, until 1½ to 1¾ times larger in bulk.

Preheat the oven to 400 degrees. Make 2 to 3 cuts ¼ inch deep across the top of the loaf with a sharp knife. Bake for 30 to 35 minutes or until the loaf sounds hollow when lightly tapped. Cool on a wire rack for 1 hour or longer before slicing.

EMILY CANNON PRUET

Nutritional Profile for this recipe on page 327.

The Junior League of Birmingham-Hugh Kaul Children's Zoo features animals native to rural and urban Alabama, such as bobcats and river otters; a barn featuring pigs, chickens, and goats; and an 8,400-gallon tank full of animals native to Alabama's streams. At its entrance stands an eighteen-foot-tall model of Red Mountain.

CREAM CHEESE AND CHIVE POTATO BREAD

An excellent way to use leftover mashed potatoes. This bread is great for sandwiches or toasted and topped with smoked salmon.

MAKES 2 (8-INCH) ROUND LOAVES

3/4 cup warm water (100 to 110 degrees)
1/4 cup (1/2 stick) butter, melted
1 tablespoon sugar
1 envelope dry yeast
8 ounces block-style cream cheese, softened
1 cup mashed cooked potatoes
1 egg, lightly beaten
4 1/2 cups all-purpose flour
2 teaspoons salt
3 tablespoons chopped fresh chives
1 egg
1 tablespoon milk

Mix the warm water, butter, sugar and yeast in a large bowl and let stand for 5 minutes or until the yeast begins to bubble. Stir in the cream cheese, mashed potatoes and 1 egg. Add 4 1/4 cups of the flour and the salt and mix until a soft dough forms. Knead the dough on a lightly floured surface for 6 minutes or until smooth and elastic, adding enough of the remaining flour, 1 tablespoon at a time, to prevent the dough from sticking to your hands. The dough will feel tacky. Knead in the chives.

Place the dough in an oiled bowl, turning to coat the surface. Let rise, covered with a lightly oiled piece of plastic wrap, in a warm place (85 degrees) free from drafts for 1 hour or until doubled in bulk. Gently press 2 fingers into the dough. If the indentation remains, the dough has risen enough.

Preheat the oven to 350 degrees. Divide the dough into 2 equal portions and shape each portion into an 8-inch round loaf on a lightly greased baking sheet. Whisk 1 egg and the milk in a bowl until blended and brush over the tops of the loaves. Make a 1/4-inch-deep cut down the center of each loaf and bake for 45 minutes or until golden brown. Remove to a wire rack to cool.

STEPHANIE GIBSON MIMS

More than fifty thousand schoolchildren visit the Children's Zoo annually and participate in educational programs and tours.

PUMPKIN WALNUT FOCACCIA WITH GRUYÈRE

This bread looks and tastes like fall. Since this recipe makes two loaves,
eat one now and freeze the remaining loaf for future use.

MAKES 16 (1-WEDGE) SERVINGS

3/4 cup milk
1/3 cup packed brown sugar
1 envelope dry yeast
3 1/2 cups bread flour
3 tablespoons butter, melted
1 cup canned pumpkin (do not use pumpkin pie filling)
1 teaspoon salt
1/2 teaspoon ground nutmeg
2 tablespoons coarse yellow cornmeal
1 cup (4 ounces) grated Gruyère cheese
1/2 cup coarsely chopped walnuts, toasted

Pour the milk into a saucepan and cook over medium heat until a thermometer registers 110 degrees; do not boil. Remove from the heat and pour into a heatproof bowl. Stir in the brown sugar and yeast and let stand for 5 minutes. Add 1 cup of the bread flour and the butter to the milk mixture and stir just until moistened. Let rise, covered loosely with plastic wrap, in a warm place (85 degrees) free from drafts for 30 minutes. Stir in the pumpkin, salt and nutmeg.

Add 2 1/4 cups of the remaining bread flour 1/4 cup at a time, stirring after each addition just until moistened. Knead the dough on a lightly floured surface for 10 minutes or until smooth and elastic, adding enough of the remaining 1/4 cup bread flour, 1 tablespoon at a time, to prevent the dough from sticking to your hands. The dough will feel sticky.

Sprinkle 2 baking sheets with the cornmeal. Divide the dough into 2 equal portions and pat each portion into a 12-inch round loaf on a prepared baking sheet. Let rise, covered loosely with lightly oiled plastic wrap, in a warm place (85 degrees) free from drafts for 1 hour or until doubled in bulk. Gently press 2 fingers into the dough. If the indentation remains, the dough has risen enough.

Preheat the oven to 425 degrees. Uncover the loaves and sprinkle evenly with the cheese and walnuts. Bake for 30 minutes or until golden brown. Let stand for 15 minutes and cut each round into 8 wedges.

Nutritional Profile for this recipe on page 327.

BeBe Rolls

MAKES 22 ROLLS

1/2 cup old-fashioned bran cereal
1/2 cup hot water
1/2 cup warm water (100 to 110 degrees)
1 envelope dry yeast (2 1/4 teaspoons)
1/2 cup vegetable oil
1/3 cup sugar
1 egg, lightly beaten
3/4 teaspoon salt
3 cups bread flour or all-purpose flour

Soak the cereal in the hot water in a large bowl until softened. Mix the warm water and yeast in a bowl and let stand for 5 minutes. Stir the oil, sugar, egg and salt into the softened cereal and blend in the yeast mixture. Add the bread flour 1 cup at a time, mixing well after each addition.

Knead the dough on a lightly floured surface until smooth and elastic. Let rise, covered, in a warm place (85 degrees) free from drafts for 1 hour or until doubled in bulk.

Preheat the oven to 350 degrees. Divide the dough into 22 equal portions and shape each portion into a ball. Arrange the balls on a baking sheet sprayed with nonstick cooking spray and bake for 22 minutes or until light brown. Remove to a wire rack. You may store the baked rolls in the freezer for up to 3 months. For testing purposes, All-Bran cereal was used.

Catherine Hall

SPOON ROLLS

MAKES 1¹/₂ DOZEN ROLLS

1 envelope dry yeast (2¹/₄ teaspoons)
1 tablespoon sugar
2 cups warm water (100 to 110 degrees)
3³/₄ cups self-rising flour
¹/₂ cup (1 stick) butter, melted
3 tablespoons sugar
1 egg

Dissolve the yeast and 1 tablespoon sugar in the warm water in a bowl and let stand for 5 minutes. Combine the yeast mixture, self-rising flour and butter in a large bowl and mix well. Stir in 3 tablespoons sugar and the egg. Chill, covered, for 8 to 10 hours.

Preheat the oven to 350 degrees. Spoon the dough into greased muffin cups, filling ²/₃ full. Bake for 25 minutes and serve immediately. The dough may be stored, covered, in the refrigerator for up to 4 days.

ELISSA HANDLEY TYSON

LUNCHEON ROLLS

MAKES 6 LARGE ROLLS, OR 1 DOZEN SMALL ROLLS

1 cup self-rising flour
¹/₂ cup milk
3 tablespoons mayonnaise
1 teaspoon sugar
¹/₂ teaspoon salt

Preheat the oven to 425 degrees. Combine the self-rising flour, milk, mayonnaise, sugar and salt in a bowl and mix just until moistened. Fill 6 large or 12 miniature greased muffin cups ¹/₂ full. Bake for 15 minutes or until golden brown, checking after 10 minutes. Serve immediately.

KIMBERLY PORTER RODGERS

SAUSAGE, APPLE AND SAGE STUFFING

*Use dry bread to prepare this stuffing. You may prepare in advance and
store, covered, in the refrigerator until just before baking.*

SERVES 8 TO 10

1/4 cup olive oil
1 pound mild Italian sausage, casings removed
1 cup chopped onion
1 apple, peeled and chopped
1/2 cup thinly sliced celery hearts
2 garlic cloves, minced
3 cups (1-inch) cubes corn bread
3 cups (1-inch) cubes dry bread
1/3 cup finely chopped fresh parsley
1 tablespoon finely chopped fresh sage
1 1/2 teaspoons salt
1 cup reduced-sodium chicken broth
6 tablespoons butter, melted
1 egg

Preheat the oven to 350 degrees. Heat 2 tablespoons of the olive oil in a large skillet over medium-high heat. Add the sausage and sauté for 8 minutes or until brown and crumbly. Remove the sausage to paper towels to drain, reserving the pan drippings. Heat the remaining 2 tablespoons olive oil with the reserved pan drippings and add the onion and apple.

Sauté for 4 minutes or until the onion is tender. Stir in the celery and garlic and sauté for 1 minute. Spoon the celery mixture into a large bowl and mix in the sausage, corn bread, dry bread, parsley, sage and salt.

Whisk the broth, butter and egg in a bowl until blended and drizzle over the bread mixture, tossing gently to combine. Spoon the stuffing into a lightly greased 9×13-inch baking dish and bake for 45 minutes or until light brown and set. Omit the salt if regular broth is used.

JOANNE MCCRARY BRASSEAL

Photograph for this recipe on page 151.

CURRIED BARLEY WITH GOLDEN RAISINS

The dish is wonderful served warm or chilled.

MAKES 4 (³/4-CUP) SERVINGS

2 cups chicken broth
1 cup pearl barley
1 teaspoon olive oil
1 teaspoon curry powder
¹/3 cup golden raisins, currants or
    dried cranberries

¹/3 cup slivered almonds, toasted
2 tablespoons chopped fresh
    flat-leaf parsley
¹/4 teaspoon salt
¹/4 teaspoon freshly ground pepper
¹/4 cup sliced green onions

Bring the broth to a boil in a 2-quart saucepan and stir in the barley. Reduce the heat to low and simmer, covered, for 10 to 15 minutes or until the barley is tender. Remove from the heat and let stand, covered, for 5 minutes; drain. Heat the olive oil in a medium nonstick skillet over medium heat. Add the curry powder and cook for 1 minute, stirring occasionally. Add the barley and toss to coat. Stir in the raisins, almonds, parsley, salt and pepper. Spoon into a serving bowl and sprinkle with the green onions.

LORI JOHNSON GOODSON

Nutritional Profile for this recipe on page 327.

TABOULI

MAKES 6 (²/3-CUP) SERVINGS

1 cup each boiling water and bulgur
¹/4 cup olive oil
¹/4 cup fresh lemon juice (1 lemon)
1 teaspoon salt
¹/2 teaspoon oregano
¹/4 teaspoon garlic powder

¹/8 teaspoon cayenne pepper
¹/4 cup chopped green onions
1 bunch parsley, chopped
1 large tomato, chopped (about 2 cups)
1 (2-ounce) can sliced black
    olives, drained

Stir the boiling water into the bulgur in a heatproof bowl and let stand, covered, for 30 minutes. Whisk the olive oil, lemon juice, salt, oregano, garlic powder and cayenne pepper in a bowl until combined. Add the green onions, parsley, tomato and olives to the bulgur and mix gently. Drizzle with the olive oil mixture and toss gently to combine. Serve with pita bread or chips.

KIM FRANKS MATTHEWS

Nutritional Profile for this recipe on page 327.

HERBED CHEESE GRITS CAKES

An excellent side dish for entertaining. The grits may be prepared up to two days in advance and stored in the refrigerator. Simply pan-fry or grill the grits cakes just before serving. Your guests will love this twist on a Southern staple.

MAKES 16 CAKES

2 cups milk
3/4 cup water
1 teaspoon salt
1 cup stone-ground grits
2/3 cup freshly grated Parmigiano-Reggiano
3/4 cup (1 1/2 sticks) unsalted butter
3 ounces cream cheese, softened
1/4 cup finely chopped fresh parsley
1 1/2 tablespoons snipped fresh chives

Combine the milk, water and salt in a medium saucepan over medium heat and bring to a boil, stirring occasionally. Add the grits gradually, whisking constantly. Reduce the heat to low and simmer for 20 minutes or until the grits are tender and the liquid is absorbed, stirring frequently. Remove from the heat and add the Parmigiano-Reggiano, 1/2 cup of the butter, the cream cheese, parsley and chives, stirring until the cheeses melt. Spread the grits mixture in a 7×11-inch dish coated lightly with nonstick cooking spray. Chill, covered, for 2 hours or until the grits mixture is set.

Invert the grits onto a flat surface and cut lengthwise into halves. Cut each half into 4 rectangles and cut each rectangle diagonally to form 16 triangles. Melt 1 tablespoon of the remaining butter in a skillet over medium heat. Add 4 cakes to the skillet and cook for 4 minutes per side or until light brown. Remove to a platter and cover to keep warm. Repeat the procedure 3 more times with the remaining butter and remaining cakes.

BEE GROVER LEWIS

Photograph for this recipe on page 151.

CHIVES

Chives have a mild flavor. They vary in size, but a good rule of thumb is, the thicker the chive, the more flavor it packs. Since chopping with a knife can tear tender chives, causing them to release moisture and turn an unappealing dark color, try using kitchen shears to snip them.

RICE BALLS

MAKES 2 DOZEN RICE BALLS

1 cup rice
2$^1/_2$ cups (10 ounces) shredded mozzarella cheese
1$^1/_2$ cups finely chopped pepperoni
1 cup ricotta cheese
$^3/_4$ cup (3 ounces) grated Parmesan cheese
1 egg, lightly beaten
$^1/_2$ teaspoon pepper
Vegetable oil for frying
2 eggs
3 tablespoons water
2 cups seasoned bread crumbs
Marinara sauce for dipping

Cook the rice using the package directions and drain. Let stand until cool. Combine the rice, mozzarella cheese, pepperoni, ricotta cheese, Parmesan cheese, 1 egg and the pepper in a bowl and mix well. Chill, covered, in the refrigerator until just before frying. Heat oil in a deep-fryer or Dutch oven. Whisk 2 eggs and the water in a bowl until blended. Shape the rice mixture into golf ball-size balls, dip in the egg wash and coat generously with the bread crumbs. Fry the rice balls in the hot oil for 1 to 1$^1/_2$ minutes or until golden brown. Drain and serve immediately with marinara sauce.

DONNA MCLEMORE COPPEDGE

ROSEMARY RICE

SERVES 4 TO 6

2 cups water
1 cup rice
3 to 4 tablespoons butter
1 tablespoon chopped fresh rosemary

Combine the water and rice in a saucepan and cook using the package directions. Melt the butter in a small skillet and sauté the rosemary in the butter. Add the rice to the rosemary mixture and toss gently to combine. Serve warm.

VIRGINIA SPECK AMASON

TOMATO RICE

SERVES 4

1 tablespoon butter
1 tablespoon olive oil
1 small sweet onion, chopped
1 large tomato, peeled and chopped
2 garlic cloves, minced
1 cup long grain rice
2 cups chicken broth
1/2 teaspoon salt
1/4 teaspoon freshly ground pepper
2 tablespoons chopped fresh basil

Heat the butter and olive oil in a 3¹/2-quart saucepan over medium heat. Add the onion to the butter mixture and sauté until tender. Stir in the tomato and garlic and cook for 5 minutes, stirring frequently. Stir in the rice and cook for 2 minutes, stirring constantly to coat.

Add the broth, salt and pepper to the rice mixture and bring to a boil. Reduce the heat to low and simmer, covered, for 20 minutes or until the rice is tender. Fluff with a fork and stir in the basil.

SHARON HILYER JONES

AUNT LOU'S BROWN RICE CASSEROLE

SERVES 6 TO 8

6 tablespoons butter
1/2 cup chopped onion
1/2 cup finely chopped celery
1 cup brown rice
1 cup pecans, broken
2 (10-ounce) cans beef consommé

Preheat the oven to 350 degrees. Melt the butter in a large saucepan and stir in the onion and celery. Sauté until tender and stir in the rice and pecans. Cook for 6 minutes or until light brown, stirring constantly.

Spoon the rice mixture into a greased 9×13-inch baking dish and pour the consommé over the top. Bake, covered, for 1 hour.

KIM FRANKS MATTHEWS

Brown Rice Pilaf

SERVES 8 TO 10

1/4 cup (1/2 stick) butter
1 bunch green onions, chopped
3 carrots, thinly sliced
2 cups brown rice
5 cups chicken broth
1/2 cup dry white wine
1/4 cup (1/2 stick) butter
1 garlic clove, minced
8 ounces mushrooms, sliced
1/2 cup chopped fresh parsley
1/4 teaspoon pepper
1 cup (4 ounces) grated Parmesan cheese
1 cup milk
2 eggs
1/2 teaspoon ground nutmeg (optional)
1/4 cup chopped green onions for garnish

Melt 1/4 cup butter in a large skillet and add the green onions and carrots. Sauté for 5 minutes or until tender. Stir in the brown rice and cook for 1 minute, stirring constantly. Add the broth and wine and bring to a boil. Reduce the heat to low and simmer, covered, for 45 minutes or until the liquid is absorbed and the rice is tender.

Melt 1/4 cup butter in a small skillet and add the garlic. Cook for 1 minute, stirring frequently. Stir in the mushrooms and cook for 5 minutes, stirring occasionally. Drain and mix in the parsley and pepper.

Preheat the oven to 350 degrees. Spread 1/2 of the rice mixture in a greased 8×12-inch baking dish. Spread with the mushroom mixture and sprinkle with 1/2 cup of the cheese. Layer with the remaining rice mixture and remaining 1/2 cup cheese. Whisk the milk, eggs and nutmeg in a bowl until blended and pour over the prepared layers. Bake for 30 minutes or until heated through. Garnish with the green onions. You may prepare in advance and store, covered, in the refrigerator. Bring to room temperature before baking.

ABBY CURRY FINNEY

WILD RICE WITH SMOKED BACON AND WILD MUSHROOMS

SERVES 8

1¹/2 pounds assorted fresh wild mushrooms
   (shiitake, cremini, oyster, porcini, etc.)
6 thick slices smoked bacon, cut crosswise into pieces
1 cup finely chopped red onion
³/4 cup chopped celery
2 garlic cloves, minced
1¹/2 cups wild rice, rinsed with cold water and drained
2¹/2 cups water
2 cups chicken broth
¹/2 cup white wine
1 bay leaf
¹/2 teaspoon salt
1 tablespoon minced fresh parsley
1 tablespoon minced fresh rosemary
1 tablespoon minced fresh thyme
¹/2 teaspoon freshly ground pepper
¹/2 cup pine nuts, toasted

Discard the tough stems from the mushrooms and break the mushrooms into bite-size pieces. Cook the bacon in a large saucepan over medium heat until brown and crisp, stirring frequently. Remove the bacon to paper towels to drain using a slotted spoon, reserving 1 tablespoon of the bacon drippings.

Add the onion, celery and garlic to the reserved pan dripping and sauté over medium heat for 5 minutes or until the onion is tender. Stir in the mushrooms, wild rice, water, broth, wine, bay leaf and salt and cover. Bring to a boil over medium heat. Reduce the heat to low and remove the cover.

Simmer for 45 to 60 minutes or until the wild rice is tender; do not stir. Drain and then stir in the parsley, rosemary, thyme and pepper. Reduce the heat to the lowest setting and heat the rice mixture for 5 minutes to remove any remaining moisture, shaking the pan frequently. Discard the bay leaf and stir in the bacon and pine nuts.

ANN ABERNETHY STEPHENS

RISOTTO WITH FALL SQUASH

Risotto is the perfect silky-smooth comfort food, especially in the fall. The beauty of this dish is you can add butternut squash or other varieties of winter squash for a splash of color, or you can omit the squash and still have a delicious side dish.

SERVES 4

6 tablespoons butter
1 1/2 cups arborio rice or other medium grain rice
2 cups (1/2-inch) cubed peeled butternut squash
2 shallots, finely chopped (about 1/4 cup)
1 garlic clove, minced
1 cup dry wine
3 cups chicken broth
1 cup water
1/2 cup (2 ounces) freshly grated
    Parmigiano-Reggiano
2 teaspoons kosher salt
1/8 teaspoon ground nutmeg
Sprig of parsley for garnish

Melt the butter in a large saucepan over medium-high heat. Add the rice and sauté for 1 minute. Stir in the squash and sauté for 1 minute. Reduce the heat to medium and add the shallots.

Sauté for 2 minutes or until the shallots are tender. Stir in the garlic and sauté for 1 minute longer. Add the wine and bring to a boil. Reduce the heat to low and simmer until the liquid is absorbed.

Bring the broth and water to a simmer in a saucepan and cover to keep warm. Add 1 cup of the hot broth mixture to the rice mixture and cook until the liquid is absorbed, stirring constantly. Repeat the procedure with the remaining hot broth mixture 1 cup at a time, cooking until the liquid is absorbed after each addition and stirring constantly. This process will take 30 to 45 minutes. Remove from the heat and add the cheese, salt and nutmeg, stirring until the cheese melts. Spoon into a serving bowl and garnish with sprig of parsley. Serve immediately.

HOLLEY CONTRI JOHNSON

Photograph for this recipe on page 150.

In 2005 the Junior League of Birmingham-Hugh Kaul Children's Zoo was awarded the Mayor's Award, "Keep Birmingham Beautiful."

WILD MUSHROOM RISOTTO

MAKES 8 CUPS

6 cups chicken broth
2 cups beef broth
1/3 cup dried porcini mushrooms
1/4 cup olive oil
1 cup finely minced yellow onion
1/4 cup finely minced shallots
8 ounces white mushrooms, chopped
1 cup arborio rice
3/4 cup dry white wine
1/4 teaspoon salt
1/2 cup (2 ounces) freshly grated
    Parmesan cheese
2 tablespoons butter
2 tablespoons (or more) chopped fresh sage
1/2 teaspoon freshly ground pepper

Combine the chicken broth and beef broth in a medium saucepan and heat for 5 minutes; do not boil. Cover to maintain the temperature. Pour 1 cup of the hot broth over the porcini mushrooms in a heatproof bowl and let stand for 30 minutes. Remove the reconstituted porcini mushrooms from the broth and chop.

Heat the olive oil in a large saucepan over medium heat and add the onion and shallots. Sauté for 3 minutes or until golden brown. Stir in the white mushrooms and sauté for 5 minutes or until the mushrooms are tender. Add the rice and stir until coated. Mix in the wine.

Add 1/2 cup of the remaining hot broth and the salt to the rice mixture and cook for 5 to 10 minutes or until the liquid is absorbed, stirring constantly. Stir in the reconstituted porcini mushrooms. Add the remaining hot broth 1/2 cup at a time, cooking until the liquid is absorbed after each addition and stirring constantly. This process will take approximately 30 minutes. The risotto is done when the rice is creamy and al dente; all of the hot broth may not be required. Remove from the heat and stir in the cheese, butter, sage and pepper. Serve immediately.

LEIGH HARDIN HANCOCK

Alabama Leadership Academy, one of the JLB's newest partners, trains school principals for implementation of new state or federal mandates and effective management. Workshops followed by visits to school sites ensure teachers have support to perform at the highest standards.

Macaroni with Tomatoes and Feta Cheese

Risotto with Fall Squash

Grains of Knowledge

PASTA PRIMER

Pasta is so versatile it can take you from elegant entertaining to quick and casual weeknight meals. If you follow the tips below, your pasta will be perfect every time.

- Always cook pasta in plenty of boiling salted water. You will need at least one gallon of water for each pound of pasta.
- Add one to two tablespoons salt to boiling water before adding the pasta. The pasta absorbs the salt as it cooks, giving the pasta itself some flavor and adding flavor to the final dish as well.
- Keep pasta from sticking by stirring the pasta in the first two to three minutes of cooking. If you stir too late, the pasta may become gummy.
- Do not add oil to the water. While oil will help prevent sticking, it will also make the pasta slippery. Sauce will not cling to slippery pasta, and therefore the pasta will not absorb the sauce.
- Prepare the sauce first, so it will be ready and waiting the minute the pasta is cooked. Hot pasta absorbs more liquid and flavor from the sauce.
- Reserve a small amount of the pasta cooking water just in case you need to add some moisture to the sauce. This starchy liquid will add body to the sauce as well.
- Resist the urge to rinse pasta unless you are using it in a casserole, pasta salad, or other cold application. Rinsing pasta rinses away any residual starch, and this will keep the sauce from clinging to the pasta.
- Cook pasta until al dente. This Italian term translates "to the tooth," meaning the pasta should still have a little resistance when you bite into it. However, if you are using pasta in a casserole, cook the pasta even less since it will finish cooking as the dish bakes.
- One pound of dry pasta cooked is the same yield as one and one-half pounds fresh pasta cooked. This yields about four to six entrée servings.
- Match pasta to the appropriate sauce: spaghetti and vermicelli (angel hair pasta) are good for smooth sauces. Shapes with waves or ridges (rigate), such as penne rigate, farfalle, fusilli, gemelli, or orecchiette work well with heartier chunky sauces since they trap the sauce. Fresh pasta works best with cream- or cheese-based sauces, but dry pasta will work as well. Always use cooked dry pasta for pasta salads and casseroles since fresh pasta is too tender.

SUGGESTED WINES:

- *Qupe Syrah 2003*
- *Domäne Wachau Grüner Veltliner 2003*
- *Bonny Doon Muscat Vin De Glaciere*

Sausage, Apple and Sage Stuffing

Herbed Cheese Grits Cakes

Melting Pot

SOUPS AND STEWS

Every cook knows that with soups and stews a little time, patience, and an occasional stirring of the pot will transform diverse stand-alone ingredients into a comforting, savory, healthy, and satisfying meal. In much the same way, Birmingham's well-documented struggle with diversity has led to changes in our city. It is now one of greater tolerance and racial harmony. Our landmark Birmingham Civil Rights Institute, looking toward Sixteenth Street Baptist Church, reminds us of the heartaches of the past. But it also directs us toward a brighter, healthier future.

Although the concept of the Civil Rights Institute was endorsed by the Birmingham City Council and Mayor David Vann as early as 1978, it did not open to the public until November 1992. And while it documents the plight of African-Americans in Birmingham, it also provides

a forum for discussion and reflections on civil and human rights worldwide. With this in mind, the 58,000-square-foot facility designed by Joseph Wetzell & Associates of Boston includes not only museum galleries but also an archive, community meeting rooms, and space for constantly changing exhibits and symposiums.

Our favorite recipes blend diverse ingredients to create a unique and often unexpected new taste. This chapter on soups and stews contains some of our best examples. Try the Pumpkin Soup on page 173 or White Bean Rosemary Soup on page 169. And with the example of the Birmingham Civil Rights Institute, our city will continue to celebrate its cultural diversity while occasionally stirring the pot.

Visit the Birmingham Civil Rights Institute at www.bcri.org.

*Birmingham Civil Rights Institute and
Sixteenth Street Baptist Church*

Chipotle Sweet Potato Soup

Soups and Stews

CONTENTS

GAZPACHO

MAKES 4 CUPS

1 cup chopped peeled tomatoes
1/2 cup finely chopped green
    bell pepper
1/2 cup finely chopped celery
1/2 cup chopped seeded
    peeled cucumber
1/4 cup finely chopped onion
2 teaspoons chopped fresh parsley

1 teaspoon minced garlic
2 cups tomato juice
2 to 3 tablespoons balsamic vinegar
2 tablespoons olive oil
1 teaspoon salt
1/2 to 1 teaspoon Worcestershire sauce
1/4 to 1/2 teaspoon pepper

Combine the tomatoes, bell pepper, celery, cucumber, onion, parsley and garlic in a large bowl and mix gently. Stir in the tomato juice, vinegar, olive oil, salt, Worcestershire sauce and pepper. Chill, covered, for 6 hours or longer before serving. Pour the gazpacho into soup mugs or ladle into soup bowls. Cut preparation time by chopping the vegetables in a food processor.

NANCY HANGER CANADA

CHILLED PEACH SOUP

A wonderfully different summer soup. This recipe highlights the flavor of Chilton County, Alabama peaches.
Because they are a delicious balance of acidity and sweetness, only a few ingredients are necessary.
Use the ripest peaches available. If you cannot find ripe peaches, adjust the honey to suit your taste. Pair with
a salad or sandwich for a light lunch or serve as a refreshing dessert soup.

MAKES 7 CUPS

2 pounds ripe peaches, peeled and
    sliced (about 4 peaches)
2/3 cup half-and-half
2/3 cup dry white wine (such as
    pinot grigio)

1/4 cup honey
3 tablespoons fresh lime juice
3/4 teaspoon freshly grated lime zest

Combine the peaches, half-and-half, wine, honey, lime juice and lime zest in a blender and process until smooth. Chill, covered, for 4 hours. Pour into crystal sherbet glasses.

LISA BELL LEWIS

Photograph for this recipe on page 177.

JANE'S CHILI

MAKES 12 CUPS

3 pounds ground round
1 pound Italian sausage, casings removed
2 onions, chopped
3 garlic cloves, minced
1 (28-ounce) can crushed tomatoes
1 (16-ounce) can kidney beans,
    drained and rinsed
1 (15-ounce) can black beans,
    drained and rinsed
1 (15-ounce) can white beans,
    drained and rinsed
3 (4-ounce) cans chopped green chiles
1/2 cup red wine
3 envelopes chili seasoning mix
1 teaspoon ground cumin

Brown the ground round and sausage in a large skillet, stirring until brown and crumbly. Drain, reserving the pan drippings. Spoon the ground round mixture into a large stockpot. Sauté the onions and garlic in the reserved pan drippings over medium heat for 5 minutes. Add the onion mixture, undrained tomatoes, beans, green chiles, wine, seasoning mix and cumin to the stockpot and mix well, adding additional wine or water if needed.

Simmer, covered, for 1 1/2 to 2 hours or to the desired consistency, stirring occasionally; remove the cover 30 minutes before the end of the cooking process if desired for a thicker consistency. Ladle into chili bowls and serve with sour cream, shredded cheese and corn muffins. You may freeze for future use. For testing purposes, Old El Paso Chili Seasoning Mix was used.

SHEILA SHEAN BLAIR

Photograph for this recipe on page 177.

VEGETABLE BEEF SOUP

MAKES 14 CUPS

2 pounds beef round or top round steak, cubed
4 (28-ounce) cans beef broth
2 (15-ounce) cans corn, drained
1 (28-ounce) can diced tomatoes with juice
1 (28-ounce) can green beans, drained
1 (15-ounce) can double beef broth
1 (10-ounce) package frozen baby lima beans
2 yellow onions, chopped
1 1/4 cups sliced carrots
1 cup chopped celery
2 bay leaves
1 teaspoon Worcestershire sauce
8 or 9 drops of Tabasco sauce
Salt and pepper to taste
2 potatoes, peeled and chopped
1 cup sliced mushrooms

Brown the beef in a large skillet, stirring frequently. Drain and add the beef, beef broth, corn, undrained tomatoes, green beans, double beef broth, lima beans, onions, carrots, celery, bay leaves, Worcestershire sauce, Tabasco sauce, salt and pepper in a stockpot and mix well. Bring to a boil over medium-high heat and reduce the heat to low.

Cook for 1 to 1 1/2 hours or until the beef is tender, stirring occasionally. Add the potatoes and mushrooms and return to a boil. Boil for 15 to 20 minutes or until the potatoes are tender, stirring occasionally. Discard the bay leaves and ladle into soups bowls.

In 2005 the JLB partnered with Schaeffer Eye Center and the Alabama Child Caring Foundation to conduct vision screenings on 316 children at Whatley Elementary and Glenn Middle Schools. As a result, 150 students with no medical insurance now have corrective lenses at no cost to their parents or guardians.

VEAL STEW

This is a great soup for a dinner party. Call your butcher to order the veal stew meat, since this cut is not always available in your local grocery store.

SERVES 6

1/4 cup (1/2 stick) butter
2 1/2 to 3 pounds veal stew meat
Salt and black pepper to taste
Cayenne pepper to taste
1 large onion, finely chopped
2 garlic cloves, minced
1/4 cup (1/2 stick) butter
1 pound fresh mushrooms, trimmed
  and quartered
1 1/2 cups beef stock
1 (8-ounce) can water chestnuts, drained
  and sliced
1/4 teaspoon ground nutmeg
1/4 teaspoon thyme
1 bay leaf
1/2 cup heavy cream or whipping cream
1 tablespoon cornstarch
2 tablespoons lemon juice
Hot cooked noodles or hot cooked rice

Preheat the oven to 375 degrees. Melt 1/4 cup butter in a large skillet and add the veal. Cook until brown on all sides, turning frequently. Season with salt, black pepper and cayenne pepper. Stir in the onion and garlic and cook for 3 minutes, stirring frequently. Spoon the veal mixture into a 3-quart baking dish.

Melt 1/4 cup butter in a skillet over high heat. Quickly sauté the mushrooms in the butter and spoon over the prepared layer. Deglaze the skillet with 1/2 cup of the stock. Pour the remaining 1 cup stock into the skillet and stir in the water chestnuts, nutmeg, thyme and bay leaf. Pour the stock mixture over the prepared layers and mix well.

Bake, covered, for 1 1/2 hours. Mix the cream, cornstarch and lemon juice in a bowl until blended and stir into the baked veal mixture. Bake for 15 minutes longer. Discard the bay leaf and ladle the stew over hot cooked noodles or rice.

LAIDE LONG KARPELES

In 2004–2005, the JLB gave $10,000 to the Sixteenth Street Baptist Church to help renovate the historic building originally constructed in 1911.

In the tradition of giving, the JLB celebrated its seventy-fifth anniversary in 1997 with a $100,000 gift to Cornerstone School, a private school for inner-city communities, to renovate its campus.

BRUNSWICK STEW

Every Brunswick stew is different. The beauty of this thick and hearty stew is you can purchase prepared meats at the supermarket or from your favorite barbecue establishment.

MAKES 14 CUPS

4 russet potatoes, chopped (2 pounds)
Salt to taste
2 tablespoons butter
2 tablespoons chopped onion
2 (15-ounce) cans small butter beans
1 (16-ounce) can stewed tomatoes
1 (15-ounce) can cream-style corn
1 (15-ounce) can whole kernel white corn
1 (10-ounce) can barbecued pork
1 (10-ounce) can barbecued beef
1 (10-ounce) package barbecued chicken
2 tablespoons Worcestershire sauce
1 tablespoon fresh lemon juice
1 teaspoon Creole seasoning

Combine the potatoes and salt with enough water to cover in a medium saucepan and bring to a boil. Boil until tender and drain. Melt the butter in a Dutch oven and stir in the onion. Sauté until tender. Stir in the undrained beans, undrained tomatoes, cream-style corn, undrained white corn, undrained barbecued pork, undrained barbecued beef and barbecued chicken.

Simmer over low heat for 1 hour or longer, stirring occasionally. Stir in the potatoes, Worcestershire sauce, lemon juice and Creole seasoning and simmer for 30 minutes longer, stirring occasionally. Ladle into soup bowls. You may add your favorite barbecue sauce to taste. For testing purposes, Lloyd's Barbeque Shredded Chicken was used.

JAN PHILLIPPI SHANNON

POSOLE

MAKES 12 CUPS

2 cups boiling water
2 ounces dried New Mexico chiles
1 teaspoon olive oil
2 pounds Boston butt roast, cut into 2-inch pieces
2 onions, chopped
3 garlic cloves, minced
1 teaspoon salt
1/2 teaspoon oregano
1/2 teaspoon ground cumin
1/2 teaspoon pepper
6 cups water
1 (4-pound) chicken
2 1/2 cups water
1 teaspoon salt
1/2 teaspoon pepper
2 (15-ounce) cans hominy, drained
1/2 cup chopped fresh cilantro

Pour the boiling water over the New Mexico chiles in a heatproof bowl and let stand for 10 minutes or until tender. Drain and cool. Remove the stems from the chiles and process the chiles in a blender until puréed.

Heat the olive oil in a large Dutch oven over medium-high heat. Brown the pork in batches in the hot oil. Drain, reserving the pan drippings. Sauté the onions, garlic, 1 teaspoon salt, the oregano, cumin and 1/2 teaspoon pepper in the reserved pan drippings for 8 minutes or until the onions are tender. Stir in the chile purée, pork and 6 cups water. Bring to a boil and reduce the heat to low.

Simmer, covered, for 1 hour, stirring occasionally. Add the chicken, 2 1/2 cups water, 1 teaspoon salt and 1/2 teaspoon pepper. Simmer for 1 hour longer, stirring occasionally. Remove the chicken to a platter and cool slightly. Pull the meat from the bones, discarding the skin and bones. Add the chicken, hominy and cilantro to the Dutch oven and cook over medium-low heat for 30 minutes, stirring occasionally. Ladle into soup bowls and serve with toppings such as thinly sliced radishes, lime wedges, chopped avocados and/or tortilla chips.

SHARON HILYER JONES

TUSCAN SAUSAGE STEW

MAKES 9 CUPS

1 tablespoon olive oil
4 (2-ounce) links chicken sausage, sun-dried
    tomato sausage and/or turkey sausage,
    coarsely chopped
1 cup sliced fresh mushrooms
1/2 cup chopped onion
3 tablespoons minced garlic
1 tablespoon chopped fresh rosemary
1 tablespoon chopped fresh basil
2 (15-ounce) cans chick-peas
1 (15-ounce) can diced garlic-roasted tomatoes
1/4 teaspoon pepper
1 (15-ounce) can chick-peas, drained
6 ounces fresh baby spinach
1/2 cup (2 ounces) shredded mozzarella cheese
1/2 cup (2 ounces) freshly grated
    Parmesan cheese

Heat the olive oil in a Dutch oven over medium-high heat and add the sausage, mushrooms, onion, garlic, rosemary and basil. Sauté until the sausage is brown. Stir in 2 cans undrained chick-peas, the undrained tomatoes and pepper. Mix in the drained chick-peas and bring to a boil, scraping down the side of the Dutch oven as needed.

Reduce the heat to low and simmer, covered, for about 10 minutes. Stir in the spinach and cook until the spinach wilts. Add the mozzarella cheese and simmer until the cheese melts. Ladle into soup bowls and sprinkle with the Parmesan cheese.

MARJORIE DAVIS-STEPHAN

Tear Italian bread or focaccia into chunks and line the bottom of the soup bowls. Ladle the Tuscan Sausage Stew over the bread and sprinkle with the Parmesan cheese.

CHICKEN AND WILD RICE SOUP

MAKES 12 CUPS

1 cup (2 sticks) butter
1 cup chopped carrots
3/4 cup chopped celery
3/4 cup chopped onion
2 quarts (8 cups) chicken broth
2 chicken bouillon cubes
1 (6-ounce) package long grain and wild
    rice mix with herbs
8 ounces fresh mushrooms, sliced
1/2 cup all-purpose flour
1 quart (4 cups) milk
3 cups chopped cooked chicken

Melt 1/4 cup of the butter in a Dutch oven and add the carrots, celery and onion. Sauté for 7 minutes or until the vegetables are tender. Stir in the broth, bouillon cubes, wild rice mix and the contents of the seasoning packet. Simmer for 30 to 40 minutes or until the rice is tender.

Melt 1/4 cup of the remaining butter in a skillet and add the mushrooms. Sauté until tender. Melt the remaining 1/2 cup butter in a saucepan and stir in the flour. Cook for 1 to 2 minutes or until bubbly, whisking constantly. Stir in the milk gradually. Cook until the sauce coats the back of a spoon, stirring constantly. Add the sauce, sautéed mushrooms and chicken to the rice mixture and cook just until thickened, stirring occasionally. Ladle into soup bowls.

KATHERINE WOOD HAMILTON

Photograph for this recipe on page 177.

Cornerstone School provides an environment of excellence in learning and character development so inner-city parents have an educational alternative for their children. Its students consistently receive better test scores than those who attend public schools in the same area.

TORTILLA SOUP

MAKES 16 CUPS

1 small onion, quartered
3 tablespoons corn oil
4 corn tortillas, finely chopped
6 garlic cloves, minced
1 tablespoon chopped fresh cilantro
2$\frac{1}{4}$ cups tomato purée
2 quarts (8 cups) chicken broth
2 teaspoons ground cumin
2 teaspoons chili powder
$\frac{1}{4}$ teaspoon cayenne pepper
2 bay leaves
2 to 3 cups shredded stewed chicken
Salt to taste
2 avocados, coarsely chopped for garnish
1 cup (4 ounces) shredded Cheddar cheese
    for garnish
3 corn tortillas, cut into strips and fried
    for garnish

Place the onion in a food processor and pulse until puréed. Heat the corn oil in a large saucepan over medium heat and add 4 chopped tortillas, the garlic and cilantro. Sauté for 2 minutes or until the tortillas are soft. Stir in the puréed onion and tomato purée and bring to a boil. Stir in the broth, cumin, chili powder, cayenne pepper and bay leaves. Bring to a boil and reduce the heat to low.

Simmer for 45 minutes, stirring frequently. Stir in the chicken and salt and simmer for 5 minutes longer or until heated through. Discard the bay leaves and ladle the soup into soup bowls. Garnish with the avocados, cheese and fried tortilla strips.

SHANNON BARNHILL LISENBY

Photograph for this recipe on page 176.

Because over half of our volunteers are employed, the JLB Corps of Volunteers was established to accommodate hectic schedules. The program makes JLB volunteers available to our community's nonprofit agencies for special events or programs.

WARM TORTELLINI SOUP

*Amazingly delicious soup that can be prepared in fifteen minutes.
Serve with a green salad and baguette slices topped with cheese. Grated Jarlsberg
is a good cheese to melt over the baguette slices. This is a quick and easy
weekday meal that will please both adults and children.*

MAKES 6 CUPS

4 cups reduced-sodium chicken broth
9 ounces fresh chicken tortellini or
     cheese tortellini
1 (15-ounce) can cannellini, drained
     and rinsed
1 (15-ounce) can diced Italian-style tomatoes
1/4 cup chopped fresh basil
11/4 tablespoons balsamic vinegar
Salt and pepper to taste
Freshly grated Parmesan cheese for garnish

Bring the broth to a boil in a stockpot over medium heat and add the pasta. Cook
for 4 minutes and stir in the beans and undrained tomatoes. Reduce the heat to
low and simmer for 5 minutes, stirring occasionally. Remove from the heat and
stir in the basil, vinegar, salt and pepper. Ladle into soup bowls and garnish with
Parmesan cheese.

ANNA BICKLEY COOPER

*"I can choose events that
fit my schedule, and with
the diversity of projects, I've
been able to see the JLB's
impact on many different
levels," says one member
of serving on the Corps of
Volunteers Committee.*

OODLES OF CHICKEN NOODLE

MAKES 12 CUPS

1 (4- to 5-pound) chicken
1 tablespoon Worcestershire sauce
1 teaspoon kosher salt
1/2 teaspoon coarsely ground pepper
8 to 9 cups water
2 cups finely chopped celery
1 cup chopped onion
1 carrot, peeled and sliced paper-thin
1 cup chopped bell pepper
1 (10-ounce) can tomato soup
1 bay leaf

1 (4-ounce) jar chopped pimentos,
   drained
1 garlic clove, crushed
16 ounces egg noodles
1 (2-ounce) can large black olives,
   drained and sliced
1 (6-ounce) can sliced mushrooms,
   drained, or 12 ounces sliced fresh
   mushrooms
1/4 cup chopped fresh parsley
Sprigs of parsley for garnish

Combine the chicken, Worcestershire sauce, salt and pepper with enough of the water to cover in a stockpot. Bring to a boil over high heat. Reduce the heat to medium-high and cook for 1 hour or until the breast meat registers 180 degrees on a meat thermometer. Remove the chicken to a platter, reserving the stock. Cool the chicken slightly and pull the meat from the bones, discarding the skin and bones.

Add the celery, onion, carrot, bell pepper, soup, bay leaf, pimentos and garlic to the reserved stock and cook over low heat for 30 minutes or until the vegetables are tender, stirring occasionally. Bring to a boil and stir in the noodles.

Cook until the noodles are almost tender using the package directions for the cooking time. Add the chicken, olives, mushrooms and 1/4 cup parsley and cook for 15 to 20 minutes or until the noodles are tender. Discard the bay leaf and ladle the soup into soup bowls. Garnish each serving with a sprig of parsley and serve with crusty French bread.

To speed up preparation time, use a rotisserie chicken. Pull the meat from the bones, discarding the skin and bones. Substitute the reserved homemade stock with a mixture of four 14-ounce cans chicken broth and 2 cups water and proceed as directed above.

PATRICIA O' BANNON MUSE

CREOLE OYSTER SOUP

This recipe was given to me by my mother-in-law, Estelle Hood of Memphis, Tennessee. It is very tasty and the oysters become very tender.

SERVES 6 TO 8

1 quart shucked oysters with liquor
6 cups cold water
1/2 cup (1 stick) butter
4 or 5 onions, finely chopped
3 to 5 garlic cloves, finely chopped
3 tablespoons all-purpose flour
2 bay leaves
2 teaspoons Tabasco sauce
1 teaspoon thyme
1/2 teaspoon pepper
Salt to taste
2 cups half-and-half

Combine the undrained oysters and cold water in a stockpot. Melt the butter in a skillet and add the onions and garlic. Cook until the onions are light brown, stirring frequently. Add the flour and stir until combined.

Add the onion mixture, bay leaves, Tabasco sauce, thyme, pepper and salt to the stockpot. Simmer, tightly covered, over low heat for 3 hours. Remove from the heat and discard the bay leaves. Stir in the half-and-half and ladle into soup bowls.

HARRIET KENNEDY COCHRANE

The JLB provides role models for children of domestic violence victims. One member had this to say about her experience with the YWCA's "Children in Crisis" program: "During one of our self-esteem exercises, a particularly quiet child was asked to write down the name of someone who was proud of him. He wrote down my name. That was an unforgettable and rewarding moment for me."

PETER'S GUMBO

SERVES 10

1 teaspoon red pepper
1 teaspoon black pepper
1 teaspoon salt
1 teaspoon Cajun seasoning
1 pound chicken, boned, skinned and
    cut into small pieces
1/2 cup olive oil
1/2 cup all-purpose flour
2 cups sliced okra
1 cup chopped onion
1 cup chopped green bell pepper
1 cup chopped red bell pepper
1/2 cup chopped green onions
3 (15-ounce) cans chicken broth
2 pounds shrimp, peeled and deveined
1 cup crab meat, shells and cartilage removed
3 bay leaves
Hot cooked rice

Mix the red pepper, black pepper, salt and Cajun seasoning in a sealable plastic bag. Add the chicken to the seasoning mixture and seal tightly. Toss to coat. Heat the olive oil in a large Dutch oven and add the chicken. Cook for 10 minutes or until cooked through. Remove to a platter using a slotted spoon, reserving the pan drippings.

Whisk the flour into the reserved pan drippings until blended. Cook over high heat until the roux is reddish brown in color, stirring constantly. Add the okra, onion, bell peppers and green onions and cook until the vegetables are tender, stirring constantly. Add the broth gradually, stirring constantly.

Return the chicken to the stockpot and add the shrimp, crab meat and bay leaves. Simmer for 1 hour, stirring occasionally. Discard the bay leaves and ladle the gumbo over hot cooked rice in bowls. You may add any variety of seafood you desire.

ANN LOWE MOORE

BABY LIMA BEAN SOUP

MAKES 8 (1-CUP) SERVINGS

1 (16-ounce) package frozen baby
    lima beans, thawed
3 tablespoons butter
1 onion, finely chopped
1 garlic clove, minced
2 1/2 cups chicken broth
1/4 teaspoon salt

1/4 teaspoon pepper
2 cups coarsely chopped trimmed
    fresh mustard greens
1 cup frozen baby peas
2 tablespoons chopped fresh chives
Salt and pepper to taste

Process 1 cup of the lima beans in a blender until puréed. Melt the butter in a 3-quart saucepan and add the onion and garlic. Cook for 6 minutes or until the onion is tender, stirring frequently. Stir in the bean purée, remaining lima beans, broth, 1/4 teaspoon salt and 1/4 teaspoon pepper. Simmer, covered, for 3 minutes, stirring occasionally. Add the mustard greens and peas and simmer, covered, for 3 minutes longer. Stir in the chives and season to taste with salt and pepper. Ladle into soup bowls.

CAROLINE STEVENS BOLVIG

Nutritional Profile for this recipe on page 327.

WHITE BEAN ROSEMARY SOUP

MAKES 8 (1-CUP) SERVINGS

4 ounces pancetta, chopped
1 onion, chopped
1 rib celery, chopped
1 carrot, chopped
2 garlic cloves, minced
3 (15-ounce) cans white beans,
    drained and rinsed

1 (32-ounce) carton chicken broth
1 (15-ounce) can diced tomatoes
1 1/2 tablespoons chopped
    fresh rosemary
1 teaspoon salt
Pepper to taste

Cook the pancetta in a large Dutch oven over medium heat for 5 minutes or until light brown, stirring frequently. Add the onion, celery, carrot and garlic and mix well. Cook for 10 minutes, stirring frequently. Add the beans, broth, undrained tomatoes, rosemary, salt and pepper and bring to a boil. Reduce the heat to low and simmer for 20 minutes, stirring occasionally. Ladle into soup bowls.

LYDA HELEN JONES

Nutritional Profile for this recipe on page 327.

CREAMY BROCCOLI SOUP

MAKES 12 CUPS

3 tablespoons butter
1 onion, chopped
1 (14-ounce) package frozen broccoli florets,
    cooked and drained
1/4 cup chopped fresh parsley
1/4 cup all-purpose flour
2 cups low-sodium chicken broth,
    at room temperature
1 cup half-and-half
1 cup 2% milk
2 tablespoons lemon juice
1/2 teaspoon kosher salt
1/2 teaspoon garlic powder
1/2 teaspoon cayenne pepper
1/4 teaspoon black pepper
1/8 teaspoon ground nutmeg
2 pounds Velveeta cheese, cubed

Melt the butter in a large saucepan and add the onion. Sauté until tender. Stir in the broccoli and parsley and simmer for 3 minutes, stirring occasionally. Sprinkle the flour over the broccoli mixture and cook over medium heat for 2 minutes or until the flour is absorbed, stirring constantly. Cool slightly and spoon the broccoli mixture into a blender.

Add enough of the broth to fill the blender 3/4 full and process until puréed. Return the purée to the saucepan and stir in the half-and-half, milk, lemon juice, salt, garlic powder, cayenne pepper, black pepper and nutmeg.

Microwave the cheese in a microwave-safe dish on Low until melted or melt in a double boiler. Stir the melted cheese into the soup and simmer for 20 to 30 minutes or to the desired consistency, stirring occasionally. Ladle into soup bowls. You may substitute 2 cups chopped cooked fresh broccoli florets for the frozen broccoli.

MARY McCUTCHEON BOLUS

The JLB set up shop next to the YWCA in 2001 and opened doors to My Sister's Closet, which offers career clothes at minimal cost to low-income women and at no cost to homeless women.

SLOW-COOKER POTATO SOUP

SERVES 8

2 potatoes, peeled and chopped into
   small pieces
3 tablespoons butter
2 cups chopped onions
1 cup water
2 tablespoons all-purpose flour
4 cups low-sodium chicken stock
1 cup water
8 ounces bacon, crisp-cooked and crumbled
1 cup half-and-half
1½ cups instant potato flakes
1 teaspoon salt
1 teaspoon pepper
½ teaspoon basil
1 cup (4 ounces) shredded Cheddar cheese
2 green onions, chopped

Combine the potatoes with enough water to cover in a saucepan and bring to a boil. Boil for 10 minutes and drain. Melt the butter in a large saucepan and add the onions. Sauté until tender. Remove the onions to a bowl using a slotted spoon, reserving the pan drippings. Stir 1 cup water and the flour into the reserved pan drippings. Cook until a roux forms, stirring constantly.

Combine the roux, cooked potatoes, stock and 1 cup water in a slow cooker and mix well. Mix in the bacon, half-and-half, potato flakes, salt, pepper and basil and cook, covered, on Low for 6 hours. Ladle into soup bowls and sprinkle with the cheese and green onions.

ELIZABETH ANNE SKINNER

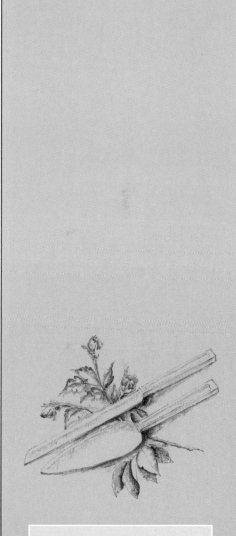

Since the opening of My Sister's Closet, the JLB has sponsored a clothes drive each year to stock the store. One year 3,854 articles of clothing and accessories were donated.

CHIPOTLE SWEET POTATO SOUP

*Chipotle chiles are smoked jalapeño chiles. They are canned and can be found in the
ethnic section in most supermarkets. Purée any remaining chiles, add a splash of fresh
lemon juice, and stir in some light mayonnaise for a spicy sandwich spread.*

MAKES 9 CUPS

1 tablespoon unsalted butter
1^1/2 cups thinly sliced onions
2 tablespoons brown sugar
1 teaspoon salt
^{1}/4 teaspoon ground cinnamon
4 garlic cloves, minced
6 cups (1-inch) chunks sweet potatoes (3 pounds)
1 chipotle chile in adobo sauce
4 cups fat-free low-sodium vegetable broth
1 cup half-and-half
3 tablespoons fresh lime juice
Sour cream for garnish
Chopped fresh chives for garnish

Melt the butter in a stockpot over medium-high heat. Add the onions, brown sugar, salt and cinnamon and sauté for 4 minutes or until the onions are light brown. Add the garlic and sauté for 1 minute. Stir in the sweet potatoes and chipotle chile and sauté for 10 minutes. Stir in the broth and bring to a boil. Reduce the heat to low.

Simmer for 25 minutes or until the sweet potatoes are tender, stirring occasionally. Remove from the heat and cool for 5 minutes. Pour ^{1}/2 of the sweet potato mixture into a blender and process until puréed. Pour the purée into a soup tureen and cover to keep warm. Repeat the process with the remaining sweet potato mixture.

Heat the half-and-half in a microwave-safe bowl on High for 30 seconds or until hot. Stir the half-and-half and lime juice into the soup and garnish with sour cream and chives.

HOPE COGEN MCINERNEY

Photograph for this recipe on page 154.

PUMPKIN SOUP

A great soup for a chilly day, but so good that you will want to eat it throughout the year.

MAKES 8 CUPS

1/4 cup (1/2 stick) butter
1 cup chopped onion
1 garlic clove, crushed
1 teaspoon curry powder
1/2 teaspoon salt
1/4 teaspoon ground coriander
1/8 teaspoon crushed red pepper
3 cups chicken broth

1 (29-ounce) can pumpkin, or
   3 1/2 cups mashed cooked
   fresh pumpkin
1 (12-ounce) can evaporated milk
1/4 cup packed light brown
   sugar (optional)
Sour cream for garnish
Chopped fresh chives for garnish

Melt the butter in a large saucepan and add the onion and garlic. Sauté for 3 to 4 minutes or until the onion is tender. Stir in the curry powder, salt, coriander and red pepper. Cook for 1 minute, stirring frequently. Add the broth and bring to a gentle boil. Boil gently for 15 to 20 minutes, stirring occasionally. Stir in the pumpkin and evaporated milk. Mix in the brown sugar for a sweeter flavor and cook for 5 minutes. Cool slightly, pour into a blender and process until creamy. Ladle the warm soup into soup bowls and garnish with sour cream and chives.

NINA HAAS DANIELS

CREAMY ITALIAN TOMATO PESTO SOUP

MAKES 9 CUPS

2 tablespoons butter
1 onion, chopped
1 garlic clove, minced
4 cups milk
3 (14-ounce) cans diced or stewed
   Italian-style tomatoes, drained

1/4 cup all-purpose flour
2 tablespoons tomato paste
Salt and pepper to taste
1 (7-ounce) jar pesto,
   at room temperature

Melt the butter in a skillet and add the onion and garlic. Sauté until the onion is tender. Heat the milk in a large stockpot until hot; do not boil. Process the onion mixture, tomatoes, flour, tomato paste, salt and pepper in a food processor or blender until smooth. Add the tomato mixture to the hot milk and bring to a boil. Reduce the heat to low and simmer for 15 minutes, stirring occasionally. Place 1 tablespoon of the pesto in each soup bowl and ladle the soup over the pesto. Serve immediately.

CHRISTINE McGRATH VELEZIS

ZUCCHINI SOUP

Great alternative to chili.

MAKES 12 CUPS

1 pound Italian sausage, casings removed
    and sausage crumbled
2 pounds zucchini, coarsely chopped
2 cups chopped celery
2 green bell peppers, chopped
1 cup chopped onion
1 (28-ounce) can diced tomatoes
1 (14-ounce) can diced tomatoes
1 (10-ounce) can tomatoes with green chiles
2 teaspoons salt
1 teaspoon Italian seasoning
1 teaspoon oregano
1 teaspoon sugar
1 teaspoon minced garlic
1/2 teaspoon basil
Grated Parmesan cheese for garnish

Brown the sausage in a skillet and drain. Sauté the zucchini, celery, bell peppers and onion in the same skillet until tender. Combine the sausage, zucchini mixture, undrained tomatoes, salt, Italian seasoning, oregano, sugar, garlic and basil in a stockpot and simmer for 1 hour, stirring occasionally. Do not be alarmed if the soup appears too thick, as additional liquid forms as the soup simmers. Ladle into soup bowls and sprinkle with cheese. Freeze for future use if desired.

GINGER GRAINGER RUEVE

Another aspect of My Sister's Closet is the donation of new and gently worn prom dresses for teens who might not otherwise be able to attend. JLB volunteers are on hand to do hair and makeup and, in partnership with the Domestic Violence Forum, present information on positive dating relationships.

ROASTED VEGETABLE MINESTRONE WITH BASIL PESTO

MAKES 6 CUPS

Basil Pesto
2 cups (3 ounces) fresh basil leaves
1/2 cup (2 ounces) freshly grated
    Parmesan cheese
1/4 cup pine nuts, toasted
2 garlic cloves, minced
1/4 teaspoon salt
3 tablespoons olive oil

Minestrone
7 ribs celery, sliced
4 large carrots, peeled and
    diagonally sliced
2 large onions, cut into 1-inch chunks
1 teaspoon salt
5 tablespoons olive oil
2 tablespoons tomato paste
1 cup red wine
4 cups beef broth
3 cups broccolini or broccoli florets
1 garlic clove, minced
1 teaspoon salt

For the pesto, combine the basil, cheese, pine nuts, garlic and salt in a food processor and process until smooth, scraping the side occasionally. Add the olive oil gradually, processing constantly until the olive oil is incorporated.

For the minestrone, preheat the oven to 500 degrees. Combine 1 cup of the celery, 1 cup of the carrots, 2 1/2 cups of the onions, 1 teaspoon salt and 2 tablespoons of the olive oil in a bowl and toss to coat. Spread the vegetable mixture in a single layer on a baking sheet and roast for 15 to 20 minutes or until the vegetables begin to brown.

Heat 1 tablespoon of the remaining olive oil in a Dutch oven over medium-high heat and add the remaining celery, remaining carrots and remaining onions. Sauté for 1 minute. Stir in the tomato paste and cook for 1 minute, stirring constantly. Add the wine and cook for 4 minutes or until the wine is absorbed, stirring occasionally. Stir in the broth and bring to a boil. Reduce the heat to low and simmer for 20 minutes or until the vegetables are tender. Strain, reserving the broth and discarding the solids.

Heat the remaining 2 tablespoons olive oil in a large saucepan over medium-high heat and add the broccolini, garlic and 1 teaspoon salt. Sauté for 3 minutes. Add the reserved broth and bring to a boil. Reduce the heat to low and simmer for 2 minutes or just until the broccolini is tender-crisp. Stir in the roasted vegetables and cook for 2 minutes or just until heated through. Ladle into soup bowls and serve with the pesto.

JOANNE MCCRARY BRASSEAL

Melting Pot

THINKING AHEAD

Use your freezer as your ultimate make-ahead strategy.

- When you have time, prepare double or triple batches of a recipe and freeze a portion for future use. Many soups and stews are ideal freezer candidates, and most double easily.
- Look for sales at the meat counter, and buy when the price is right. Simply freeze fresh chicken, beef, or pork if you do not plan to cook it within two days after purchase.
- When grilling, throw extra steaks, pork chops, or chicken on the grill. Eat some and freeze a portion for later use. You can even chop or shred the extra, divide in individual freezer bags, and remove as needed to add to pastas, soups, or stews.
- The two biggest enemies of frozen food are air and moisture because they can cause freezer burn. Airtight containers are a must.
- Stock up on seasonal items and store in the freezer. For example, buy fresh black-eyed peas and other shell beans or fresh cranberries when available. The peas will require blanching before freezing, but the cranberries, like most fruit, can go straight into the freezer.
- Use a permanent marker to label food before freezing. Include the name of the item, date frozen, number of servings, temperature and length of time required for baking, and any other necessary information, or keep a freezer inventory. Casseroles, soups, meats, vegetables, and fruit can be itemized and kept handy.

- **FREEZER GUIDE**
  Cooked Beef: steak, hamburger, and roasts—up to three months
  Cooked Pork: chops, ham, ribs, roasts, and bacon—up to three months
  Cooked Chicken: whole and chicken pieces—up to four months
  Uncooked Beef:
    Steaks—up to twelve months
    Ground Meat—up to nine months
    Roasts—up to four months
  Uncooked Pork:
    Chops and roasts—up to twelve months
    Ribs—up to three months
    Ham and bacon—up to one month
  Uncooked Chicken:
    Whole—up to twelve months
    Chicken pieces—up to nine months

Tortilla Soup

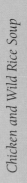
Chicken and Wild Rice Soup

Jane's Chili

CHILI SUPPER

SUGGESTED WINES:
- *Mason Napa Valley*
  Sauvignon Blanc 2004
- *Seghesio Sonoma Zinfandel 2004*
- *Marietta Old Vine Red*

Chilled Peach Soup

Center Stage

MAIN DISHES

Thanksgiving dinner, holiday gatherings, tailgate parties, neighborhood picnics, and especially the family supper table all demand an eye-catching and delicious entrée to be featured front and center. Whether it is Shrimp with Peanut Sauce on page 234, Lime Soy Tuna Steaks on page 230, Artichoke Chicken Pizza on page 220, or Pepper Chutney Beef Tenderloin on page 182, the star of the show takes a bow in this chapter.

Our main dishes that set the stage for the rest of the meal are appropriately showcased at Birmingham's "Showplace of the South"—the Alabama Theatre for the Performing Arts. This landmark theatre, built by Paramount Studios, is accented by a gold-leaf ceiling, crystal chandeliers, and cantilevered box seats.

Due to a fifteen-year (and ongoing) fund-raising effort spearheaded by Cecil Whitmire, the palatial interior,

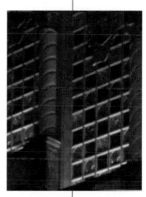

first opened to the public in 1927, was completely restored in 1998. Featuring "The Mighty Wurlitzer" pipe organ, the theatre now advertises classic old movies as well as concerts and theatrical performances, hosting more than three hundred events annually.

Cooking is a performance art. But it takes a great script for a memorable performance. Our recipes have been rehearsed in front of our most demanding and honest critics— our families and friends— and they have received stellar reviews. From the magnificent to the modest, you will find that the recipes in this chapter set the stage for the best supporting elements.

Visit Alabama Theatre at www.alabamatheatre.com or purchase the book *Alabama Theatre, Showplace of the South*, available in the theatre office.

Roasted Cornish Hens with
Wild Rice Stuffing

Main Dishes

CONTENTS

PEPPER CHUTNEY BEEF TENDERLOIN

SERVES 10

1 (3- to 4-pound) beef tenderloin, trimmed
3/4 cup unsweetened pineapple juice
1/2 cup Dale's steak seasoning
1/3 cup Worcestershire sauce
1/3 cup port
1/4 cup lemon juice
2 teaspoons seasoned salt
1 teaspoon black pepper
1 teaspoon lemon pepper
1 teaspoon dry mustard
2 teaspoons freshly ground black pepper
4 or 5 slices bacon
1 (9-ounce) jar chutney

Place the tenderloin in a heavy-duty sealable plastic bag or shallow dish. Whisk the pineapple juice, steak seasoning, Worcestershire sauce, wine, lemon juice, seasoned salt, 1 teaspoon black pepper, the lemon pepper and dry mustard in a bowl and pour over the tenderloin. Seal tightly and turn to coat. Marinate in the refrigerator for 8 hours, turning occasionally. Drain the tenderloin, reserving the marinade. Bring the marinade to a boil in a small saucepan and set aside.

Preheat the oven to 425 degrees. Rub the tenderloin generously with 2 teaspoons freshly ground black pepper and place on a rack in a shallow roasting pan. Arrange the bacon slices over the top and roast for 45 to 50 minutes or until a meat thermometer inserted in the thickest portion registers 135 degrees, basting occasionally with the reserved marinade.

Spoon the chutney evenly over the tenderloin and roast for 5 to 10 minutes longer or until a meat thermometer inserted in the thickest portion registers 145 degrees for medium-rare or 160 degrees for medium. Remove the tenderloin to a platter and let stand for 10 minutes before slicing. For testing purposes, Crosse & Blackwell Major Grey's Chutney was used.

CATHY CRISS ADAMS

SLOW-COOKER POT ROAST

SERVES 6

1 (3-pound) boneless beef chuck roast
2 large garlic cloves, sliced
1/4 cup all-purpose flour
1/2 teaspoon salt
1/2 teaspoon pepper
1/3 cup olive oil
1 1/2 cups red wine
1 onion, sliced
1 (8-ounce) can tomato sauce
1 tablespoon brown sugar
1 teaspoon oregano
1 teaspoon prepared horseradish
1 teaspoon prepared mustard
1 bay leaf
8 small red potatoes, peeled
    (about 1 1/2 pounds)
8 carrots, peeled and quartered
3 ribs celery, chopped

Cut the roast into halves and make small slits in the top of each half. Insert a garlic slice into each slit. Coat the roast with a mixture of the flour, salt and pepper. Heat the olive oil in a large skillet and brown the roast on all sides in the hot oil.

Place the roast in a 6-quart slow cooker and add the wine and onion. Mix the tomato sauce, brown sugar, oregano, prepared horseradish, prepared mustard and bay leaf in a bowl and pour over the roast. Add the potatoes, carrots and celery and cook, covered, on Low for 8 hours. Discard the bay leaf before serving.

LeAnn Holifield Cox

FAST TIPS FOR SLOW COOKING

- *One hour on High equals two hours on Low.*

- *Do not remove the lid except to add ingredients. It takes about twenty minutes to return to the original temperature.*

- *Vegetables generally cook slower than most meats. Thinly slice vegetables and arrange near the side or bottom.*

- *Cut whole chickens and cuts of meat over two pounds into halves to ensure even cooking.*

- *Cook poultry and meat on High for one hour and then reduce to Low unless the recipe calls for browning the meat first. This speeds up the time it takes the meat to reach a safe temperature.*

GRANDMOTHER'S TEXAS BARBECUED BRISKET

Long, slow cooking makes this brisket fall-off-the-fork tender.

SERVES 8

2 teaspoons celery salt
1 teaspoon garlic powder
1 teaspoon onion salt
1 (3- to 4-pound) beef brisket
1/2 cup barbecue sauce
2 tablespoons ketchup
2 tablespoons Worcestershire sauce
1/2 teaspoon liquid smoke

Mix the celery salt, garlic powder and onion salt in a bowl and rub evenly over the brisket. Combine the barbecue sauce, ketchup, Worcestershire sauce and liquid smoke in a bowl and mix well. Brush the barbecue sauce mixture over the brisket and wrap in heavy-duty foil. Chill for 8 hours or longer.

Preheat the oven to 300 degrees. Arrange the foil-wrapped brisket in a heavy roasting pan and bake for 5 hours or until the brisket is tender. Slice or shred as desired. For testing purposes, Ollie's Barbecue Sauce was used.

JULIE GRIMES BOTTCHER

The Bargain Carousel, our 1,000-family garage sale, began in 1981, and until 2004 was held every two years. The garage sale is now held annually because of its successful fundraising record.

WEEKNIGHT FLANK STEAK

This is a great and easy weeknight dish, and the leftovers make delicious sandwiches. For a different flavor, add one tablespoon honey and one minced garlic clove to the marinade.

MAKES 6 (4-OUNCE) SERVINGS

1 (2-pound) flank steak
1/3 cup chopped green onions
1 1/2 tablespoons soy sauce
1 1/2 tablespoons canola oil
Grated zest and juice of 1 lemon
1 teaspoon freshly ground pepper
1/2 teaspoon Italian seasoning

Arrange the steak in a 9×13-inch dish and sprinkle with the green onions. Whisk the soy sauce, canola oil, lemon zest, lemon juice, pepper and Italian seasoning in a bowl and pour over the steak. Marinate, covered with plastic wrap, in the refrigerator for 8 hours.

Preheat the grill to 350 to 400 degrees or to medium-high. Remove the steak and green onions from the marinade and discard the marinade. Arrange the steak topped with the green onions on the grill rack. Grill, covered with the grill lid, for 7 to 8 minutes per side or to the desired degree of doneness. Let stand for 5 minutes and cut diagonally across the grain into thin slices.

LISA BELL LEWIS

Nutritional Profile for this recipe on page 327.

The first Bargain Carousel generated $42,000. By 2005 the JLB celebrated a profit of $339,206 with more than 15,000 people coming to shop. All proceeds go into community projects that promote the well-being of women and children.

HOMEMADE FAJITAS

SERVES 6

1 (1½-pound) flank steak or skirt steak
½ cup orange juice
¼ cup tequila (optional)
¼ cup vegetable oil
Juice of 2 limes
2 tablespoons Worcestershire sauce
2 tablespoons steak marinade
3 green onions, minced
4 garlic cloves, minced
½ teaspoon pepper
2 tablespoons vegetable oil
2 onions, sliced
2 green bell peppers, sliced
Flour tortillas, heated
Toppings: shredded lettuce, chopped tomatoes,
    sour cream, shredded Cheddar cheese

Place the steak in a large heavy-duty sealable plastic bag. Mix the orange juice, tequila, ¼ cup oil, the lime juice, Worcestershire sauce, steak marinade, green onions, garlic and pepper in a bowl and pour over the steak. Seal tightly and turn to coat. Marinate in the refrigerator for 8 hours or longer, turning occasionally. Drain, reserving the marinade. Bring the marinade to a boil in a small saucepan and set aside.

Preheat the grill to 400 to 500 degrees or to high and grill the steak for 6 to 8 minutes per side, basting frequently with the reserved marinade. Heat 2 tablespoons oil in a large skillet over medium-high heat and add the onions and bell peppers. Cook until tender, stirring frequently.

Slice the steak into thin strips and arrange the steak, onion mixture and tortillas on a preheated fajita skillet. Serve immediately with lettuce, tomatoes, sour cream and cheese. For testing purposes, Moore's Original Marinade was used.

MARY T. WILLET MILLER

STEAK PIZZAIOLA

SERVES 4

3 tablespoons olive oil
1 yellow onion, julienned
3 tomatoes, peeled and chopped
1/2 cup sliced mushrooms
2 garlic cloves, minced

2 or 3 basil leaves
3/4 teaspoon salt
3/4 teaspoon oregano
1/2 teaspoon pepper
1 1/2 pounds sirloin steak, 1 inch thick

Heat 1 tablespoon of the olive oil in a small saucepan over medium heat and add the onion. Sauté until tender and stir in the tomatoes, mushrooms, garlic, basil, 1/2 teaspoon of the salt, the oregano and 1/4 teaspoon of the pepper. Reduce the heat to low and simmer, partially covered, for 15 minutes or until thickened and of a sauce consistency, stirring frequently. Discard the basil leaves.

Heat the remaining 2 tablespoons olive oil in a large skillet. Sprinkle the remaining 1/4 teaspoon salt and remaining 1/4 teaspoon pepper over the steak and add to the hot oil. Cook until the desired degree of doneness, turning once or twice. Remove the steak to a platter and let stand for 5 minutes or until cool to the touch. Cut into thin slices. Drizzle the sauce over the steak and serve immediately.

LISA GOOLDRUP COSTANZO

BEER AND NUT GREEK BURGERS

SERVES 8

2 pounds extra-lean ground beef
1/3 cup beer
1 envelope onion soup mix
1 to 2 tablespoons pine nuts, chopped

1/3 teaspoon Greek seasoning
1/4 teaspoon garlic salt
1/4 teaspoon pepper
Hamburger buns, lightly toasted

Preheat the grill to 350 to 400 degrees or to medium-high. Combine the ground beef, beer, soup mix, pine nuts, Greek seasoning, garlic salt and pepper in a bowl and mix well. Shape the ground beef mixture into 8 patties.

Arrange the patties on the grill rack and grill for 15 minutes, turning once. Serve on toasted buns with feta cheese, roasted red peppers and spinach if desired. For testing purposes, Lipton Onion Soup Mix was used.

HALLIE TRIMMIER GIBBS

ENCHILADA CASSEROLE

*Lauren compares this dish to a Mexican lasagna and adds that it is
a good way to sneak spinach into your family meal. If you prefer more heat,
use Pepper Jack cheese or add sliced jalapeño chiles.*

SERVES 6 TO 8

1 (10-ounce) package frozen chopped spinach,
    thawed and drained
1^1/$_2$ pounds lean ground beef
^{1}/$_2$ onion, chopped
1 garlic clove, minced
^{1}/$_2$ teaspoon ground cumin
^{1}/$_2$ teaspoon ground red pepper
Salt and black pepper to taste
1 (14-ounce) can diced Mexican-style tomatoes
1 (8-ounce) can tomato sauce
1 (4-ounce) can diced green chiles
Juice of 1 lime
1 teaspoon sugar
10 (6-inch) corn tortillas, quartered
^{1}/$_2$ cup (1 stick) butter, melted
2 cups (8 ounces) shredded Monterey Jack
    cheese or Cheddar cheese
1 cup sour cream

Squeeze any excess moisture from the spinach. Brown the ground beef with the onion, garlic, cumin, red pepper, salt and black pepper in a skillet, stirring until the ground beef is crumbly; drain. Stir in the spinach, undrained tomatoes, tomato sauce, green chiles, lime juice and sugar. Simmer, covered, for 10 minutes, stirring occasionally.

Preheat the oven to 350 degrees. Dip the tortilla quarters in the melted butter. Arrange ^{1}/$_2$ of the tortillas in a greased 9×13-inch baking dish. Spread with ^{1}/$_2$ of the ground beef mixture and sprinkle with ^{1}/$_2$ of the cheese. Layer with the remaining tortillas, sour cream, remaining ground beef mixture and remaining cheese and bake for 30 minutes.

LAUREN LAWS CONNER

Tears of joy are witnessed by JLB members as people from the community find much-needed, reasonably priced items at Bargain Carousel, such as a stove for a hot meal, a warm coat, or a magical Walt Disney book to entice a young reader to improve his or her reading skills.

LASAGNA

SERVES 6

1 pound ground beef
2 garlic cloves, minced
1 (8-ounce) can tomato sauce
1 (6-ounce) can tomato paste
3 tomato paste cans water
1 envelope spaghetti seasoning mix
3 cups cottage cheese
1 egg, beaten
1 teaspoon chopped fresh parsley
8 no-boil lasagna noodles
1 pound mozzarella cheese, thinly sliced
Grated Parmesan cheese to taste

Brown the ground beef with the garlic in a skillet over medium-high heat, stirring until the ground beef is crumbly; drain. Mix the tomato sauce, tomato paste, water and seasoning mix in a bowl and add to the ground beef mixture. Simmer for 15 minutes, stirring occasionally.

Preheat the oven to 350 degrees. Mix the cottage cheese, egg and parsley in a bowl. Spread 1/3 of the ground beef mixture in a 9×13-inch baking dish sprayed with nonstick cooking spray. Layer with 1/2 of the noodles, 1/2 of the cottage cheese mixture and 1/2 of the mozzarella cheese. Top with 1/2 of the remaining ground beef mixture, the remaining noodles, remaining cottage cheese mixture and remaining mozzarella cheese. Spread with the remaining ground beef mixture and sprinkle with Parmesan cheese. Bake, covered, for 30 minutes. Remove the cover and bake for 30 minutes longer. For testing purposes, McCormick's Italian Spaghetti Seasoning Mix was used.

JILL DeWITT ACOSTA

THE SKINNY ON GROUND BEEF

If a package is labeled ground beef, it must contain no more than 30 percent fat. Labels normally indicate the cut of beef that has been ground: ground chuck, ground round, or ground sirloin. Ground sirloin is the leanest—sometimes it's labeled "extra lean" with about 10 to 15 percent fat. Ground round—which may be labeled "lean"—is normally about 20 percent fat. Ground chuck is the highest with up to 30 percent fat.

Decide which you will purchase based on price, personal preference, and the recipe you're preparing. For example, if you're browning beef and pouring off the drippings, go ahead and buy the extra-lean sirloin with less fat from the start. If you're making chili, ground round or ground chuck will lend the most flavor.

FALL CASSEROLE

SERVES 8 TO 10

8 ounces small elbow macaroni
1 pound ground chuck
1 onion, chopped
1 garlic clove, minced
1 green bell pepper, chopped
8 ounces fresh mushrooms, sliced

1/2 cup pimento-stuffed green
    olives, sliced
1 (10-ounce) can tomato purée
Salt and pepper to taste
2 cups (8 ounces) shredded sharp
    Cheddar cheese

Preheat the oven to 350 degrees. Cook the pasta using the package directions and drain. Brown the ground chuck with the onion and garlic in a Dutch oven over medium-high heat, stirring until the ground chuck is crumbly; drain. Stir in the bell pepper, mushrooms and olives and simmer for 3 minutes, stirring frequently. Mix the tomato purée with enough water to measure 2 cups and add to the ground chuck mixture. Season to taste with salt and pepper and stir in 1 1/2 cups of the cheese. Spoon the ground chuck mixture into a lightly greased 9×13-inch baking dish and bake for 25 minutes. Sprinkle with the remaining 1/2 cup cheese and bake for 5 minutes longer.

HEATHER BRYANT ANTHONY

BEST-EVER GOURMET MEAT LOAF

SERVES 4

1 pound ground round
1 cup soft fresh bread crumbs
3/4 cup chopped fresh basil
1/2 cup ketchup
1/2 cup oil-pack sun-dried
    tomatoes, chopped

1/2 cup finely chopped onion
1/2 cup (2 ounces) shredded
    provolone cheese
2 eggs, beaten
2 garlic cloves, chopped
1/3 cup ketchup

Preheat the oven to 350 degrees. Line a 5×9-inch loaf pan with foil. Combine the ground round, bread crumbs, basil, 1/2 cup ketchup, the sun-dried tomatoes, onion, cheese, eggs and garlic in a bowl and mix well. Shape the ground round mixture into a loaf in the prepared loaf pan and spread with 1/3 cup ketchup. Bake for 1 hour.

VIRGINIA BAXLEY WINN

Photograph for this recipe on page 247.

MEAT LOVER'S SPAGHETTI SAUCE

MAKES 12 CUPS

8 ounces ground beef
8 ounces ground pork
8 ounces ground chicken or ground turkey
6 to 8 slices bacon, chopped
1 large onion, chopped
2 ribs celery, chopped
1 (18-ounce) can diced tomatoes
1 (14-ounce) jar artichoke hearts, drained and chopped
1 (14-ounce) can stewed tomatoes
1 (6-ounce) can tomato paste
1 (2-ounce) can sliced black olives, drained
1 cup dry red wine
1/2 cup sliced pimento-stuffed green olives
2 teaspoons coarsely ground black pepper
1 teaspoon oregano, crushed
1 teaspoon basil, crushed
1/2 teaspoon ground red pepper
1 bay leaf
Hot cooked pasta

Mix the ground beef, ground pork, ground chicken, bacon, onion and celery in a large Dutch oven. Cook over medium-high heat until the ground beef, ground pork and ground chicken are crumbly and are no longer pink, stirring frequently; drain. Stir in the undrained diced tomatoes, artichokes, undrained stewed tomatoes, tomato paste, black olives and wine. Add the green olives, black pepper, oregano, basil, red pepper and bay leaf and mix well. Bring to a boil and then reduce the heat to low.

Simmer for 1 hour or to the desired consistency, stirring occasionally. Discard the bay leaf and spoon the sauce over hot cooked pasta on a serving platter. Sprinkle with grated Parmesan cheese if desired.

LEIGH HARDIN HANCOCK

MARINATED LAMB CHOPS

SERVES 2

3/4 cup balsamic vinegar
1/3 cup mint jelly
1/3 cup fresh mint leaves, chopped

4 (4-ounce) lamb loin chops
Salt and pepper to taste

Mix the vinegar and jelly in a small saucepan and cook just until the mixture comes to a boil, stirring occasionally. Remove from the heat and stir in the mint leaves. Season the lamb chops with salt and pepper and place in a sealable plastic bag or shallow dish. Pour the vinegar mixture over the chops and seal tightly. Turn to coat and marinate in the refrigerator for 2 hours, turning occasionally.

Coat the grill rack with nonstick cooking spray and preheat the grill to 350 to 400 degrees or to medium-high. Drain the chops, discarding the marinade. Arrange the chops on the prepared grill rack. Grill for 7 to 9 minutes per side or to the desired degree of doneness.

LESLIE BERRY MCLEOD

ROSEMARY LAMB

To save time, ask the butcher to trim the lamb racks.

SERVES 4 TO 6

3 tablespoons red wine vinegar
2 tablespoons sugar
2 tablespoons Dijon mustard
1 tablespoon minced garlic
1 1/2 tablespoons chopped
     fresh rosemary

1 teaspoon kosher salt
1 teaspoon cracked pepper
1/2 cup extra-virgin olive oil
2 racks of lamb, trimmed, or
     3 lamb loin chops

Combine the vinegar, sugar, Dijon mustard, garlic, rosemary, salt and pepper in a bowl and mix well. Add the olive oil gradually, whisking constantly until the oil is incorporated. Pour the vinegar mixture over the lamb in a shallow dish and turn to coat. Marinate, covered, in the refrigerator for 8 hours or longer, turning occasionally. Preheat the grill to 350 to 400 degrees or to medium-high. Drain the lamb, discarding the marinade, and grill for 5 to 6 minutes per side or until a meat thermometer inserted in the thickest portion registers 150 degrees for medium-rare.

MARY SPOTSWOOD BOX

ROSEMARY GINGER PORK TENDERLOIN

MAKES 8 (3-OUNCE) SERVINGS

2 (1-pound) pork tenderloins, trimmed	3 tablespoons chopped fresh rosemary
1 (12-ounce) jar apricot preserves	2 tablespoons chopped fresh ginger
1 (5-ounce) bottle light teriyaki sauce	

Place the tenderloins in a large heavy-duty sealable plastic bag or in a shallow dish. Mix the preserves, teriyaki sauce, rosemary and ginger in a bowl and pour over the tenderloins. Seal tightly and turn to coat. Marinate in the refrigerator for 30 minutes or for up to 8 hours, turning occasionally. Drain the tenderloins, reserving the marinade. Preheat the oven to 425 degrees. Bring the reserved marinade to a boil in a small saucepan and set aside. Arrange the tenderloins in a baking pan and bake for 25 minutes or until a meat thermometer inserted in the thickest portion registers 155 degrees, basting frequently with the reserved marinade. Remove from the oven and let stand, covered, for 10 minutes or until a meat thermometer registers 160 degrees.

KATHRYN LAVALLET TORTORICI

Nutritional Profile for this recipe on page 327.

PORK MEDALLIONS IN CREAMY MUSTARD SAUCE

This is a wonderful recipe for a cold winter night. Serve with wild rice and grilled asparagus.

SERVES 4

1 pork tenderloin, cut into 1¹/₂-inch slices	¹/₄ cup vegetable oil
Salt and pepper to taste	²/₃ cup dry white wine
¹/₂ cup all-purpose flour	²/₃ cup sour cream
	1¹/₂ teaspoons Dijon mustard

Sprinkle the pork with salt and pepper and coat lightly with the flour. Heat the oil in a heavy skillet over medium-high heat. Sauté the pork in the hot oil for 5 minutes per side or until light brown and cooked through. Remove the pork to a platter and cover to keep warm. Heat the wine in the skillet, stirring with a wooden spoon to loosen any browned bits from the bottom of the skillet. Reduce the heat to medium-low and stir in the sour cream. Cook for 2 minutes or until thickened and of a sauce consistency, stirring constantly. Remove from the heat and stir in the Dijon mustard. Serve the sauce over the pork.

MITZI MUNGER IRELAND

HOLIDAY PORK TENDERLOIN

SERVES 3

1 (8- to 10-ounce) pork tenderloin
Salt and pepper to taste
1$1/2$ tablespoons butter
$1/2$ cup chopped onion
1 tablespoon chopped fresh rosemary
$1/2$ cup low-sodium chicken broth
$1/3$ cup whole cranberry sauce
1 tablespoon balsamic vinegar

Preheat the oven to 450 degrees. Sprinkle the tenderloin with salt and pepper. Melt $1/2$ tablespoon of the butter in a large ovenproof skillet over medium-high heat. Brown the pork on all sides in the butter and bake for 8 to 10 minutes or until a meat thermometer inserted in the thickest portion registers 155 degrees. Remove from the oven and let stand, covered, for 10 minutes or until a meat thermometer registers 160 degrees.

Melt the remaining 1 tablespoon butter in a heavy skillet over medium-high heat and add the onion and rosemary. Sauté for 3 minutes or until the onion is tender. Stir in the broth, cranberry sauce and vinegar and cook for 2 minutes or until the cranberry sauce melts, whisking constantly.

Remove the tenderloin to a serving platter and pour the pan juices into the cranberry mixture. Bring to a boil and boil for 6 minutes or until the sauce coats the back of a spoon, stirring occasionally. Slice the tenderloin as desired and serve with the cranberry sauce.

NANCY BEAIRD BROMBERG

ENTERTAIN WITH EASE

The adage "practice makes perfect" is good advice to follow when entertaining. If you plan to serve a new dish, give it a practice run one to two weeks before the dinner party. This will give you an opportunity to find out where to purchase all of the ingredients, tweak the flavors if necessary, practice any new techniques involved, and think about beautiful garnishes as well. You can also work out the timing of the recipe and plan what steps can be prepared ahead.

TEXAS-STYLE CHALUPA

*My mother discovered this recipe when she lived in Texas. It is a
fun dish for company that may be prepared in advance.*

SERVES 10 TO 12

1 pound dried pinto beans
1 (3-pound) center-cut boneless pork roast
7 cups water
1 onion, chopped
1 (4-ounce) can chopped green chiles
1 (2-ounce) jar diced pimento, drained
2 garlic cloves, minced
2 tablespoons chili powder
1 tablespoon salt
1 tablespoon ground cumin
1 teaspoon oregano
Corn chips
Toppings: diced avocado, sliced green onions,
    shredded lettuce, salsa, shredded Cheddar
    cheese, chopped cucumber, chopped
    tomato, sour cream

Sort and rinse the beans. Combine the beans, pork, water, onion, green chiles,
pimento, garlic, chili powder, salt, cumin and oregano in a Dutch oven and bring
to a boil. Reduce the heat to low and simmer, covered, for 3 hours or until the
pork is tender, stirring occasionally.

Remove the pork to a platter and shred with a fork. Return the shredded pork
to the Dutch oven and cook for 1 1/2 hours longer or until thickened, stirring
occasionally. Serve over corn chips with the desired toppings.

ANNE STARNES FINCH

*The JLB introduced The
Market as a new fundraiser
in October 2005. Vendors
from all over the U.S. came
to display their goods just in
time for the busy holiday
shopping season.*

CAROLINA BARBECUED PORK

SERVES 8

1 onion, thickly sliced
1/4 cup packed brown sugar
1 tablespoon paprika
2 teaspoons salt
2 teaspoons celery salt
2 teaspoons chili powder
1 teaspoon black pepper
1 (3- to 5-pound) boneless pork butt, trimmed
    and cut into halves
3/4 cup apple cider vinegar
4 teaspoons Worcestershire sauce
1 1/2 teaspoons granulated sugar
1 teaspoon garlic salt
1 teaspoon black pepper
1/2 teaspoon dry mustard
1/4 teaspoon ground red pepper
Hamburger buns

Arrange the onion slices over the bottom of a 6-quart slow cooker. Mix the brown sugar, paprika, salt, celery salt, chili powder and 1 teaspoon black pepper in a bowl. Rub the brown sugar mixture over the surface of the pork and place in the prepared slow cooker.

Combine the vinegar, Worcestershire sauce, granulated sugar, garlic salt, 1 teaspoon black pepper, the dry mustard and red pepper in a bowl and mix well. Pour 1/2 of the vinegar sauce over the pork and cook, covered, on High for 1 hour. Reduce the heat to Low and cook for 6 hours longer. Shred the pork and drizzle with the remaining vinegar sauce if desired. Serve on hamburger buns topped with your favorite coleslaw.

JEANNE REID SHEARER

Photograph for this recipe on page 246.

196

CRISPY BAKED PORK CHOPS WITH LEMON WINE SAUCE

SERVES 4

2 pork chops, butterflied
1 cup dry bread crumbs
1/2 cup (2 ounces) grated Parmesan cheese
1/4 teaspoon salt
1/4 teaspoon pepper
1 cup milk
2 eggs
3 tablespoons vegetable oil
1 (14-ounce) can chicken broth
1/2 cup dry white wine
2 tablespoons lemon juice
1 (10-ounce) package frozen green peas
1/4 cup water
1 teaspoon cornstarch
Lemon wedges for garnish

Cut the pork chops lengthwise into halves. Mix the bread crumbs, cheese, salt and pepper in a shallow dish. Whisk the milk and eggs in a shallow dish until blended. Dip the chops in the egg mixture and coat with the bread crumb mixture. Heat the oil in a large skillet over medium heat and add the chops.

Cook for 5 minutes and turn. Cook for 5 minutes longer or until brown. Add the broth and cook, covered, for 30 minutes or until the chops are tender. Remove the chops to a platter and cover to keep warm, reserving the pan juices.

Add the wine and lemon juice to the reserved pan juices and bring to a boil. Boil for 2 minutes. Stir in the peas and cook, covered, over medium heat for 5 minutes or until the peas are tender. Remove the peas with a slotted spoon and spoon the peas around the chops, reserving the wine mixture. Whisk the water and cornstarch in a bowl until blended and stir into the reserved wine mixture. Bring to a boil and cook until thickened, stirring occasionally. Drizzle the wine sauce over the chops and garnish with lemon wedges.

MARY McCUTCHEON BOLUS

PORK CHOPS WITH BLACKBERRY, JALAPEÑO AND RED WINE SAUCE

SERVES 4

Pork Chops
1/2 cup salt
1/2 cup sugar
4 thick-cut bone-in pork chops
Crushed fresh sage stalks
Freshly ground pepper
2 to 3 tablespoons olive oil

Blackberry, Jalapeño and Red Wine Sauce
12 ounces fresh blackberries
1/4 cup cider vinegar
1/4 cup sugar
1 jalapeño chile, minced
1/16 teaspoon salt
2 cups red wine (such as cabernet sauvignon)
1 teaspoon butter

For the pork chops, combine the salt and sugar in a 1-gallon sealable plastic bag and add enough water to fill 2/3 full. Add the pork chops and sage to the brine and seal tightly. Chill for 6 to 10 hours; the longer the better.

Preheat the oven to 350 degrees. Drain the chops, pat dry and season with pepper. Heat the olive oil in a large ovenproof skillet over high heat. Sear the chops on 1 side in the hot oil for 5 minutes or until golden brown; turn. Bake for 15 to 20 minutes or until cooked through. Remove from the oven and let rest, covered with foil, for 5 minutes.

For the sauce, combine the blackberries, vinegar, sugar, jalapeño chile and salt in a small saucepan and cook for 15 minutes or until the mixture is reduced by 3/4, stirring frequently. Stir in the wine and cook for 10 minutes or until the mixture is reduced by 1/2, stirring frequently. Blend in the butter just before serving and serve with the chops.

MARY SPOTSWOOD BOX

STUFFED PORK CHOPS WITH PARMESAN SAUCE

SERVES 6

1 (10-ounce) package frozen chopped spinach,
   thawed and drained
2 tablespoons olive oil
1/2 cup finely chopped mushrooms
1/2 cup finely chopped onion
1/4 cup finely chopped carrots
2 garlic cloves, minced
1/2 cup herb-seasoned or Italian-style bread crumbs
1/3 cup fat-free plain yogurt
1/16 teaspoon red pepper flakes
6 (1-inch-thick) rib pork chops
Salt and black pepper to taste
1/4 cup fat-free plain yogurt
1/4 cup milk
1/4 cup (1 ounce) shredded Parmesan cheese
1/8 teaspoon garlic powder
1/8 teaspoon basil
1/8 teaspoon sage
1/16 teaspoon ground red pepper

Press any excess moisture from the spinach and place in a bowl. Heat the olive oil in a medium saucepan over medium heat and add the mushrooms, onion, carrots and garlic. Sauté for 5 minutes or until the vegetables are tender. Add the sautéed mixture to the spinach and mix well. Stir in the bread crumbs, 1/3 cup yogurt and the red pepper flakes.

Preheat the oven to 350 degrees. Make a pocket in each pork chop and sprinkle the chops with salt and black pepper. Spoon about 1/6 of the bread crumb mixture into each pocket and secure with wooden picks. Brown the chops on both sides in a nonstick skillet and arrange in a single layer in a baking pan.

Mix 1/4 cup yogurt, the milk, cheese, garlic powder, basil, sage and red pepper in a bowl and spoon the yogurt mixture over the chops. Bake for 30 minutes or until cooked through.

LYNN COMPTON CHAPMAN

SWEET-AND-SPICY PORK CHOPS

*Our testers recommend serving these chops with mashed potatoes,
so the additional sauce could spill over onto them.*

SERVES 4

2 tablespoons vegetable oil
4 (1-inch-thick) bone-in pork chops
1 large onion, sliced
1 cup (or more) orange juice
2 tablespoons brown sugar
1 tablespoon lemon juice
1/2 to 1 teaspoon ground ginger
1/2 teaspoon poultry seasoning
1/2 teaspoon marjoram
1/2 cup seedless golden raisins
Salt and pepper to taste

Heat the oil in a large skillet and add the pork chops. Cook until brown on both sides. Remove the chops to a platter, reserving the pan drippings. Cook the onion in the reserved pan drippings until tender. Stir in the orange juice, brown sugar, lemon juice, ginger, poultry seasoning, marjoram, raisins, salt and pepper.

Return the chops to the skillet and cook, covered, over low heat for 1 hour or until the chops are cooked through, adding additional orange juice as needed for the desired consistency and stirring occasionally.

CAROLYN RITCHEY KING

ONIONS

Onions are easily divided into two categories: green onions and dry onions. Green onions are simply immature plants harvested before a mature bulb forms, whereas dry onions are mature bulbs with an edible interior and dry papery outer skin. With so many varieties, shapes, and sizes, use the guide below to help you select the right onion for the job.

Yellow-skinned onions (except sweet varieties) tend to have the strongest flavor and should be used for cooking.

White onions are the most versatile. Since they have a somewhat mild flavor and a bit more natural sugar than yellow-skinned, these onions are often eaten raw, especially in Mexican food, such as salsa. White onions are also good in cooked dishes. ➤

200

BARBECUED DRY-RUBBED PORK RIBS

SERVES 4

Mopping Sauce
2 cups cider vinegar
1/4 cup packed dark brown sugar
2 tablespoons Worcestershire sauce
2 teaspoons kosher salt
1/2 teaspoon freshly ground pepper
1 onion, thinly sliced and separated into rings
3 garlic cloves, crushed
1 jalapeño chile, sliced (optional)

Pork Ribs
1/4 cup sweet paprika
3 tablespoons ground cumin
2 tablespoons kosher salt
1 1/2 tablespoons dark brown sugar
2 teaspoons onion powder
2 teaspoons ground red pepper
1 teaspoon celery salt
1 teaspoon garlic salt
2 racks baby back ribs

For the sauce, combine the vinegar, brown sugar, Worcestershire sauce, salt and pepper in a bowl and mix until the sugar and salt dissolve. Stir in the onion, garlic and jalapeño chile.

For the ribs, prepare a hot fire by stacking charcoal on 1 side of the grill, leaving the other side empty. For gas grills, light only 1 side. Coat the grill rack with nonstick cooking spray.

Mix the paprika, cumin, salt, brown sugar, onion powder, red pepper, celery salt and garlic salt in a bowl. Rub the seasoning mixture over the ribs and arrange the ribs over direct heat.

Grill for 10 minutes or until brown. Turn the ribs and place over indirect heat. Grill, covered with the grill lid, for 2 1/2 hours or until the meat begins to pull away from the bone, turning and brushing with the sauce every 30 minutes.

MARY SPOTSWOOD BOX

Red onions are actually a purplish-red color, and they have a mild flavor. Best eaten raw, red onions work well in salads or quick-cooked dishes that allow them to maintain their glorious color. They turn a grayish-brown color when cooked for any length of time.

Sweet onions include varieties such as Vidalia, Walla Walla, Maui, and Texas Sweet 1015. These onions have a high natural sugar content, so they're best eaten raw. However, these are a great choice for making caramelized or grilled onions because the natural sugars will brown.

Green onions are also known as scallions, spring onions, or salad onions. Raw green onions have a sweet delicate flavor, but they will stand up to quick cooking and grilling as well.

DAVE'S FAVE PIZZA

*To shorten preparation time, use a jar of roasted red bell
peppers instead of roasting your own.*

SERVES 4 TO 6

1 red bell pepper
1 yellow bell pepper
1 onion, sliced
3 tablespoons olive oil
1 pound Italian sausage, casings removed
2 (10-ounce) packages whole wheat pizza crusts
1 (7-ounce) jar pesto
1 cup (4 ounces) shredded mozzarella cheese
2 ounces goat cheese, crumbled
Grated Parmesan cheese to taste

Preheat the oven to 450 degrees. Toss the bell peppers and onion with the olive oil in a bowl until coated. Arrange the onion slices and bell peppers on a baking sheet and roast for 10 minutes, turning occasionally. Let stand until cool. Cut the bell peppers into strips, discarding the seeds and membranes. Maintain the oven temperature.

Brown the sausage in a large skillet over medium heat, stirring until crumbly; drain. Arrange the pizza crusts on a baking sheet and spread evenly with the pesto. Sprinkle each crust with 1/2 cup of the mozzarella cheese. Top evenly with the sausage, bell peppers and onion. Sprinkle with the goat cheese and Parmesan cheese and bake for 7 to 8 minutes or until the cheese melts. For testing purposes, Boboli Pizza Crusts were used.

LESLIE BERRY MCLEOD

Oven Jambalaya

SERVES 8

1 pound andouille, sliced
4 cups chopped cooked chicken
1/2 cup (1 stick) butter, melted
1 pound converted rice
1 (14-ounce) can beef broth
1 (10-ounce) can tomato sauce

1 (10-ounce) can French onion soup
1 green bell pepper, chopped
1 bunch green onions, chopped
  (about 1/4 cup)
1 tablespoon Creole seasoning

Preheat the oven to 375 degrees. Brown the sausage in a Dutch oven and drain. Add the chicken, butter, rice, broth, tomato sauce, soup, bell pepper, green onions and Creole seasoning to the sausage and mix well.

Spoon the sausage mixture into a lightly greased 9×13-inch baking dish and bake, covered, for 1 1/4 hours, stirring occasionally. Sprinkle with additional Creole seasoning before serving if desired. For testing purposes, Uncle Ben's Rice was used.

Lauren Zito Palermo

Great Grilled Venison

SERVES 6

6 venison tenderloin fillets
8 ounces cream cheese, softened
1 tablespoon chopped fresh oregano
1 1/2 teaspoons minced garlic

1 1/2 teaspoons minced onion
1/2 teaspoon kosher salt
1/2 teaspoon freshly ground pepper
6 slices bacon

Preheat the grill to high. Pound the fillets between sheets of waxed paper until flattened. This step may be omitted if the venison is already tenderized.

Mix the cream cheese, oregano, garlic, onion, salt and pepper in a bowl. Spread 2 to 3 tablespoons of the cream cheese mixture on each fillet and roll to enclose the filling. Wrap each roll with a slice of bacon and secure with wooden picks. Arrange the rolls on the grill rack and grill until seared on all sides. Decrease the heat to low and grill until the desired degree of doneness, turning occasionally.

Nancy Bedsole Bynon

DUCK CONFIT

This is a twist on a traditional French method for cooking duck. Use this succulent duck in pasta dishes, to make fillings for Mexican dishes such as enchiladas or quesadillas, or serve shredded atop mashed potatoes.

SERVES 4 TO 6

4 duck legs with thighs attached
$1^1/2$ tablespoons kosher salt
$3/4$ teaspoon freshly ground pepper
$1/2$ cup extra-virgin olive oil
8 garlic cloves, crushed
15 sprigs of thyme
1 lemon, thinly sliced
Zest of 1 orange
$1/2$ cup extra-virgin olive oil
$1/2$ cup (1 stick) unsalted butter
$1/3$ cup bacon drippings

Place the duck in a sealable plastic bag and sprinkle with the salt and pepper, squeezing the bag to distribute the seasonings evenly. Add $1/2$ cup olive oil, the garlic, thyme, lemon and orange zest and seal tightly. Turn to coat and marinate in the refrigerator for 24 hours, turning occasionally.

Preheat the oven to 200 degrees. Heat $1/2$ cup olive oil, the butter and bacon drippings in a Dutch oven over medium heat. Discard the lemon slices and add the duck and marinade to the butter mixture. Bake, covered, for $2^1/2$ hours or until the duck is cooked through. Allow the duck to cool in the oil mixture and chill for 24 hours. Remove the duck from the oil mixture and pull the meat from the bones, discarding the skin and bones.

JULIE GRIMES BOTTCHER

DUCK CONFIT WITH ORECCHIETTE AND BUTTERNUT SQUASH

SERVES 4

1/4 cup (1/2 stick) butter
3 shallots, cut into halves and thinly sliced
2 cups (1-inch) chunks butternut squash
3 garlic cloves, minced
1 cup less-sodium fat-free chicken broth
1 teaspoon kosher salt
1/4 teaspoon crushed red pepper flakes
2 1/2 cups shredded Duck Confit (page 204)
8 ounces orecchiette, cooked
1/3 cup chopped fresh flat-leaf parsley
3 tablespoons chopped fresh thyme

Melt the butter in a large skillet over medium-high heat and add the shallots. Sauté for 1 minute. Stir in the squash and garlic and sauté for 3 minutes. Mix in the broth, salt and red pepper flakes and bring to a boil. Reduce the heat to low.

Simmer for 12 minutes or until most of the liquid is absorbed and the squash is tender, stirring occasionally. Stir in the duck and cook for 2 minutes or until heated through. Add the hot cooked pasta and cook for 1 minute or until heated through. Spoon into a serving bowl and sprinkle with the parsley and thyme. Serve immediately.

JULIE GRIMES BOTTCHER

GARLIC

The most pungent allium, garlic is widely available year-round. Ranging in size and color, three varieties are the most common. White or American garlic has the strongest flavor, while the lavender-skinned Mexican and Italian garlic are milder. Larger heads of garlic, such as elephant garlic, tend to have the mildest flavor of all.

Crushing or chopping garlic releases the flavor. To lightly perfume a sauce, soup, or stew, add whole or largely sliced garlic cloves to the pan. If it's a more assertive flavor you're after, crush or mince the garlic to release more natural oils and therefore, more of the characteristic garlicky bite.

When shopping for garlic, avoid heads with green shoots growing out the end. This is a sign of age, and old garlic will have an unpleasant bitter flavor.

DUCK BREAST WITH CHERRY BALSAMIC SAUCE

SERVES 4

4 boneless duck breast halves
2 tablespoons olive oil
2 tablespoons honey
1 tablespoon fresh lime juice
1 teaspoon grated lime zest
2 teaspoons grated fresh ginger
1¹/₂ teaspoons Thai chile paste
2 garlic cloves, minced
2 tablespoons olive oil
1 teaspoon kosher salt
¹/₃ cup balsamic vinegar
1 (10-ounce) package fresh or frozen cherries or
    frozen blackberries
¹/₂ cup less-sodium fat-free chicken broth
¹/₄ cup orange liqueur

Place the duck in a sealable plastic bag. Mix 2 tablespoons olive oil, the honey, lime juice, lime zest, ginger, chile paste and garlic in a bowl and pour over the duck. Seal tightly and turn to coat evenly. Marinate in the refrigerator for 1 hour, turning once.

Heat 2 tablespoons olive oil in a large skillet over medium-high heat. Drain the duck, reserving the marinade. Sprinkle the duck with the salt and arrange skin side down in the hot oil. Sauté for 2 minutes or until brown; turn. Cook for 6 minutes or to the desired degree of doneness. Remove the duck to a platter and cover to keep warm, reserving the pan drippings. Depending on the thickness of the duck breasts, you may finish cooking the duck in a 400-degree oven for 7 minutes to prevent overbrowning.

Add the vinegar to the reserved pan drippings and scrape the bottom of the skillet with a metal spatula to loosen any browned bits. Cook for 2 minutes or until most of the liquid evaporates. Stir in the reserved marinade, cherries, broth and liqueur and bring to a boil. Reduce the heat to low.

Simmer for 15 minutes, stirring occasionally. Cool slightly and pour into a blender. Process until smooth. Strain the sauce through a fine mesh sieve into a bowl, discarding the solids. Serve the sauce with the duck.

CARI LORENTZ SOUTH

ROASTED QUAIL STUFFED WITH BACON AND CORN BREAD

SERVES 6

1¹/3 cups cornmeal
1/3 cup all-purpose flour
1 teaspoon baking powder
3 slices bacon, chopped
1 bunch scallions, sliced
3 cups buttermilk
1 egg, lightly beaten
1/2 teaspoon kosher salt
1/2 teaspoon pepper

5 tablespoons vegetable oil
1/2 cup finely chopped onion
1/4 cup finely chopped carrots
1/4 cup finely chopped celery
4 sprigs of thyme
1/2 teaspoon kosher salt
1/2 teaspoon pepper
1/2 cup chicken broth
6 semi-boneless quail

Preheat the oven to 350 degrees. Mix the cornmeal, flour and baking powder in a bowl. Cook the bacon in a skillet until brown and crisp and add the scallions. Cook for 1 to 2 minutes or until the scallions are tender. Add the bacon mixture, buttermilk and egg to the cornmeal mixture and mix well. Stir in 1/2 teaspoon salt and 1/2 teaspoon pepper. Coat a cast-iron skillet with 2 tablespoons of the oil and add the cornbread mixture to the prepared skillet. Bake for 30 minutes. Remove the corn bread to a wire rack and let stand until cool. Crumble the corn bread into a large bowl. Increase the oven temperature to 400 degrees.

Heat 1 tablespoon of the remaining oil in a skillet and add the onion, carrots and celery. Sauté until the vegetables are tender but not brown. Stir the sautéed vegetables into the crumbled corn bread. Add the thyme, 1/2 teaspoon salt and 1/2 teaspoon pepper and mix well. Add just enough of the broth to moisten and mix well.

Heat the remaining 2 tablespoons oil in an ovenproof skillet. Spoon about 2 tablespoons of the corn bread mixture into each quail cavity. Form the quail into the natural shape, tucking in the legs, and place breast side down in the hot oil. Sauté for 3 minutes or until brown. Turn and sauté for 2 minutes longer. Roast for 8 minutes or until cooked through.

IDIE AND CHRIS HASTINGS, HOT & HOT FISH CLUB IN SOUTHSIDE

ROASTED CORNISH HENS WITH WILD RICE STUFFING

SERVES 4

Cornish Hens
4 fresh Cornish hens
Salt and freshly ground pepper to taste
2 tablespoons olive oil
2 tablespoons butter
1 tablespoon cornstarch
1/2 cup currant jelly
1/4 cup apple cider vinegar
2 tablespoons fresh lemon juice
1 teaspoon salt
6 whole cloves

Wild Rice Stuffing and Assembly
1/4 cup (1/2 stick) butter
8 ounces fresh mushrooms, sliced
2 ribs celery, finely chopped
4 green onions, finely chopped
1 (6-ounce) package long grain and
    wild rice with seasoning packet
2 cups water

For the hens, season the outside of the hens with salt and pepper to taste and rub with the olive oil. Place the hens in a shallow dish or sealable plastic bag and chill for 3 to 4 hours.

Melt the butter in a saucepan over low heat and whisk in the cornstarch until smooth. Whisk the jelly, vinegar, lemon juice and 1 teaspoon salt in a bowl until blended and add to the saucepan. Stir in the cloves and bring to a boil. Cook for 1 minute or until of a glaze consistency, stirring frequently. Remove from the heat and discard the cloves. Divide the glaze into 2 equal portions, reserving 1 portion for basting and the remaining portion to serve with the hens.

For the stuffing, melt the butter in a skillet over medium-high heat and add the mushrooms, celery and green onions. Sauté for 5 minutes and stir in the rice, seasoning packet and water. Bring to a boil and reduce the heat to low. Simmer for 15 minutes or until the liquid is absorbed. The rice may be crunchy, but it will continue to cook as the hens roast.

Preheat the oven to 350 degrees. Arrange the hens breast side up in a roasting pan and spoon approximately 1 cup of the stuffing into each hen. Roast for 70 minutes or until the hens test done, basting twice with 1 portion of the reserved glaze. Remove the hens to serving plates and let stand for 10 minutes. Serve with the remaining reserved warm glaze.

ZOË PROFERIS CASSIMUS

Photograph for this recipe on page 180.

CHICKEN CARRIE

SERVES 4 TO 6

1 (3½-pound) chicken
Salt and freshly ground pepper to taste
1 lemon, cut into halves
5 sprigs of flat-leaf parsley
3 sprigs of rosemary
2 garlic cloves
6 tablespoons olive oil
5 shallots, quartered
1 large onion, sliced
1 red bell pepper, cut into 1-inch pieces
1 yellow bell pepper, cut into 1-inch pieces
1 sweet potato, peeled and cut into
    1-inch pieces
10 garlic cloves

Preheat the oven to 425 degrees. Discard the giblets and neck from the chicken cavity. Season the inside cavity and outside surface of the chicken with salt and pepper and stuff the cavity with the lemon, parsley, rosemary and 2 garlic cloves. Tie the legs together with kitchen twine if desired and rub the outside surface of the chicken with 2 tablespoons of the olive oil.

Drizzle 2 tablespoons of the remaining olive oil into a large roasting pan and heat in the oven for 5 minutes or until the oil is hot. Remove the pan from the oven and arrange the chicken breast side up in the hot oil. Bake for 45 minutes.

Toss the shallots, onion, bell peppers, sweet potato and 10 garlic cloves with the remaining 2 tablespoons olive oil in a bowl until coated and season with salt and pepper. Add the vegetable mixture to the roasting pan and bake for 45 minutes longer or until a meat thermometer inserted into the leg joint registers 170 degrees, stirring the vegetables halfway through the baking process. Let stand for 10 minutes. Slice the chicken as desired and serve with the vegetables.

LESLIE BERRY MCLEOD

SLOW-COOKER CHICKEN AND DUMPLINGS

*Frozen dumpling sheets are located in the frozen food section of most
supermarkets, near the frozen pastas and frozen bread dough. Two cups dried wide
egg noodles may be substituted for the dumplings if necessary.*

SERVES 6

1 (3^1/2-pound) chicken, skin removed and chicken cut up
1 cup sliced peeled carrots (about 3)
1 cup chopped onion
2 ribs celery, chopped
4 bay leaves
2 tablespoons parsley flakes
2 teaspoons Greek seasoning
1 teaspoon salt
^{1}/2 teaspoon garlic powder
Freshly ground pepper to taste
6 cups water
1 (12-ounce) package frozen dumplings

Place the chicken in a slow cooker and add the carrots, onion, celery, bay leaves, parsley flakes, Greek seasoning, salt, garlic powder and pepper. Pour the water over the top and cook, covered, on Low for 6 to 8 hours or until the chicken is tender.

Remove the chicken to a platter and cool slightly. Shred the chicken, discarding the bones. Remove the solids from the broth using a slotted spoon, reserving the carrots and discarding the remaining vegetables and bay leaves. Increase the heat to High and add the dumplings to the broth. Cook for 20 to 30 minutes or until the dumplings are cooked through. Return the chicken and carrots to the slow cooker and cook for 10 minutes longer or until heated through. For testing purposes, Mary Hill Frozen Dumplings were used.

HOLLY HOLMES WILLIAMS

GRILLED RASPBERRY CHICKEN

If you want a sauce for the chicken, double the marinade and reserve half.
Boil the reserved marinade for two minutes before serving.

MAKES 6 (1 CHICKEN BREAST AND 1 CUP COUSCOUS) SERVINGS

1/2 cup raspberry preserves
3 tablespoons apple cider vinegar
2 garlic cloves, minced
1/2 teaspoon pepper
6 bone-in chicken breasts
1 (5-ounce) package chicken-flavor couscous
2 cups watercress (optional)

Mix the preserves, vinegar, garlic and pepper in a shallow dish. Add the chicken to the preserves mixture and turn to coat. Marinate, covered, in the refrigerator for 1 hour, turning after 30 minutes.

Prepare a hot fire by stacking the charcoal on 1 side of the grill, leaving the other side empty. For gas grills, light only 1 side. Coat the grill rack with nonstick cooking spray and arrange the chicken skin side down on the grill rack over direct heat.

Grill for 10 minutes or until brown. Turn the chicken and place over indirect heat. Grill for 35 minutes or until a meat thermometer inserted in the thickest portion registers 170 degrees. Prepare the couscous using the package directions and spread an even layer of the couscous on a serving platter. Top with the chicken and arrange the watercress around the edge of the platter.

SHERI SUMMERFORD COOK

Nutritional Profile for this recipe on page 327.

CHICKEN WITH MUSTARD CREAM SAUCE

This dish is tasty enough for company, but quick enough for weeknight dinners, and I always serve it on a bed of Sautéed Spinach with Garlic. Whole grain mustard gives the dish a tang, but Dijon mustard will work as a substitute.

SERVES 4

4 (6-ounce) boneless skinless chicken breasts
Salt and freshly ground pepper to taste
3 tablespoons olive oil
1 shallot, chopped
2 garlic cloves, minced
3/4 cup less-sodium chicken broth
1/4 cup heavy cream or whipping cream
1 tablespoon whole grain mustard
Sautéed Spinach with Garlic (sidebar)

Pound the chicken breasts 1/2 inch thick between sheets of heavy-duty plastic wrap. Sprinkle with salt and pepper. Heat 2 tablespoons of the olive oil in a skillet over medium-high heat and add the chicken. Sauté for 4 minutes per side or until brown. Remove the chicken to a platter and cover to keep warm, reserving the pan drippings.

Heat the remaining 1 tablespoon olive oil with the reserved pan drippings over low heat. Add the shallot and cook for 3 minutes, stirring frequently. Stir in the garlic and cook for 1 minute. Increase the heat to high and add the broth. Bring to a boil.

Cook for 4 minutes or until the liquid is reduced by 1/2, stirring frequently. Stir in the cream and mustard and return the chicken to the skillet. Cook for 2 minutes or until the chicken is cooked through. Spoon equal portions of the Sautéed Spinach with Garlic on 4 serving plates and arrange 1 chicken breast on each portion. Drizzle with the mustard sauce and serve immediately.

ANNA BICKLEY COOPER

Serve Chicken with Mustard Cream Sauce over **Sautéed Spinach with Garlic**. *Melt 1 tablespoon butter in a skillet over medium-high heat and add 1 minced garlic clove. Sauté for 30 seconds and add 10 ounces fresh baby spinach. Season to taste with salt and pepper and sauté for 2 minutes or until the spinach wilts. Remove from the heat and sprinkle with 1 1/2 teaspoons fresh lemon juice. Serve immediately.*

CITRUS BASIL CHICKEN

SERVES 4

1¹/2 cups orange juice
¹/2 cup lemon juice
¹/3 cup olive oil
¹/4 cup loosely packed fresh basil leaves
2 teaspoons honey
1 teaspoon salt
¹/2 teaspoon ground nutmeg
4 (6-ounce) boneless skinless chicken breasts
1 teaspoon salt
¹/4 cup (¹/2 stick) butter
¹/4 cup slivered almonds

Combine the orange juice, lemon juice, ¹/4 cup of the olive oil, the basil and honey in a blender and process until smooth. Pour the orange juice mixture into a large sealable plastic bag and add 1 teaspoon salt, the nutmeg and chicken. Seal tightly and turn to coat. Marinate in the refrigerator for 1 hour, turning at least once.

Preheat the oven to 400 degrees. Drain the chicken, reserving the marinade. Sprinkle the chicken with 1 teaspoon salt. Heat the remaining olive oil in a large skillet over medium high heat and add the chicken. Sauté for 4 minutes per side or until brown. Arrange the chicken in a lightly greased 7×11-inch baking dish and drizzle with the reserved marinade. Bake, covered with foil, for 30 minutes or until the chicken is cooked through.

Melt the butter in a small skillet over medium-high heat and add the almonds. Cook for 3 to 4 minutes or until toasted, stirring frequently. Remove from the heat and spoon 1 tablespoon of the almond mixture over each chicken breast.

PAIGE WILLIAMS GOLDMAN

Serve Citrus Basil Chicken with a mixed green salad drizzled with Herb Vinaigrette on page 110, Rosemary Rice on page 144, and steamed asparagus.

GATHER AROUND

1. *Plan a celebratory dinner the night before school begins to focus on new beginnings and goals for the new school year.*

2. *Out of the blue, plan a surprise for your family, and prepare their favorite meal, complete with candlelight and an extra-special table setting. This is a great way to tell your children they are doing well in school, or reward your husband for an accomplishment at work.*

3. *When there is no time to prepare dinner, order out. However, serve the food on dinner plates and sit at the table as a family.*

4. *Change the location of the family dinner table. Eat in the dining room, foyer, patio, or set up a family picnic on a quilt in the backyard.* ➤

MUSTARD AND BROWN SUGAR CHICKEN

SERVES 6

6 boneless skinless chicken breasts
1/2 cup packed brown sugar
6 tablespoons olive oil
1/4 cup cider vinegar
3 garlic cloves, crushed
3 tablespoons coarse grain mustard
2 tablespoons fresh lime juice
1 1/2 tablespoons fresh lemon juice
1 1/2 teaspoons salt
Freshly ground pepper to taste
Hot cooked rice

Arrange the chicken in a single layer in a 7×11-inch baking dish. Mix the brown sugar, olive oil, vinegar, garlic, coarse grain mustard, lime juice, lemon juice, salt and pepper in a bowl and pour over the chicken, turning to coat. Marinate, covered, in the refrigerator for 4 hours, turning occasionally.

Preheat the oven to 350 degrees. Bake the chicken in the marinade for 40 minutes. Spoon the hot cooked rice onto a serving platter and top with the chicken. Drizzle with the hot marinade.

MARY CARSON BAKER LARUSSA

GRILLED CHICKEN WITH WHITE SAUCE

SERVES 6

Chicken
2 tablespoons olive oil
3 garlic cloves, minced
2 teaspoons kosher salt
1 teaspoon finely chopped fresh rosemary
3/4 teaspoon freshly ground pepper
6 bone-in chicken breasts

White Sauce
2/3 cup mayonnaise
1/4 cup apple cider vinegar
3 tablespoons buttermilk
1 tablespoon sugar
1/2 small garlic clove, crushed
1/4 teaspoon salt
1/4 teaspoon freshly ground pepper
1/8 teaspoon dry mustard

For the chicken, prepare a hot fire by stacking charcoal on 1 side of the grill, leaving the other side empty. For gas grills, light only 1 side. Mix the olive oil, garlic, salt, rosemary and pepper in a bowl until of a paste consistency.

Carefully loosen the skin from the chicken by inserting your fingers, gently pushing between the skin and breast meat. Rub the spice paste evenly over the breast meat and reposition the skin. Arrange the chicken skin side down over direct heat and grill for 10 minutes or until brown. Turn the chicken and place over indirect heat. Grill for 35 minutes longer or until the chicken is cooked through.

For the sauce, combine the mayonnaise, vinegar, buttermilk, sugar, garlic, salt, pepper and dry mustard in a bowl and mix well. Serve with the chicken.

KRISTIN DENSON SARTELLE

Photograph for this recipe on page 246.

5. When you know a day is going to be hectic, cook dinner in the morning or maybe the night before.

6. Write in your cookbook like you mark in your Bible. Record events or even menus. It will be a treasured book for you and your family.

7. Invite children or grandchildren, boyfriends or husbands to your kitchen while you are cooking. Show them how to cook and let them in on the fun.

8. Plan theme nights and dress the part to make dinner a bit more interesting and exciting. This may encourage children to try foods they wouldn't ordinarily touch.

ROSEMARY-CRUSTED STUFFED BREAST OF BONELESS CHICKEN WITH SHAVED VIRGINIA HAM AND FRESH MOZZARELLA

SERVES 2

2 thin slices Virginia ham
1 teaspoon Creole mustard
1/4 cup (1 ounce) shredded fresh mozzarella cheese
8 basil leaves
1/4 cup dry white wine
2 tablespoons extra-virgin olive oil
1 teaspoon chopped fresh rosemary
2 (6-ounce) boneless skinless chicken breasts
Salt and freshly ground pepper to taste

Coat the grill rack with oil and preheat the grill. Spread the ham slices evenly with the Creole mustard and sprinkle with the cheese and basil. Roll the slices starting with the small end to enclose the filling. Whisk the wine, olive oil and rosemary in a bowl.

Cut a 1-inch-wide pocket in middle of each chicken breast half and brush the inside of the pocket with the wine mixture. Insert 1 ham roll into each pocket. Brush the surface of the chicken with the remaining wine mixture and sprinkle with salt and pepper.

Arrange the chicken on the prepared grill rack and grill over direct heat for 8 minutes per side or until the chicken is cooked through.

DARRYL BORDEN, BOMBAY CAFÉ IN LAKEVIEW

CHICKEN TORTILLA CASSEROLE

*Monterey Jack cheese gives this dish a mild flavor. Substitute with
Pepper Jack cheese to add a bit more heat.*

SERVES 6

1 tablespoon butter
1 pound boneless skinless chicken breasts,
    cut into bite-size pieces
1/4 cup chopped onion
1 garlic clove, minced
1 (15-ounce) can tomato sauce
1 (8-ounce) can tomato sauce
1 (4-ounce) can chopped green chiles
1 tablespoon chili powder
1 teaspoon ground cumin
1/2 teaspoon salt
1/4 teaspoon freshly ground pepper
2 cups sour cream
2 cups (8 ounces) shredded Cheddar cheese
1 cup (4 ounces) shredded Monterey Jack cheese
1/4 cup chopped fresh cilantro
15 (6-inch) corn tortillas
2 cups drained canned whole kernel corn
1 cup (4 ounces) shredded Cheddar cheese
Chopped fresh cilantro for garnish

Melt the butter in a large skillet over medium heat and add the chicken, onion and garlic. Sauté for
8 minutes. Stir in the tomato sauce, green chiles, chili powder, cumin, salt and pepper and reduce the
heat to low. Simmer for 15 minutes, stirring occasionally.

Preheat the oven to 375 degrees. Combine the sour cream, 2 cups Cheddar cheese, the Monterey Jack
cheese and 1/4 cup cilantro in a bowl and mix well. Line the bottom of a lightly greased 2 1/2- to 3-quart
baking dish with 1/3 of the tortillas, tearing the tortillas as needed to completely cover the bottom. Layer
with 1/3 of the chicken mixture, 1/3 of the corn and 1/3 of the sour cream mixture. Repeat the process
2 more times with the remaining tortillas, remaining chicken mixture, remaining corn and remaining
sour cream mixture. Sprinkle with 1 cup Cheddar cheese and bake for 25 minutes or until the cheese
melts. Let stand for 10 minutes before serving. Garnish with chopped cilantro.

AMY HASSIG SMITH

MEXICAN CHICKEN AND RICE

SERVES 4 TO 6

1 tablespoon vegetable oil
1 pound boneless skinless
    chicken breasts, cut into
    bite-size pieces
1 small onion, chopped
1 red bell pepper, chopped
1/8 teaspoon salt
1/8 teaspoon pepper

1 (16-ounce) package frozen corn
1 cup salsa
1/2 cup chicken broth
2 cups hot cooked rice
1 (2-ounce) can chopped olives
1/2 cup (2 ounces) shredded
    Cheddar cheese
1 teaspoon chopped fresh cilantro

Heat the oil in a large skillet over medium heat and add the chicken, onion, bell pepper, salt and pepper. Cook until the chicken is cooked through, stirring frequently. Add the corn, salsa and broth and bring to a boil. Stir in the rice and olives and cover. Remove from the heat and let stand for 5 minutes. Fluff with a fork and sprinkle with the cheese and cilantro. Cover and let stand until the cheese melts.

MOLLY CAMERON MARTIN

OVEN CHICKEN KABOBS

SERVES 6

Wooden skewers
1/2 cup olive oil
1/2 cup dry white wine
1 tablespoon chopped fresh parsley
1/4 teaspoon salt
1/4 teaspoon freshly ground
    black pepper
1/8 teaspoon crushed red pepper

6 boneless skinless chicken breasts,
    cut into 1-inch pieces
    (about 2 1/2 pounds)
3/4 cup fresh bread crumbs
3/4 cup (3 ounces) freshly grated
    Parmesan cheese
1/4 cup (1/2 stick) butter, melted
2 tablespoons lemon juice

Immerse wooden skewers in water and soak for 30 minutes. Drain and pat dry. Mix the olive oil, wine, parsley, salt, black pepper and red pepper in a bowl. Add the chicken and stir until coated. Marinate, covered, in the refrigerator for 1 hour, stirring occasionally. Preheat the broiler or grill. Drain the chicken, discarding the marinade. Toss the bread crumbs and cheese in a shallow dish and coat the chicken with the crumb mixture. Thread the coated chicken on the skewers and broil on a rack in a broiler pan or grill over hot coals for 8 minutes or until the chicken is cooked through, turning once. Remove the kabobs to a platter and drizzle with a mixture of the butter and lemon juice.

NANCY BEAIRD BROMBERG

CURRY CHICKEN

Thai chiles or bird chiles are fiery hot, so be sure to remove the pods before serving. They are occasionally available fresh at the supermarket, but you will definitely find them at Asian markets.

SERVES 4 TO 6

8 boneless skinless chicken thighs
Salt and freshly ground pepper to taste
1/4 cup olive oil
2 large onions, chopped
4 garlic cloves, minced
1 tablespoon grated fresh ginger
1 (28-ounce) can diced tomatoes
2 tablespoons Indian curry powder
2 Thai chiles or bird chiles
1 (13-ounce) can unsweetened coconut milk
4 to 6 sprigs of cilantro
4 cups hot cooked white rice

Sprinkle the chicken with salt and pepper. Heat the olive oil in a large skillet over medium-high heat and add the chicken. Cook for 6 minutes per side or until golden brown. Remove the chicken to a platter using a slotted spoon, reserving the pan drippings.

Cook the onions, garlic and ginger in the reserved pan drippings until the onions are tender, stirring frequently. Stir in the undrained tomatoes, curry powder and Thai chiles. Cook over low heat for 30 minutes or longer, stirring occasionally. Stir in the coconut milk and cook for 15 minutes. You may purée the sauce at this point for a thinner consistency if desired. Return the chicken to the skillet and cook for 15 to 30 minutes longer or until the chicken is cooked through and the sauce is the desired consistency, stirring occasionally. Remove from the heat and discard the chiles.

Place 1 sprig of cilantro in the bottom of each of 4 to 6 tea cups and press the hot rice into the cups. Invert the rice onto serving plates and serve with the chicken and sauce. For variety, substitute peeled deveined shrimp for the chicken. The cooking time will decrease as the shrimp will cook more quickly.

ELIZABETH BAIRD CRAWFORD

ARTICHOKE CHICKEN PIZZA

This pizza also makes a great appetizer.

SERVES 4

1 (14-ounce) can artichoke hearts, drained
1¹/2 tablespoons mayonnaise
1 deep-dish pizza crust
1¹/2 cups chopped cooked chicken
2 tablespoons olive oil
¹/2 green bell pepper, sliced
¹/2 red bell pepper, sliced
1 plum tomato, chopped
1 tablespoon chopped fresh basil
2 cups (8 ounces) shredded mozzarella cheese
¹/2 cup (2 ounces) shredded Parmesan cheese
1 cup (4 ounces) crumbled feta cheese

Preheat the oven to 400 degrees. Process the artichokes and mayonnaise in a food processor until smooth. Place the crust on a baking sheet or baking stone and spread the artichoke mixture evenly over the crust. Sprinkle with the chicken.

Heat the olive oil in a large skillet over medium-high heat and add the bell peppers, tomato and basil. Sauté until the bell peppers are tender. Spread the bell pepper mixture over the prepared layers and sprinkle with the mozzarella cheese, Parmesan cheese and feta cheese. Bake for 15 minutes or until the cheeses melt.

LEE HARCROW TAPSCOTT

When a recipe calls for chopped cooked chicken, shorten preparation time by using a rotisserie chicken. They are available in the deli section of most supermarkets in a variety of flavors. Pick the flavor that best suits your recipe. Generally one rotisserie chicken yields three cups chopped chicken.

SOUTHWESTERN TURKEY WITH CHILI-CUMIN GLAZE AND SPICY GRAVY

SERVES 12

Turkey

3/4 cup (1 1/2 sticks) butter, softened
3 tablespoons chopped fresh cilantro
4 garlic cloves, minced
2 chipotle chiles in adobo
    sauce, minced
1 tablespoon ground cumin
1 1/2 teaspoons grated lime zest
1 1/2 teaspoons fresh lime juice
1 teaspoon salt
1 (12-pound) turkey
2 teaspoons salt

Spicy Gravy

2 tablespoons butter
1/2 cup chopped onion
1 garlic clove, minced
2 cups heavy cream or
    whipping cream
1 chipotle chile in adobo
    sauce, minced
1 tablespoon fresh lime juice
Salt to taste

For the turkey, preheat the oven to 450 degrees. Combine the butter, cilantro, garlic, chipotle chiles, cumin, lime zest, lime juice and 1 teaspoon salt in a mixing bowl and beat at medium speed until combined. Carefully insert your fingers between the skin and flesh of the turkey to loosen the skin and rub the butter mixture over the flesh. Reposition the skin and sprinkle 2 teaspoons salt evenly over the surface of the turkey.

Arrange the turkey breast side up in a roasting pan and roast for 20 minutes. Baste with the pan drippings. Reduce the oven temperature to 350 degrees and roast for 1 hour and 45 minutes or until a meat thermometer inserted in the leg joint registers 170 degrees, basting with the pan drippings every 30 minutes. Remove the turkey to a platter and let stand for 10 minutes before slicing, reserving 1/2 cup of the pan drippings for the gravy.

For the gravy, melt the butter in a medium saucepan and add the onion and garlic. Sauté for 2 minutes. Stir in the cream and chipotle chile and bring to a boil. Reduce the heat to low and simmer for 20 minutes or until the mixture is reduced by 1/2, stirring occasionally. Stir in the reserved pan drippings and cook for 1 minute longer. Remove from the heat and stir in the lime juice. Season to taste with salt. Serve with the turkey.

JULIE GRIMES BOTTCHER

OLIVE AND SAGE TURKEY BREAST

This is a perfect recipe for casual entertaining. You can prepare the olive tapenade and stuff the turkey one day in advance. Wrap tightly and chill until just before roasting. Look for fresh or frozen boneless turkey breasts in the supermarket.

MAKES 8 (4^1/$_2$-OUNCE) SERVINGS

1/2 cup walnuts, toasted
1/2 cup large green olives, pitted
1/2 cup kalamata olives, pitted
2 tablespoons fresh sage leaves
2 garlic cloves
1 1/2 teaspoons grated orange zest
1/2 teaspoon salt
1/4 teaspoon crushed red pepper
1/4 cup extra-virgin olive oil
1 teaspoon salt
1 teaspoon freshly ground black pepper
1 (4-pound) boneless turkey breast
2 tablespoons extra-virgin olive oil

Preheat the oven to 450 degrees. Combine the walnuts, olives, sage, garlic, orange zest, 1/2 teaspoon salt and the red pepper in a food processor and process until coarsely chopped. Add 1/4 cup olive oil gradually, processing constantly until smooth. Add 1 teaspoon salt and the black pepper and process until blended.

Cut the turkey lengthwise to but not through into halves and open like a book. Lay between sheets of heavy-duty plastic wrap and pound 1/2 inch thick. Spread the olive oil mixture evenly over the cut side of the turkey, leaving a 1/2-inch border around the edges. Beginning with the long edge, roll as for a jelly roll and secure with kitchen twine. Cut the roll crosswise into halves to form two 8-inch-long rolls.

Pour 2 tablespoons olive oil into a roasting pan and heat in the oven for 5 minutes. Arrange the turkey halves in the hot oil and roast for 20 minutes. Turn the turkey halves over and reduce the oven temperature to 350 degrees. Roast for 25 minutes longer or until a meat thermometer inserted in the thickest portions of the rolls registers 165 degrees. Let stand for 10 minutes before slicing.

CATHERINE HALL

Nutritional Profile for this recipe on page 327.

BAKED SNAPPER WITH TOMATO SALSA

*I was looking for something new since my family was tired of chicken
every night. This is what I came up with, and we love it. This dish has a great
fresh taste and is an easy way to cook fish at home.*

SERVES 4

1/2 cup olive oil
1 tomato, chopped
1 small yellow onion, chopped
3 tablespoons fresh lemon juice
1 teaspoon chopped fresh parsley

1 teaspoon chopped fresh dill weed
1 teaspoon salt
1/4 teaspoon freshly ground pepper
4 (6-ounce) snapper fillets or
     grouper fillets

Preheat the oven to 350 degrees. Mix 1/4 cup of the olive oil, the tomato, onion, lemon juice, parsley, dill weed, salt and pepper in a bowl. Cut 4 medium pieces of heavy-duty foil and drizzle 1 tablespoon of the remaining olive oil over each piece.

Arrange 1 fillet in the center of each piece of foil and top each with 1/4 of the tomato mixture. Bring the edges of the foil over the fillets and seal tightly. Arrange the packets on a baking sheet and bake for 20 minutes or until the fillets flake easily when tested with a fork.

KATHERINE WOOD HAMILTON

BAKED SOLE WITH PARMESAN CRUMBS

SERVES 4

4 (6-ounce) sole fillets or
     flounder fillets
Salt and freshly ground pepper to taste
1/2 cup coarse fresh bread crumbs

3/4 cup (3 ounces) grated
     Parmigiano-Reggiano
1/4 cup (1/2 stick) butter, melted
2 tablespoons olive oil

Preheat the oven to 425 degrees. Season the fillets with salt and pepper and arrange in a single layer in a greased 9×13-inch baking dish. Toss the bread crumbs, cheese, butter and olive oil in a bowl and spread the crumb mixture over the fillets. Bake for 15 minutes or until the topping is golden brown. Let stand for 5 minutes before serving.

EVELYN BRITTON STUTTS

PAN-FRIED CORNMEAL CATFISH

SERVES 4

1/4 cup coarse cornmeal
2 teaspoons sweet paprika
1 teaspoon onion powder
3/4 teaspoon garlic salt
1/4 teaspoon celery salt
1/4 teaspoon cayenne pepper
1 1/2 teaspoons kosher salt
4 (6-ounce) catfish fillets
1/4 cup (1/2 stick) unsalted butter
3 tablespoons chopped fresh parsley for garnish

Mix the cornmeal, paprika, onion powder, garlic salt, celery salt and cayenne pepper in a bowl and mix well. Sprinkle the salt over both sides of the fillets and coat with the cornmeal mixture.

Melt the butter in a large skillet over medium-high heat and add the fillets. Sauté for 4 minutes or until brown. Turn the fillets and sauté for 3 minutes longer or until the fillets flake easily when tested with a fork. Remove the fillets to a serving platter and drizzle with the pan juices. Garnish with the parsley.

CARI LORENTZ SOUTH

To skin a fish fillet, place it skin side down on a clean cutting board. Starting at the tail end, slip the blade of a long sharp knife between the fish flesh and the skin, holding down firmly with your other hand. Gently push the blade along at a 30-degree angle, separating the fillet from the skin.

PECAN-CRUSTED BASA

Basa is a fish that is imported from Vietnam. A member of the catfish family, basa has a similar flavor and texture to Southern catfish, but is slightly milder. You may substitute catfish, tilapia, or grouper for the basa.

SERVES 4

4 (6-ounce) basa fillets
1/4 cup olive oil
1/4 cup apple cider vinegar
3/4 cup salted pecans
2 slices whole wheat bread
2 tablespoons butter, melted
2 tablespoons Dijon mustard
1 1/2 tablespoons maple syrup
Chopped fresh parsley

Rinse the fillets and pat dry. Arrange the fillets in a single layer in a 3-quart baking dish and drizzle with the olive oil and vinegar, turning to coat. Marinate, covered, in the refrigerator for 1 hour, turning occasionally.

Toast the pecans in a skillet over medium-high heat until light brown, stirring frequently. Cool slightly and finely crush. Toast the bread and crumble.

Preheat the oven to 450 degrees. Drain the fillets, discarding the marinade. Mix the butter, Dijon mustard and syrup in a bowl and brush over the fillets in the baking dish. Toss the pecans and bread crumbs in a bowl and sprinkle over the top. Sprinkle with parsley and bake for 10 minutes or until the fillets flake easily when tested with a fork.

KATHRYN LAVALLET TORTORICI

FISH TALES

Fortunately Birmingham is close enough to the Gulf that we get fresh (never frozen) fish regularly. Of course, seasons affect availability, but you should be able to get fresh fish throughout the year.

Fillets and steaks are the most common and best way to buy fish. Don't buy anything more than one day old—especially if you don't plan to cook it the same night. You can always ask when the fish came in.

Try to make the fish counter your last stop before going directly home. Cook the fish within twenty-four hours. You can also freeze it. (See "Thinking Ahead" on page 176 for tips.) Keep the fish as cold as possible until you are ready to cook, but don't store it in direct contact with ice.

GRILLED SALMON WITH SOUR CREAM HORSERADISH SAUCE

SERVES 4

Salmon
1 (2-pound) salmon fillet, cut into 4 equal
  portions
1¹/2 tablespoons olive oil
1 teaspoon garlic powder
Salt and freshly ground pepper to taste
8 teaspoons chopped fresh dill weed
1 tablespoon honey

Sour Cream Horseradish Sauce
1 cup sour cream
1 tablespoon chopped fresh dill weed
2 teaspoons lemon juice
2 teaspoons Worcestershire sauce
1 teaspoon prepared horseradish
Salt and freshly ground pepper to taste

For the salmon, prepare a grill with heat on only 1 side. Place the fillets skin side down on a plate and drizzle with the olive oil. Sprinkle evenly with the garlic powder, salt and pepper. Top each with 2 teaspoons of the dill weed.

Arrange the fillets skin side down on the grill rack and grill for 10 minutes. Carefully turn the fillets with 2 spatulas and remove the skin. Grill for 3 minutes longer. Remove to a platter dill side up and drizzle with the honey.

For the sauce, combine the sour cream, dill weed, lemon juice, Worcestershire sauce, prepared horseradish, salt and pepper in a bowl and mix well. Serve with the salmon.

WENDY WOODEN BARZE

The texture of the fish's flesh is what determines how it should be cooked. Below is a guide grouping fish by texture, with suggested cooking methods.

DELICATE

Delicate fish respond best to gentle cooking methods such as braising, poaching, pan-frying, or baking. They flake very easily and have a soft texture when cooked. These fish are traditionally sold as fillets. Sole, flounder, cod, and orange roughy are all examples of delicate fish.

MEDIUM (FLAKY WHITE FISH)

Firmer when cooked than delicate fish, these are by far the most versatile fish to cook. Any medium-fleshed fish can be used when your recipe specifies "flaky white fish." ➤

SALMON BLTs

The addition of salmon to this classic sandwich makes for a delicious and hearty summer fare. Dress up the dish by serving the grilled salmon fillet without the hamburger buns. Simply crumble the bacon, chop the tomatoes, and serve over the top of the salmon along with the flavored mayonnaise on the side.

SERVES 4

1/2 cup mayonnaise
1 tablespoon minced green onion
1 teaspoon fresh lemon juice
1/4 teaspoon tarragon
Salt and freshly ground pepper to taste
4 (6-ounce) salmon fillets
1 tablespoon olive oil
4 hamburger buns
4 leaves green lettuce
8 thick slices smoked bacon, crisp-cooked
    and drained
2 ripe tomatoes, sliced

Mix the mayonnaise, green onion, lemon juice and tarragon in a bowl and season to taste with salt and pepper. Chill, covered, in the refrigerator.

Preheat the grill or broiler. Brush the surface of the fillets with the olive oil and sprinkle with salt and pepper. Grill over hot coals or broil on a rack in a broiler pan for 4 minutes per side or to the desired degree of doneness.

Spread about 1 tablespoon of the mayonnaise mixture over the cut sides of the buns. Arrange 1 lettuce leaf on the bottom half of each bun and top each with 1 fillet. Layer each with 2 slices of the bacon and 1 or 2 tomato slices. Sprinkle with salt and pepper and top with the remaining bun halves. Serve immediately.

ANNE STARNES FINCH

Try baking, broiling, braising, or pan-frying. Many of these fish, such as halibut, grouper, mahi mahi, and salmon, will even stand up to grilling. Snapper, walleye, tilapia, freshwater bass and trout are further examples of medium-fleshed fish.

FIRM

Firm texture and full flavor go hand in hand. Most fish in this category can be accurately described as meaty, and as the description might imply, these fish will stand up to assertive flavors and high heat cooking. Firm-fleshed fish are perfect for grilling, broiling, or sautéing. Tuna, swordfish, triggerfish, and amberjack are all examples of firm fish.

TRIGGERFISH FILLETS WITH LEMON BUTTER SAUCE

This recipe is based on one I love from the Destin Ice House. Triggerfish has spotty availability, so if you find it at your local fish market, snap it up. Since they are delicious prepared in the same manner, soft-shell crabs make a good substitute for triggerfish when they are fresh and in season. Otherwise, you may use fresh grouper fillets.

SERVES 4

1/2 cup cornmeal
1/2 cup all-purpose flour
4 (6- to 8-ounce) triggerfish fillets
Salt and freshly ground pepper to taste
1/2 cup milk
1/2 cup (1 stick) butter
1/2 cup dry white wine
4 teaspoons lemon juice
3 green onions, chopped

Mix the cornmeal and flour in a shallow dish. Season the fillets with salt and pepper, dip in the milk and coat with the cornmeal mixture. Melt 1/2 cup butter in a skillet large enough to hold all 4 fillets and add the fillets.

Cook over medium heat until the fillets are light brown on the bottom, shaking the skillet occasionally to keep the fillets from sticking. Carefully lift the fillets with a large spatula and turn. Cook until brown on the remaining side. Remove the fillets to a heated serving platter, reserving the pan drippings.

Increase the heat to medium-high and add the desired amount of additional butter to the reserved pan drippings. Cook just until the butter begins to brown, stirring constantly with a wooden spoon to release any browned bits from the bottom of the skillet. Stir in the wine, lemon juice and green onions and cook until slightly thickened, stirring frequently. Drizzle over the fillets and serve immediately.

GINGER GRAINGER RUEVE

Sunshine School at Children's Hospital helps children continue their education during hospitalization. Elimination of funding put the school at risk, but the JLB's commitment of $300,000 helped in the effort of saving the school, which in 2005 served 1,148 children from forty-eight Alabama counties.

CEDAR-PLANKED TROUT WITH LEMON AND WALNUT BROWN BUTTER

Baking fish on a wood plank is a great way to infuse a subtle smoky flavor, and the plank makes for an effortless yet impressive presentation. This technique works for most varieties of fish, chicken breasts, or pork chops.

SERVES 4

1 cedar plank
4 rainbow trout fillets
1 1/2 teaspoons kosher salt
3/4 teaspoon freshly ground pepper
2 tablespoons butter, melted
1/4 cup finely chopped fresh parsley
2 tablespoons finely chopped fresh tarragon
8 sprigs of thyme
12 (1/8-inch) lemon slices
1/4 cup (1/2 stick) butter
1/4 cup chopped walnuts
2 tablespoons chopped fresh parsley
    for garnish

Immerse the cedar plank in water and soak for 30 minutes. Pat dry with paper towels. Position an oven rack in the center of the oven and preheat the oven to 425 degrees.

Heat the plank in the oven for 10 minutes or until hot. Sprinkle the fillets with the salt and pepper and brush with 2 tablespoons butter. Sprinkle with 1/4 cup parsley and the tarragon. Arrange 2 sprigs of thyme across the top of each fillet and fan 3 lemon slices over each. Place the fillets on the hot plank and bake for 25 minutes or until the fillets flake easily when tested with a fork. Discard the thyme.

Heat 1/4 cup butter in a small saucepan over medium heat for 6 minutes or until light brown and fragrant, stirring occasionally. Remove from the heat and stir in the walnuts, swirling to coat. Garnish the trout with 2 tablespoons parsley and serve with the brown butter.

CATHERINE HALL

TAKE THE PLANK

Wood planks can be purchased from most gourmet kitchen stores and come in a wide variety of woods such as hickory, cedar, maple, and alder. Follow these simple steps when using a plank.

1. Soak the plank in water for about thirty minutes before grilling.

2. Allow the grill to get hot.

3. Place the plank directly over the flame for about five minutes.

4 Turn the plank over with the charred side facing up.

5. Arrange the meat in a single layer to provide an intense smoky flavor.

LIME SOY TUNA STEAKS

SERVES 4

4 (6-ounce) tuna steaks,
    1 to 1¹/2 inches thick
1/3 cup soy sauce
1/4 cup fresh lime juice
1/4 cup canola oil
1/4 cup chopped green onions

1 tablespoon Dijon mustard
2 teaspoons finely grated lime zest
2 garlic cloves, minced
1/2 teaspoon (or more) freshly
    ground pepper

Place the steaks in a sealable plastic bag. Whisk the soy sauce, lime juice, canola oil, green onions, Dijon mustard, lime zest, garlic and pepper in a bowl and pour over the steaks. Seal tightly and turn to coat. Marinate in the refrigerator for 3 hours, turning occasionally. Preheat the grill or broiler. Grill over hot coals or broil on a rack in a broiler pan for 3 to 4 minutes per side or to the desired degree of doneness.

LISA BELL LEWIS

PARSLIED CLAMS AND HARICOTS VERTS OVER FETTUCCINI

MAKES 6 (1 CUP CLAM SAUCE AND 1 CUP PASTA) SERVINGS

16 ounces fettuccini
1/4 cup (1/2 stick) butter
1 cup chopped peeled tomato
1/4 cup finely chopped shallots
3 garlic cloves, minced
1/2 teaspoon salt
1 cup dry white wine

1 (8-ounce) bottle clam juice
42 littleneck clams, scrubbed and
    rinsed (about 2 pounds)
8 ounces haricots verts, trimmed and
    cut into halves
1 cup chopped fresh flat-leaf parsley

Cook the pasta using the package directions. Drain and cover to keep warm. Melt the butter in a Dutch oven over medium-high heat and add the tomato, shallots, garlic and salt. Sauté for 3 minutes and stir in the wine and clam juice. Stir in the clams and bring to a boil. Reduce the heat to low. Simmer, covered, for 5 minutes or until the clams begin to open. Add the haricots verts and cook, covered, for 2 minutes or until the beans are tender-crisp. Remove from the heat and stir in the parsley. Spoon 1 cup of the sauce over 1 cup of the pasta on each of 6 serving plates.

JULIE GRIMES BOTTCHER

Nutritional Profile for this recipe on page 327.

CRUSTLESS CRAB MEAT PIE

SERVES 8 TO 10

2 tablespoons butter
8 ounces mushrooms, sliced
4 eggs
1 cup sour cream
1 cup small curd cottage cheese
1/4 cup all-purpose flour
1/4 teaspoon salt
6 drops of Tabasco sauce
12 ounces fresh lump crab meat, shells and
    cartilage removed
2 cups (8 ounces) grated Gruyère cheese or
    shredded Swiss cheese
1/2 cup chopped green onions
Paprika for garnish

Preheat the oven to 350 degrees. Melt the butter in a skillet and add the mushrooms. Sauté until tender and drain on a paper towel. Place the mushrooms in a large bowl. Combine the eggs, sour cream, cottage cheese, flour, salt and Tabasco sauce in a blender or food processor and process until smooth.

Add the sour cream mixture to the mushrooms and mix well. Fold in the crab meat, Gruyère cheese and green onions. Spoon the crab meat mixture into a lightly greased 10-inch pie plate and bake for 45 minutes or until a knife inserted in the center comes out clean. Let stand for 5 minutes before slicing. Sprinkle with paprika and cut into wedges.

GRACE WALRAVEN PADGETT

LOBSTER POTPIE

*The addition of lobster takes this Southern comfort food upscale. Substitute two lobster tails
for the whole live lobster if you prefer, or shrimp will work in a pinch. The recipe directs to bake the
potpies in individual serving dishes, but you may prepare family style in one large baking dish.*

SERVES 4 TO 6

1 (1¹/2- to 2-pound) live lobster
Salt to taste
¹/2 cup (1 stick) unsalted butter
1 cup (¹/4-inch) pieces peeled
   russet potato
³/4 cup quartered pearl onions
¹/2 cup chopped carrots
¹/4 cup finely chopped celery
¹/2 cup sherry or dry white wine

2 tablespoons all-purpose flour
1¹/2 cups heavy cream or
   whipping cream
3 sprigs of thyme
¹/2 cup frozen green peas, thawed
1¹/4 teaspoons kosher salt
¹/2 teaspoon freshly ground pepper
1¹/2 tablespoons chopped fresh thyme
1 sheet frozen puff pastry, thawed

Place the lobster in boiling salted water in a large stockpot and cook for 8 minutes. Remove the lobster to a platter, reserving 3 cups of the cooking liquid. Let stand until cool. Remove the tail and claws from the lobster, discarding the body. Remove the meat from the tail and claws, reserving the shells. Chop the meat.

Melt ¹/4 cup of the butter in a stockpot and add the reserved shells. Sauté for 5 minutes. Stir in the reserved cooking liquid and bring to a boil. Cook for 8 minutes or until the mixture is reduced to 2 cups. Strain, reserving the liquid and discarding the solids. Wipe the stockpot clean with paper towels.

Melt the remaining ¹/4 cup butter in the stockpot and add the potato, onions and carrots. Sauté for 4 minutes and stir in the celery. Sauté for 2 minutes and stir in the sherry. Bring to a boil and cook for 4 minutes or until the liquid evaporates. Add the flour and cook for 1 minute. Gradually stir in the reserved reduced cooking liquid, cream and sprigs of thyme. Bring to a boil and reduce the heat to low.

Simmer for 15 minutes or until thickened, stirring frequently. Discard the sprigs of thyme and stir in the lobster meat, peas, 1¹/4 teaspoons salt and the pepper. Cook for 3 minutes or until heated through. Remove from the heat and stir in the chopped thyme.

Preheat the oven to 400 degrees. Divide the lobster mixture evenly among four to six 10-ounce ramekins or ovenproof soup bowls, filling each ²/3 full. Cut the pastry to fit over the top of the lobster mixture and drape the pastry over each ramekin. Arrange the ramekins on a baking sheet and bake for 30 minutes or until puffed and golden brown. Serve immediately.

CATHERINE HALL

STEAMED SCALLOP PACKETS WITH SUMMER VEGETABLES

This is an easy and delicious summer recipe. Use a mix of yellow and red tomatoes for a beautiful presentation. It is terrific served with rice to soak up all of the flavorful juices.

SERVES 6

2 shallots, thinly sliced	3 cups shredded fresh spinach
3/4 cup dry white wine	(optional)
2 tablespoons butter, cut into 6 slices	1 cup fresh or frozen corn kernels
2 tablespoons extra-virgin olive oil	3/4 cup chopped fresh basil
2 1/4 pounds sea scallops	Salt and freshly ground pepper to taste
2 pints cherry or grape tomatoes	

Preheat the grill to medium. Cut six 18×20-inch pieces of heavy-duty foil. Place 1/6 of the shallots, 2 tablespoons of the wine, 1 slice of the butter and 1 teaspoon of the olive oil on each sheet of foil. Top evenly with the scallops, tomatoes, spinach, corn and basil. Sprinkle with salt and pepper. Bring the sides of the foil together to form rectangles and grill for 10 minutes or until the steam inflates the packets and you hear the juices bubbling. Open the foil packets carefully and pour into soup bowls.

EVELYN BRITTON STUTTS

SAUTÉED SHRIMP

SERVES 2 TO 3

6 tablespoons butter	1 pound large shrimp, peeled
2 cups (1-inch) cubes sourdough bread	and deveined
4 ounces sliced fresh cremini or baby	3 tablespoons sherry
bella mushrooms	3 tablespoons lemon juice
1/4 cup chopped green onions	Salt and freshly ground pepper to taste

Melt 2 tablespoons of the butter in a large skillet over medium-high heat. Add the bread cubes and cook for 8 minutes or until toasted on all sides, stirring frequently. Remove the bread cubes to a platter, reserving the pan drippings. Melt the remaining 4 tablespoons butter with the reserved pan drippings over medium-high heat and add the mushrooms and green onions. Sauté for 8 minutes or until the mushrooms are tender. Add the shrimp and cook for 3 minutes or until the shrimp turn pink. Stir in the sherry and lemon juice and cook for 1 minute. Remove from the heat and season to taste with salt and pepper. Add the bread cubes and toss to combine. Serve immediately.

JAN PHILLIPPI SHANNON

SHRIMP WITH PEANUT SAUCE

SERVES 8

1/4 cup sliced green onions
4 garlic cloves, minced
3/4 cup no-salt-added chicken broth
5 tablespoons creamy peanut butter
2 tablespoons reduced-sodium soy sauce
2 tablespoons lemon juice
2 teaspoons chili powder
2 teaspoons brown sugar
1/2 teaspoon ground ginger
2 pounds large shrimp, peeled and deveined

Sauté the green onions and garlic in a skillet coated with nonstick cooking spray over medium heat for 3 minutes. Add the broth, peanut butter, soy sauce, lemon juice, chili powder, brown sugar and ginger and mix well. Reduce the heat to low.

Simmer for 10 minutes, stirring frequently. Remove from the heat and let stand until cool. Add the shrimp and toss to coat. Marinate, covered, in the refrigerator for 1 hour or longer. Drain the shrimp, discarding the marinade.

Preheat the broiler. Thread the shrimp on metal skewers and arrange on a rack in a broiler pan. Broil for 4 minutes per side or until the shrimp turn pink.

CARI LORENTZ SOUTH

The Alabama Child Caring Foundation provides health insurance for children of low-income families who are not eligible for government programs. In 2003, a JLB gift of $60,000 was granted to the foundation to provide health insurance to one thousand children on the organization's waiting list.

SPICY GRILLED SHRIMP WITH MANGO SALSA

Salsa is best if prepared in advance so the flavors have a chance to mingle.
Adjust the heat level of the salsa to suit your family's taste by adding more jalapeño
chiles or omitting them altogether. For a clever and slightly more formal presentation, arrange
the shrimp around the edges of martini glasses and fill the glasses with the salsa.

MAKES 4 (3 OUNCES SHRIMP AND 1/2 CUP SALSA) SERVINGS

Mango Salsa

1 ripe mango, peeled and chopped
1/2 cup finely chopped red onion
1/4 cup fresh lime juice
2 tablespoons chopped fresh cilantro
1 tablespoon grated lime zest
1/2 jalapeño chile, seeded and minced

Shrimp

Wooden skewers
2 tablespoons olive oil
2 tablespoons fresh lime juice
1 1/2 teaspoons grated lime zest
1/8 teaspoon crushed red pepper flakes
1/2 teaspoon salt
1 pound medium shrimp, peeled and deveined

For the salsa, combine the mango, onion, lime juice, cilantro, lime zest and jalapeño chile in a bowl and mix well. Chill, covered, for 2 hours or longer.

For the shrimp, soak wooden skewers in water for 30 minutes. Drain and pat dry. Mix the olive oil, lime juice, lime zest, red pepper flakes and salt in a bowl. Add the shrimp and toss to coat. Marinate, covered, in the refrigerator for 30 minutes, stirring occasionally.

Preheat the grill. Drain the shrimp, discarding the marinade. Thread the shrimp on the soaked skewers and arrange on the grill rack over direct heat. Grill for 3 minutes per side or until the shrimp are firm and pink. Serve the shrimp with the salsa.

LeAnn Holifield Cox

Nutritional Profile for this recipe on page 327.

STUFFED SHRIMP

SERVES 6 TO 8

3 tablespoons butter
1 1/2 cups chopped onions
1 green bell pepper, finely chopped
1 pound lump crab meat, shells and
    cartilage removed
1/3 cup Italian-style bread crumbs
1/4 cup mayonnaise
1/2 teaspoon salt
1/4 teaspoon freshly ground pepper
24 jumbo shrimp, peeled, deveined
    and butterflied
3/4 teaspoon salt
1/4 teaspoon freshly ground pepper

Preheat the oven to 350 degrees. Melt the butter in a skillet over medium-high heat and add the onions and bell pepper. Sauté for 5 minutes or until the onions are tender. Remove from the heat and stir in the crab meat, bread crumbs, mayonnaise, 1/2 teaspoon salt and 1/4 teaspoon pepper.

Sprinkle the shrimp with 3/4 teaspoon salt and 1/4 teaspoon pepper. Mound some of the crab meat mixture in each shrimp and press gently to close. Arrange the shrimp stuffing side up on a baking sheet. Bake for 12 minutes or until the shrimp turn pink and the stuffing is light brown.

SANDY BOLEN BALLARD

To honor the YWCA of Central Alabama's 100th anniversary, the JLB gave a gift of $100,000 to subsidize families whose children attend YWCA day care and to help the center become accredited.

SHRIMP CAKES

For an interesting twist on familiar crab cakes, this recipe uses shrimp. Have the shrimp peeled, deveined, and steamed at the fish counter to save time. Prepare large cakes to serve as a main dish atop salad greens, or smaller cakes for an appetizer course. The recipe works just as well with one pound of jumbo lump crab meat.

SERVES 4

1/4 cup butter (1/2 stick) butter
1/2 cup chopped onion
1/2 cup chopped celery
1 pound shrimp, cooked, peeled and chopped
1/3 cup fine dry bread crumbs
1/2 cup mayonnaise
2 tablespoons minced fresh parsley
1/2 teaspoon Old Bay seasoning
1/2 teaspoon Worcestershire sauce
Tabasco sauce to taste
Salt and freshly ground pepper to taste
1/3 cup fine dry bread crumbs
2 tablespoons butter
Lemon wedges

Melt 1/4 cup butter in a skillet and add the onion and celery. Sauté until tender and spoon into a bowl. Stir the shrimp and 1/3 cup bread crumbs into the onion mixture. Mix the mayonnaise, parsley, Old Bay seasoning, Worcestershire sauce, Tabasco sauce, salt and pepper in a bowl and stir into the shrimp mixture.

Shape the shrimp mixture into 8 cakes and arrange in a single layer on a baking sheet lined with waxed paper. Chill, covered with plastic wrap, for 1 to 4 hours.

Coat the cakes with 1/3 cup bread crumbs. Melt 2 tablespoons butter in a heavy skillet over medium heat and add the cakes. Cook for 2 to 3 minutes per side or until golden brown. Serve the cakes warm with lemon wedges or Lemon Butter Sauce (sidebar).

LAIDE LONG KARPELES

LEMON BUTTER SAUCE

Sauté 2 minced garlic cloves in 1/2 cup butter in a small saucepan for 1 minute. Whisk in 1 1/2 tablespoons cornstarch until combined. Stir in 1/2 cup dry white wine and bring to a boil. Cook for 1 minute or until thickened, stirring constantly. Remove from the heat and stir in 1 tablespoon fresh lemon juice, 3 chopped green onions, 1/2 teaspoon salt and 1/4 teaspoon ground red pepper. Serve with Shrimp Cakes. Omit the cornstarch for a simple butter sauce that pairs well with most any fish.

HEATHER ALLEN BROWN

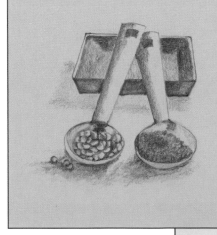

SHRIMP WITH FETA CHEESE OVER ANGEL HAIR PASTA

SERVES 4

1 pound medium shrimp, peeled and deveined
1/4 cup fresh lemon juice
1/4 cup olive oil
3/4 cup finely chopped green onions
1 tablespoon minced garlic
5 plum tomatoes, peeled and chopped (about 2 cups)
1/4 cup clam juice
3 tablespoons butter
1 teaspoon basil
1/2 teaspoon oregano
1/4 teaspoon kosher salt
1/4 cup white wine
3/4 cup crumbled feta cheese
12 ounces angel hair pasta

Toss the shrimp and lemon juice in a bowl. Heat the olive oil in a skillet over medium-high heat and add the green onions and garlic. Sauté until the green onions are tender. Stir in 1 1/2 cups of the tomatoes and bring to a boil. Reduce the heat to medium-low and simmer, covered, for 20 minutes, stirring occasionally. Stir in the clam juice and simmer for 5 minutes longer.

Preheat the oven to 350 degrees. Melt the butter in a skillet over medium heat. Add the shrimp and sauté for 5 minutes or until the shrimp turn pink. Pour the tomato mixture into a shallow 2-quart baking dish. Place the remaining tomatoes in the center of the tomato mixture and surround with the shrimp. Sprinkle the basil, oregano and salt over the shrimp and drizzle with the wine. Sprinkle with the feta cheese and bake for 15 minutes or until heated through. Cook the pasta using the package directions and drain. Spoon the shrimp mixture over the hot pasta on a serving platter and serve immediately.

NANCY BEDSOLE BYNON

ROASTED RED PEPPER AND PESTO
SHRIMP OVER PASTA

SERVES 4 TO 6

12 to 16 ounces angel hair pasta
1 (12-ounce) jar roasted red peppers, drained
8 ounces cream cheese, softened
1/2 cup chicken broth
1/2 teaspoon salt
1/4 teaspoon red pepper
1/4 cup prepared fresh pesto
2 pounds deveined peeled cooked fresh shrimp

Cook the pasta using the package directions. Drain and cover to keep warm. Combine the roasted peppers, cream cheese and broth in a blender and process until smooth. Spoon the roasted pepper mixture into a large skillet and cook over medium to medium-high heat until heated through. Stir in the salt and red pepper and bring to a boil.

Cook for 4 minutes, stirring frequently. Remove from the heat and stir in the pesto. Stir in the shrimp and simmer for 4 minutes or until heated through. Serve immediately over the hot cooked pasta.

HOLLY HOLMES WILLIAMS

Photograph for this recipe on page 246

GREEK RICE AND SHRIMP BAKE WITH FETA CHEESE CRUMB TOPPING

SERVES 6 TO 8

Feta Cheese Crumb Topping
3/4 cup fresh bread crumbs
3/4 cup crumbled feta cheese
2 tablespoons chopped fresh parsley

Shrimp Bake
2 1/2 cups chicken broth
1 1/4 cups white rice
2 tablespoons olive oil
1 onion, chopped
2 garlic cloves, finely chopped
1 teaspoon oregano
1/2 teaspoon hot red pepper flakes
1/2 teaspoon salt
2 large tomatoes, chopped
1 red bell pepper, chopped
1/2 cup kalamata olives, coarsely chopped
2 tablespoons chopped pepperoncini chiles
1 pound large shrimp, peeled and deveined

For the topping, toss the bread crumbs, feta cheese and parsley in a bowl.

For the shrimp bake, bring the broth to a boil in a saucepan over high heat and stir in the rice. Reduce the heat to low and simmer, covered, for 20 minutes or until the rice is tender. Let stand until cool. Preheat the oven to 375 degrees. Heat the olive oil in a large nonstick skillet over medium heat and add the onion, garlic, oregano, red pepper flakes and salt. Cook for 4 minutes, stirring occasionally. Stir in the tomatoes and bell pepper and cook for 3 minutes. Add the olives, pepperoncini chiles and rice and mix well.

Spoon the rice mixture into a lightly greased shallow 3-quart baking dish and arrange the shrimp over the top. Bake for 20 minutes or until the shrimp are almost done. Sprinkle with the topping and bake for 10 minutes longer or until the shrimp turn pink and the topping is light brown.

EVELYN BRITTON STUTTS

GRILLED ROYAL RED SHRIMP KABOBS

*Royal Red shrimp are a deep water species with a sweet flavor reminiscent
of lobster. These large shrimp are so named because they are often a bright red color. Serve over
saffron rice with a spinach salad for a colorful and tasty meal.*

SERVES 4

Wooden skewers
1/4 cup chopped fresh parsley
3 tablespoons olive oil
1 1/2 tablespoons fresh lemon juice
2 garlic cloves, minced
Grape tomatoes
1 large onion, cut into 2-inch pieces
1 large yellow bell pepper, cut into 2-inch pieces
1 1/2 pounds Royal Red shrimp,
    peeled and deveined
1/2 teaspoon salt
1/2 teaspoon freshly ground pepper

Soak wooden skewers in water for 30 minutes. Mix the parsley, olive oil, lemon juice and garlic in a small bowl. Thread the tomatoes, onion, bell pepper and shrimp alternately on the wooden skewers and sprinkle with the salt and pepper. Brush with the olive oil mixture and arrange on a platter. Chill, covered, for up to 2 hours.

Preheat the grill. Arrange the skewers on the grill rack and grill for 2 minutes per side or until the shrimp turn pink and are no longer translucent, turning occasionally.

HARRIET KENNEDY COCHRANE

CHIMICHURRI

Chimichurri is an all-purpose Argentinean condiment, much like ketchup is in America. This delicious herb sauce, made with olive oil, vinegar, herbs, and lots of chopped fresh parsley, pairs equally well with grilled meats and a variety of vegetables. Use fresh flat-leaf parsley for the best flavor.

MAKES ABOUT 2 CUPS

1 cup packed fresh flat-leaf
   parsley leaves
1/4 cup finely minced purple onion
4 garlic cloves
1/2 cup extra-virgin olive oil
1/4 cup red wine vinegar

2 tablespoons water
1 teaspoon kosher salt
1 teaspoon fresh lemon juice
1/2 teaspoon oregano
1/4 teaspoon cayenne pepper
1/4 teaspoon red pepper flakes

Combine the parsley, onion and garlic in a food processor and process until finely chopped, scraping the side of the bowl several times. Spoon the parsley mixture into a bowl and whisk in the olive oil, vinegar, water, salt, lemon juice, oregano, cayenne pepper and red pepper flakes.

Let stand for 30 minutes before serving to allow the flavors to develop. Store, covered, in the refrigerator for several days.

SUSAN CARTER HANCOCK

CRANBERRY CHERRY RELISH

*Prepare this relish at least one day in advance to allow the flavors to meld.
Be sure to grate the orange before juicing.*

MAKES 4 CUPS

1 pound fresh cranberries
2 cups sugar
1/2 cup fresh orange juice

1/2 cup cranberry juice
Finely grated zest of 1 orange
1 cup dried cherries

Combine the cranberries, sugar, orange juice, cranberry juice and orange zest in a large saucepan and mix well. Bring to a boil over medium heat and boil for 10 minutes or until the cranberries pop.

Skim off the foam with a metal spoon and stir in the cherries. Let stand until cool. Store, covered, in the refrigerator for up to 1 month.

EVELYN BRITTON STUTTS

TERIYAKI GLAZE

Great to serve with grilled chicken or tuna steaks.

MAKES 3/4 CUP

1/4 cup water
2 tablespoons dark brown sugar
2 tablespoons Asian sesame oil
1 tablespoon rice vinegar
1 tablespoon sherry
1 tablespoon sesame seeds

3 green onions, finely chopped
2 garlic cloves, minced
1 teaspoon grated fresh ginger
1/4 teaspoon salt
1/4 teaspoon pepper

Combine the water, brown sugar, sesame oil, vinegar, sherry, sesame seeds, green onions, garlic, ginger, salt and pepper in a medium saucepan and cook over low heat until heated through, stirring occasionally. Cook for 10 minutes longer or until thickened and of a glaze consistency, stirring occasionally.

KIMBERLY PORTER RODGERS

BARBECUE SAUCE

MAKES 2 CUPS

1 1/2 cups ketchup
1/4 cup vinegar
3 tablespoons brown sugar
2 tablespoons Worcestershire sauce
1 small onion, finely chopped
1 tablespoon minced garlic

1 tablespoon molasses
1 teaspoon prepared mustard
1 teaspoon fresh lemon juice
1/4 teaspoon salt
1/4 teaspoon Tabasco sauce
1/8 teaspoon ground red pepper

Combine the ketchup, vinegar, brown sugar, Worcestershire sauce, onion, garlic, molasses, prepared mustard and lemon juice in a large saucepan and mix well. Stir in the salt, Tabasco sauce and red pepper. Bring to a boil and reduce the heat to low.

Simmer for 40 to 50 minutes or to the desired consistency, stirring occasionally. Let stand until cool. Store in an airtight container in the refrigerator.

SUSAN CARTER HANCOCK

CUCUMBER SAUCE

This sauce is delicious served over fish, and children love it as a dip.

MAKES 1¹/2 CUPS

¹/2 cup mayonnaise	¹/2 cup chopped cucumber
¹/2 cup sour cream	¹/2 cup chopped red onion
¹/2 teaspoon salt	¹/2 cup chopped tomato

Combine the mayonnaise, sour cream and salt in a bowl and mix well. Stir in the cucumber, onion and tomato. Chill, covered, for 1 hour or longer before serving.

JILL DEWITT ACOSTA

DEWANA'S GREAT GRILLING SAUCE

A wonderful cook and former neighbor from Tuscaloosa gave me this recipe as a young newlywed in the 1970s. It remains a favorite.

MAKES 4¹/2 CUPS

2 cups Worcestershire sauce	1 tablespoon sugar
1 cup strong black coffee	1 tablespoon salt
1 cup ketchup	³/4 tablespoon pepper

Combine the Worcestershire sauce, coffee, ketchup, sugar, salt and pepper in a bowl and mix well. Use immediately or store, covered, in the refrigerator for up to 2 weeks. Use as a marinade and/or basting sauce with steaks. Or, marinate a 3-pound pot roast in the sauce and cook the roast in the sauce in a Dutch oven over low heat until the desired degree of doneness.

SUSAN MEADOWS LEACH

Nana's Rémoulade Sauce

MAKES 2 CUPS

1 cup mayonnaise
1 cup Creole mustard
1¹/2 tablespoons lemon juice
1 teaspoon Cognac
1 teaspoon grated onion

1 teaspoon dry sherry
¹/2 teaspoon anchovy paste
¹/8 teaspoon Tabasco sauce
¹/4 teaspoon Worcestershire sauce

Combine the mayonnaise, Creole mustard, lemon juice, brandy, onion, sherry, anchovy paste, Tabasco sauce and Worcestershire sauce in a bowl and mix well. Chill, covered, for several hours before serving. Serve with shrimp, fried fish or Shrimp Cakes on page 237.

KELLI NELSON JETMUNDSEN

Citrus Marinade for Chicken and Pork

MAKES 1¹/2 CUPS

¹/2 cup white wine vinegar
¹/2 cup extra-virgin olive oil
¹/3 cup orange juice
2 tablespoons soy sauce

1 tablespoon chopped fresh thyme, or
   1 teaspoon dried thyme
¹/2 teaspoon freshly ground pepper
¹/2 teaspoon Worcestershire sauce
¹/2 teaspoon Tabasco sauce

Whisk the vinegar, olive oil, orange juice, soy sauce, thyme, pepper, Worcestershire sauce and Tabasco sauce in a bowl until combined. Pour the marinade over 6 bone-in chicken breasts or two 1-pound pork tenderloins in a sealable plastic bag. Seal tightly and marinate in the refrigerator for 5 hours, turning occasionally. Drain, reserving the marinade. Bring the marinade to a boil in a small saucepan and baste the chicken or pork during the grilling process.

PATRICIA LISENBY HAND

Main Dishes

QUICK FIXES

Grilled Chicken with White Sauce

Boneless skinless chicken breasts are a staple in most kitchens, and it is easy to run out of ideas to jazz up your weeknight dinners. Here is a solution that requires just one pan and takes less than thirty minutes. Season chicken breasts with salt and pepper and coat with flour. Cook in butter or vegetable oil in a skillet over medium-high heat for six minutes per side or until cooked through. Remove the chicken to a platter and cover to keep warm. Then add a few additional ingredients, simmer briefly, and dinner is served.

- **MARSALA SAUCE**
  Melt 1/4 cup butter in the skillet over medium-high heat. Stir in 2 1/2 cups sliced mushrooms and sauté for 6 minutes. Add 1 minced garlic clove and sauté for 1 minute. Stir in 1 1/4 cups marsala and 3/4 cup reduced-sodium chicken broth and bring to a boil, scraping the bottom of the skillet with a wooden spoon to loosen any browned bits. Reduce the heat and simmer for 10 minutes or until reduced by half. Spoon the sauce over the chicken and sprinkle with grated Parmesan cheese.
  Lisa Gooldrup Costanzo

- **MUSTARD TARRAGON SAUCE**
  Melt 1 1/2 tablespoons butter in the skillet over medium-high heat. Add 1/3 cup chopped shallots and sauté for 1 minute. Add 1/3 cup dry vermouth and stir to loosen any browned bits on the bottom of the skillet. Stir in 1/2 cup heavy cream or whipping cream and 2 tablespoons whole grain mustard and bring to a boil. Reduce the heat and simmer for 3 minutes or until slightly thickened, stirring constantly. Return the chicken to the skillet and cook for 1 minute or until heated through. Sprinkle with 2 1/2 tablespoons chopped fresh tarragon.
  Nancy Beaird Bromberg

- **BALSAMIC AND THYME ONION SAUCE**
  Melt 2 tablespoons butter in the skillet over medium-high heat. Add 2 cups thinly sliced red onions, 1 tablespoon brown sugar and 1/2 teaspoon salt and sauté for 4 minutes. Stir in 1 cup reduced-sodium chicken broth and 3 tablespoons balsamic vinegar and bring to a boil. Cook for 7 minutes or until the onion is tender, stirring frequently and adding additional broth if necessary for the desired consistency. Stir in 2 teaspoons chopped fresh thyme and serve over the chicken.
  Jeannie Tatum Pate

- **BOURBON MAPLE SAUCE**
  Melt 2 tablespoons butter in the skillet over medium-high heat. Stir in 1/3 cup finely chopped sweet onion and cook for 3 minutes, stirring constantly. Add 1/4 cup bourbon and bring to a boil, scraping the bottom of the skillet with a wooden spoon to loosen any browned bits. Cook for 2 minutes and add 1/2 cup reduced-sodium chicken broth, 2 tablespoons maple syrup and 1/4 teaspoon salt. Bring to a boil and boil for 3 minutes or until the sauce is reduced to 1/2 cup, stirring frequently. Serve the sauce with the chicken.

Carolina Barbecued Pork

Roasted Red Pepper and Pesto Shrimp over Pasta

- ### HERBED GOAT CHEESE SAUCE
  Melt 1 tablespoon butter in the skillet over medium-high heat. Add $1/4$ cup finely chopped shallots and sauté for 2 minutes. Add 1 minced garlic clove and sauté for 1 minute. Stir in $1/2$ cup dry white wine and $3/4$ cup reduced-sodium chicken broth and scrape the bottom of the skillet with a wooden spoon to loosen any browned bits. Bring to a boil and boil for 5 minutes or until the mixture is reduced by half, stirring frequently. Remove from the heat and stir in 3 ounces crumbled goat cheese, 2 tablespoons chopped fresh parsley and 2 tablespoons chopped fresh chives. Drizzle over the chicken.

- ### HONEY MUSTARD WINE SAUCE
  Heat 2 tablespoons olive oil in the skillet over medium heat. Add 1 minced garlic clove and cook for 1 minute or until fragrant but not brown. Stir in $3/4$ cup dry white wine and scrape the bottom of the skillet with a wooden spoon to loosen any browned bits. Cook for 3 minutes and whisk in 2 tablespoons Dijon mustard and 2 tablespoons honey. Cook for 2 minutes and add the chicken to the skillet. Cook for 2 minutes or until heated through. Garnish with chopped fresh rosemary.

  Lyda Helen Jones

WEEKNIGHT SUPPER   MENU

SUGGESTED WINES:
- *Robert Sinskey
  Los Carneros Merlot 2001*
- *Le Rigeoulet en Provence Red*
- *Stags Leaf Napa Valley
  Viognier 2003*

Best-Ever Gourmet Meat Loaf

Health Fare

VEGETABLES

Plant a vegetable garden, snap some pea pods, dig some potatoes, or marvel at a bean stalk, and then raise a glass to an often underappreciated part of the food triangle—the vegetable. With an ever expanding variety of tastes, textures, and colors, properly prepared vegetables are making a comeback. Substitute Cheater's Corn Pudding on page 262 for pasta. Or serve colorful Roasted Beets with Spicy Orange Glaze on page 258. We think these will tempt even the pickiest eaters.

Everyone's heard that if we eat our vegetables we improve our health. But we are exceptionally fortunate to have the medical center at the University of Alabama Birmingham (UAB) if we need a little extra help. The thirty-six-year-old comprehensive metropolitan university and medical center encompasses eighty-two city blocks and is often referred to as the backbone of employment and research not just in Birmingham, but throughout the South.

Eleven programs from UAB are ranked in the annual "America's Best Hospitals" section of 2005 *U.S. News & World Report*. And in just a few decades, UAB has evolved into a world-renowned research university and health-care center, Alabama's single largest employer, and an engine of revitalization for the city of Birmingham. UAB is focused on the future of teaching, research, community service, and health care.

We encourage you to try these tasty vegetable recipes. Even squash may surprise you after trying Squash Tomato Pie with Feta Cheese on page 272. Here's to your health: "Salud! À Votre Santé!" And know that UAB is right here in Birmingham promoting educational, physical, and economic health as well.

Visit the University of Alabama Birmingham at www.uab.edu.

The Hillman Building at UAB Hospital

Clockwise: Martha's Sweet Potato Soufflé,
Norman's Creamed Spinach,
Best Squash Casserole

Vegetables

ARTICHOKE BROCCOLI CASSEROLE

This sauce is great over broccoli, brussels sprouts, or other vegetables in the cabbage family. It is quick and easy.

SERVES 6

1 (16-ounce) package chopped
    broccoli florets, or 1 head
    chopped fresh broccoli (5 cups)
Salt to taste
1 (7-ounce) can artichoke hearts,
    drained and chopped into
    bite-size pieces

1/2 cup slivered almonds, toasted
1/2 cup mayonnaise
1/4 cup (1 ounce) grated
    Parmesan cheese
1/4 cup (1/2 stick) butter, melted
2 teaspoons fresh lemon juice
1/4 teaspoon celery salt

Preheat the oven to 350 degrees. Cook the broccoli in boiling salted water in a saucepan for 4 to 6 minutes or until tender-crisp and drain. Arrange the broccoli and artichokes in a buttered 2-quart baking dish. Reserve 2 tablespoons of the almonds and sprinkle the remaining almonds over the top. Combine the mayonnaise, cheese, butter, lemon juice and celery salt in a bowl and mix well. Spread the mayonnaise mixture over the prepared layers and sprinkle with the reserved 2 tablespoons almonds. Bake for 20 minutes or until heated through.

HOLLY HOLMES WILLIAMS

ASPARAGUS BUNDLES

MAKES 4 (4-OUNCE) SERVINGS

1 pound fresh asparagus spears
1 tablespoon olive oil
1 garlic clove, minced
1 teaspoon kosher salt

1 teaspoon freshly ground pepper
Tops of 1 bunch green onions,
    cut into strips
Pimentos (optional)

Preheat the oven to 400 degrees. Snap off the thick woody ends of the asparagus spears and discard. Blanch the asparagus in boiling water in a saucepan for 2 to 3 minutes and drain. Toss the asparagus, olive oil, garlic, salt and pepper in a shallow dish until coated. Arrange the asparagus and green onions in a roasting pan and bake for 8 to 10 minutes or to the desired degree of crispness. To serve, bundle 3 or 4 asparagus spears and tie with 1 green onion strip. Place a pimento slice on top of the tie for color and serve immediately.

HEATHER ALLEN BROWN

Nutritional Profile for this recipe on page 327.

ASPARAGUS TART

A very pretty and easy side dish to prepare.

SERVES 6 TO 8

1 (9-inch) refrigerator pie pastry
1 pound asparagus spears
2 thick slices hickory-smoked bacon
1 tablespoon butter
1/4 cup chopped sweet onion
1/4 cup chopped red bell pepper
4 ounces cream cheese, softened
1/2 cup mayonnaise
1/2 cup half-and-half
2 tablespoons all-purpose flour
2 eggs
2 cups (8 ounces) shredded Swiss cheese
1 cup (4 ounces) grated Parmesan cheese

Preheat the oven to 350 degrees. Fit the pie pastry into a lightly greased tart pan and bake for 5 to 7 minutes. Let stand until cool. Maintain the oven temperature.

Snap off the thick woody ends of the asparagus spears and discard. Cut the spears into 3-inch pieces. Bring 1 inch of water to a boil in a saucepan and place the asparagus in a steamer basket over the boiling water. Steam, covered, for 4 to 6 minutes or until tender-crisp and drain.

Cook the bacon in a skillet over medium-high heat until crisp. Remove the bacon to a paper towel to drain, reserving the pan drippings. Cool the bacon and crumble. Melt the butter with the reserved pan drippings and add the onion and bell pepper. Sauté until tender.

Combine the cream cheese, mayonnaise, half-and-half, flour and eggs in a mixing bowl and beat until blended. Stir in the bacon, onion mixture and Swiss cheese. Arrange the asparagus in the baked shell and pour the cream cheese mixture over the top. Sprinkle with the Parmesan cheese and bake for 30 to 35 minutes or until a knife inserted near the center comes out clean.

MICHELLE LIKOS KELLY

Photograph for this recipe on page 277.

BLACK BEAN TART

SERVES 6

Follow these simple instructions for seeding a jalapeño chile. Rinse the jalapeño chile, cut lengthwise into halves, and discard the seeds. Be sure to wash your hands with soap and water after handling any chile, or simply wear kitchen gloves while handling chiles.

Potato Crust
2 cups frozen shredded hash brown potatoes, thawed
3 tablespoons butter, melted
1/2 teaspoon each salt and pepper

Bean Filling
1 tablespoon vegetable oil
1 red bell pepper, finely chopped (about 1 cup)
1/2 cup finely chopped purple onion
1 (15-ounce) can black beans, drained and rinsed
1 (15-ounce) can whole kernel corn, drained
2 jalapeño chiles, seeded and finely chopped
1/2 teaspoon ground cumin
1/2 teaspoon chili powder
1 1/2 cups (6 ounces) shredded Monterey Jack cheese
1 teaspoon chopped fresh cilantro

Creamy Lime Topping
1 cup sour cream
2 teaspoons fresh lime juice
1/4 teaspoon each salt and pepper
Chopped fresh cilantro for garnish

For the crust, preheat the oven to 350 degrees. Press the potatoes between paper towels to remove any excess moisture. Mix the potatoes, butter, salt and pepper in a bowl. Pat the potato mixture over the bottom and up the side of a greased 9-inch pie plate and bake for 20 to 25 minutes or until light brown. Maintain the oven temperature.

For the filling, heat the oil in a skillet and add the bell pepper and onion. Sauté until tender and remove from the heat. Stir in the beans, corn, jalapeño chiles, cumin and chili powder. Fold in the cheese and cilantro. Spoon the bean mixture into the potato crust and bake for 20 minutes. Cool in the pan on a wire rack for 10 minutes.

For the topping, mix the sour cream, lime juice, salt and pepper in a bowl. Top the tart with the topping and garnish with the cilantro.

CAROLYN AMOS FREEMAN

GARLIC-ROASTED GREEN BEANS AND SHALLOTS WITH HAZELNUTS

Chopped hazelnuts are a great flavor match for green beans, and a refreshing departure from the more expected almonds.

MAKES 6 (1/2-CUP) SERVINGS

6 shallots
1 pound fresh green beans, trimmed
5 garlic cloves, coarsely chopped
3 tablespoons extra-virgin olive oil
1 teaspoon kosher salt
1/2 teaspoon freshly ground pepper
1/4 cup finely chopped fresh flat-leaf parsley
1/4 cup coarsely chopped toasted hazelnuts
1 teaspoon finely grated lemon zest

Position an oven rack in the center of the oven and preheat the oven to 450 degrees. Cut each shallot lengthwise into 1/4-inch slices. Combine the shallots, beans, garlic and olive oil in a bowl and toss to coat. Sprinkle with the salt and pepper and toss again.

Spoon the bean mixture into a 10×15-inch baking dish and roast for 18 to 20 minutes or until the vegetables are light brown and tender, stirring once. Mix the parsley, hazelnuts and lemon zest in a bowl and sprinkle over the top, tossing to mix. Serve immediately.

JULIE GRIMES BOTTCHER

Nutritional Profile for this recipe on page 327.

Outdoor play improves academic performance and encourages social development, but many schools do not have proper playground equipment. The JLB is committed to building one new playground each year through 2010.

HARICOTS VERTS WITH ROASTED GARLIC BUTTER

*Roasted garlic has a creamy texture and pairing it with butter makes
for an intensely flavorful combination. Prepare the garlic butter up to two days in
advance and toss with the hot haricots verts just before serving.*

MAKES 6 (4 OUNCES BEANS WITH 2 TEASPOONS SAUCE) SERVINGS

1 head garlic
2 tablespoons finely chopped shallots
1/4 teaspoon salt
4 teaspoons butter, softened
2 teaspoons chopped fresh rosemary
11/2 pounds haricots verts
1 tablespoon salt

Preheat the oven to 350 degrees. Remove the white papery skin from the garlic head; do not peel or separate the cloves. Wrap the garlic head in foil and bake for 1 hour. Cool for 10 minutes and separate the cloves. Squeeze to extract the garlic pulp and discard the skins.

Combine the garlic pulp, shallots, 1/4 teaspoon salt, butter and rosemary in a bowl and mix well. Add the beans and 1 tablespoon salt to enough boiling water to cover in a medium saucepan and cook for 2 minutes or until tender-crisp. Drain and toss the hot beans with the butter mixture. If these tiny French green beans are not available, substitute with fresh green beans and cook for 2 to 3 minutes longer or until tender-crisp.

JULIE GRIMES BOTTCHER

Nutritional Profile for this recipe on page 327.

Ranch-Hand Beans

This is a great alternative to baked beans.

SERVES 10 TO 12

8 ounces ground beef
1/4 cup chopped onion
8 ounces Polish sausage
5 slices bacon
2 (16-ounce) cans pork and beans
1/3 cup ketchup
1/4 cup packed light brown sugar
2 tablespoons molasses
1 1/2 teaspoons Worcestershire sauce
1 1/2 teaspoons prepared mustard
1/4 teaspoon salt
1/4 teaspoon pepper
1/4 teaspoon ground cumin

Brown the ground beef with the onion in a skillet, stirring until the ground beef is crumbly; drain. Cut the sausage into 1/4-inch slices and brown on both sides in a skillet; drain. Cook the bacon in a skillet until brown and crisp. Drain and cool slightly. Crumble the bacon.

Combine the pork and beans, ketchup, brown sugar and molasses in a Dutch oven and mix well. Stir in the Worcestershire sauce, prepared mustard, salt, pepper and cumin. Add the ground beef mixture, sausage and bacon and mix well. Simmer the mixture for 20 to 30 minutes or to the desired consistency, stirring occasionally.

Nellah Bailey McGough

ROASTED BEETS WITH SPICY ORANGE GLAZE

MAKES 4 (1/2-CUP) SERVINGS

6 small fresh beets, peeled
 and chopped
1 tablespoon olive oil
1/4 teaspoon salt
1/8 teaspoon pepper
1/3 cup fresh orange juice

3 tablespoons hot jalapeño jelly
1/2 teaspoon freshly grated orange zest
1/4 teaspoon salt
1/8 teaspoon pepper
1 tablespoon olive oil

Preheat the oven to 425 degrees. Toss the beets, 1 tablespoon olive oil, 1/4 teaspoon salt and 1/8 teaspoon pepper in a bowl. Spread the beet mixture on a foil-lined baking sheet and roast for 30 to 40 minutes or until the beets are tender, stirring occasionally. Combine the orange juice, jelly, orange zest, 1/4 teaspoon salt and 1/8 teaspoon pepper in a small saucepan and cook over medium-low heat for 7 to 12 minutes or until the mixture is the consistency of a thick glaze, stirring occasionally. Toss the hot beets, 1 tablespoon olive oil and the hot glaze in a bowl until coated and serve immediately.

KATHERINE ADAMS MCKNIGHT

Nutritional Profile for this recipe on page 327.

BROCCOLI AU GRATIN

SERVES 6 TO 8

2 heads broccoli
1 (10-ounce) can cream of
 shrimp soup
1/2 cup heavy cream or
 whipping cream
1/2 cup tomato juice

2 tablespoons butter
1/2 cup plain bread crumbs
1 cup (4 ounces) shredded sharp
 Cheddar cheese
1/8 teaspoon paprika
Salt and pepper to taste

Preheat the oven to 400 degrees. Steam the broccoli for 8 to 10 minutes or until bright green and tender. Cool slightly and cut into bite-size pieces. Arrange the broccoli in a 7×11-inch baking dish. Combine the soup, cream and tomato juice in a small saucepan and cook just until heated through, stirring occasionally. Pour the soup mixture over the broccoli. Melt the butter in a small skillet and add the bread crumbs. Cook until toasted, stirring frequently. Sprinkle the bread crumbs over the prepared layers and top with the cheese, paprika, salt and pepper. Bake for 10 to 15 minutes or until bubbly.

ELIZABETH HAMITER FERGUSON

ROASTED BRUSSELS SPROUTS WITH CITRUS AND WALNUTS

SERVES 4 TO 6

1¹/2 pounds fresh brussels sprouts
    (about 32)
1 tablespoon olive oil
¹/2 teaspoon salt
2 tablespoons butter, melted
2 tablespoons fresh lemon juice

1 tablespoon fresh orange juice
1 teaspoon sugar
³/4 teaspoon grated orange zest
¹/4 teaspoon freshly ground pepper
¹/2 cup walnuts, toasted and chopped

Preheat the oven to 450 degrees. Line a baking sheet with foil and spray with nonstick cooking spray. Boil the brussels sprouts in enough water to cover in a saucepan for 5 minutes. Drain and cut the sprouts into halves. Arrange the sprouts on the prepared baking sheet, drizzle with the olive oil and sprinkle with the salt. Toss to coat. Roast for 8 to 10 minutes or until light brown, stirring once. Mix the butter, lemon juice, orange juice, sugar, orange zest and pepper in a large bowl. Add the brussels sprouts to the butter mixture and toss gently to coat. Stir in the walnuts and serve immediately.

RAMI MARIE PERRY

SPICY CABBAGE

SERVES 8

4 slices bacon
1 onion, chopped
1 garlic clove, minced
1 (14-ounce) can diced tomatoes
1 (4-ounce) can spicy vegetable
    juice cocktail
1 teaspoon Tabasco sauce, or to taste

3 (10-ounce) packages angel hair
    cabbage slaw
1 (14-ounce) can chicken broth
1 to 2 teaspoons Cajun seasoning, or
    to taste
¹/4 cup sugar

Cook the bacon in a skillet until brown and crisp. Drain and crumble the bacon. Sauté the onion and garlic in a large nonstick skillet until the onion is tender. Stir in the bacon, undrained tomatoes, vegetable juice cocktail and Tabasco sauce. Simmer for 15 minutes, stirring occasionally. Add the slaw, broth and Cajun seasoning and mix well. Simmer, covered, for 30 minutes, adding the sugar after 15 minutes and stirring occasionally.

NINA HAAS DANIELS

ROASTED CARROTS AND PARSNIPS WITH SHALLOT AND HERB BUTTER

*Roasted carrots and parsnips come alive with flavor in this delicious
herb butter. It is easy to prepare extra and store in the freezer for up to three months.
Use the butter on hot fresh rolls, tossed with rice or pasta for a quick side dish,
or brush over grilled or roasted meats in place of a sauce.*

SERVES 4

Roasted Vegetables
5 large carrots, peeled (about 1 pound)
4 large parsnips, peeled (about 1 pound)
1 tablespoon olive oil
2 teaspoons kosher salt
1/2 teaspoon freshly ground pepper

Shallot and Herb Butter
1/4 cup (1/2 stick) unsalted butter, softened
2 tablespoons minced shallots
2 tablespoons finely chopped fresh chives
1 tablespoon finely chopped fresh rosemary
2 teaspoons chopped fresh thyme
1 garlic clove, minced
1/2 teaspoon kosher salt

For the vegetables, position an oven rack in the center of the oven and preheat the oven to 450 degrees. Cut the carrots and parsnips into matchsticks, 2 inches long and 1/4 inch thick. Toss the carrots and parsnips with the olive oil in a bowl. Sprinkle with the salt and pepper and toss again. Spoon the vegetables into a small roasting pan with 2-inch sides and roast for 35 minutes or until the vegetables are light brown, stirring once.

For the butter, combine the butter, shallots, chives, rosemary, thyme, garlic and salt in a small bowl and mix well. Toss the hot roasted vegetables with the herb butter in a serving bowl until coated and serve immediately. Or, you may serve the herb butter on the side with the roasted vegetables.

BEATY EVANS COLEMAN

Photograph for this recipe on page 276.

SAUTÉED COLLARD GREENS WITH HAM AND ONIONS

*Look for one-pound packages of chopped collard greens in your supermarket.
It will save time and effort in the kitchen.*

SERVES 8

1 tablespoon olive oil
4 ounces ham, chopped (about 1 1/2 cups)
1 cup chopped onion
2 pounds fresh collard greens, trimmed and
    coarsely chopped
1 teaspoon salt
1 teaspoon crushed red pepper flakes
6 ounces salt pork
2 cups low-sodium chicken broth
1/2 cup white wine
1/4 cup apple cider vinegar
1/2 cup (1 stick) unsalted butter

Heat the olive oil in a Dutch oven over medium-high heat and add the ham and onion. Sauté for 4 minutes or until light brown. Stir in the collard greens, salt and red pepper flakes and sauté for 4 minutes or until the collard greens are slightly wilted. Add the salt pork, broth, wine and vinegar and bring to a boil. Reduce the heat to low.

Simmer, covered, for 1 1/2 hours, stirring occasionally. Add the butter and cook for 10 minutes longer, stirring occasionally. Discard the salt pork and spoon the collard greens into a serving bowl.

JULIE GRIMES BOTTCHER

AUNT MAGGIE'S CORN CASSEROLE

SERVES 6

2 (9-ounce) cans white Shoe Peg corn, drained
1/2 cup (1 stick) butter
2 tablespoons all-purpose flour
1 cup heavy cream or whipping cream
1/2 teaspoon salt
1/2 teaspoon pepper

Preheat the oven to 350 degrees. Pour the corn into a 2-quart baking dish. Melt the butter in a saucepan over medium heat and stir in the flour. Cook until smooth and bubbly, stirring constantly. Add the cream, salt and pepper and cook for 10 to 12 minutes or until thickened and the consistency of a sauce, stirring frequently. Pour the sauce over the corn and stir to combine. Bake for 45 to 60 minutes or until bubbly.

DENISE CALDERARO MODLING

CHEATER'S CORN PUDDING

Good and easy side dish!

SERVES 10

1 (8-ounce) package corn muffin mix
1 (14-ounce) can whole kernel corn, drained
1 (10-ounce) package frozen cream-style corn
1 cup sour cream
2 eggs, lightly beaten
1/2 cup (1 stick) butter, melted
1/2 cup (2 ounces) shredded Cheddar cheese
6 to 8 slices bacon, crisp-cooked and crumbled

Preheat the oven to 350 degrees. Spray ten 1/2-cup ramekins or one 7×11-inch baking pan with nonstick cooking spray. Combine the muffin mix, whole kernel corn, cream-style corn, sour cream, eggs and butter in a bowl and mix just until moistened.

Fill the prepared ramekins 3/4 full and sprinkle with the cheese and bacon. Bake for 20 to 30 minutes or until the centers are set. If using a baking pan, bake for 40 to 60 minutes or until the center is set.

JEANNE REID SHEARER

COMPANY CORN PUDDING

Firm and smooth. A great soufflé look.

SERVES 6

1 tablespoon butter
1¹/2 tablespoons all-purpose flour
2 cups fresh corn kernels
 (from about 4 ears)
1³/4 cups half-and-half

3 eggs
1 tablespoon sugar
1 teaspoon salt
2 cups heavy cream or
 whipping cream

Preheat the oven to 325 degrees. Coat a 2-quart soufflé dish with the butter and sprinkle with the flour, tilting the dish to ensure even coverage. Combine 1 cup of the corn and the half-and-half in a blender and process until smooth. Add the eggs, sugar and salt and pulse just to combine.

Mix the corn mixture, remaining 1 cup corn and the cream in a bowl. Pour into the prepared soufflé dish and bake for 70 minutes or until the center of the pudding barely moves when the pan is lightly touched. Let stand for 10 minutes before serving.

LORETTA GLEASON KELLER

Photograph for this recipe on page 277.

FRIED OKRA

SERVES 4 TO 5

1 pound fresh or frozen okra (4 cups)
¹/4 cup all-purpose flour
¹/4 cup milk

1 cup cornmeal
Salt and pepper to taste
Vegetable oil for frying

Cut the okra into ¹/2-inch pieces. Place the okra in a 1-gallon sealable plastic bag and add the flour. Seal tightly and toss to coat. Pour the milk into the bag and seal tightly. Turn the bag until the okra is completely coated. Remove the okra to another 1-gallon sealable plastic bag and add the cornmeal. Seal tightly and toss to coat. Season to taste with salt and pepper.

Preheat oil in a deep skillet and add the okra. Fry until medium brown in color and drain on paper towels. Serve immediately.

NANCY BEDSOLE BYNON

BAKED VIDALIA ONIONS

SERVES 4

4 large Vidalia onions
1/4 cup (1/2 stick) butter, cut into 4 tablespoons
1 teaspoon salt
1/4 teaspoon pepper
1 cup (4 ounces) freshly shredded Parmesan cheese

Preheat the oven to 400 degrees. Peel the onions, leaving the root end intact. Cut each onion into eighths, cutting to but not through the root end. Arrange each onion on a lightly greased piece of foil. Press 1 tablespoon of the butter into the center of each onion and sprinkle evenly with the salt, pepper and cheese. Enclose the onions with the foil and seal tightly. Arrange the foil-wrapped onions in a 9×13-inch baking dish and bake for 1 hour or until tender.

ALLISON BERMAN WEIL

FRIED ONION RINGS

This is a very light batter and is delicious with a variety of vegetables, such as zucchini and other types of squash. This recipe will serve a large number of guests.

SERVES 18

1 (12-ounce) can light beer
1 1/2 cups all-purpose flour
1 teaspoon sugar
Vegetable oil for frying
3 large yellow onions, thinly sliced and separated into rings
1/2 teaspoon salt
1/8 teaspoon pepper

Whisk the beer, flour and sugar in a large bowl until blended and let stand for about 1 hour. Heat oil in a large deep skillet until a drop of water sizzles; during the frying process adjust the temperature as required to keep the onions from burning. Dip the onion slices in the batter until coated, allowing the excess to drip off. Fry the onion rings in batches in the hot oil until golden brown, turning occasionally for even browning; do not crowd the skillet. Drain on brown grocery sacks lined with 2 layers of paper towels. Sprinkle with the salt and pepper and serve immediately, or keep warm in a 250-degree oven.

MITZI MUNGER IRELAND

Photograph for this recipe on page 277.

TARRAGON SUGAR SNAP PEAS

This is a new and refreshing method for preparing sugar snap peas.

SERVES 4

1 pound fresh or frozen sugar snap peas
2 teaspoons butter
2 teaspoons finely chopped shallots
2 teaspoons chopped fresh tarragon
2 teaspoons chopped fresh parsley
1/2 teaspoon grated lemon zest
1/4 teaspoon salt
1/8 teaspoon pepper

Trim the ends of the peas, removing any tough strings. Melt the butter in a skillet and add the peas. Sauté for 10 to 15 minutes or until tender-crisp. Stir in the shallots, tarragon, parsley, lemon zest, salt and pepper. Heat for 1 to 2 minutes, stirring frequently. You may substitute asparagus for the peas, or add along with the peas.

HOLLEY CONTRI JOHNSON

Nutritional Profile for this recipe on page 327.

GOLDEN POTATO AND BOURSIN GRATIN

SERVES 8 TO 10

2 cups heavy cream or whipping cream
5 ounces garlic and herb boursin cheese
3 tablespoons minced shallots
2 1/2 pounds unpeeled Yukon gold potatoes,
    cut into 1/4-inch slices (about 7 potatoes)
Salt and freshly ground pepper to taste

Preheat the oven to 400 degrees. Combine the cream, cheese and shallots in a saucepan and cook over medium heat for 5 minutes or until the cheese melts and the mixture is combined, stirring constantly. Arrange 1/2 of the potato slices slightly overlapping in a greased 9×13-inch baking dish. Sprinkle generously with salt and pepper and pour 1/2 of the cheese sauce over the potatoes. Layer with the remaining potato slices and sprinkle generously with salt and pepper. Spread the remaining cheese sauce over the prepared layers and bake for 50 to 60 minutes or until the top is golden brown and the potatoes are tender.

LEIGH HARDIN HANCOCK

BUTTERMILK RANCH MASHED POTATOES

You can mash the potatoes or leave cubed. It is a great recipe to serve when you need a starch to round out the meal.

SERVES 8 TO 10

5 pounds red potatoes, cut into 1-inch cubes
1/2 teaspoon kosher salt
1 cup buttermilk
1/2 cup (1 stick) butter, softened
1 envelope buttermilk ranch salad dressing mix
1/4 cup chopped fresh chives
1 teaspoon kosher salt
1/2 teaspoon freshly ground pepper

Combine the potatoes and 1/2 teaspoon salt with enough water to cover in a Dutch oven and bring to a boil. Reduce the heat to medium-low and simmer for 20 minutes or until the potatoes are tender; drain.

Return the potatoes to the Dutch oven and cook over low heat for 1 minute or until any remaining moisture evaporates. Remove from the heat and mash the potatoes with a potato masher or hand mixer until the desired consistency. Stir in the buttermilk, butter, salad dressing mix, chives, 1 teaspoon salt and the pepper until blended. Serve immediately.

LYDA HELEN JONES

Ever mindful of childhood obesity issues, the JLB installed a fitness-oriented playground at Wilson Elementary School in 2005 so children can get in shape while having fun.

MARTHA'S SWEET POTATO SOUFFLÉ

For special occasions you may double the recipe.

SERVES 6 TO 8

Pecan Topping
2 tablespoons butter
1 cup chopped pecans
1/2 cup packed brown sugar

Sweet Potatoes and Assembly
4 large sweet potatoes
1 cup (2 sticks) unsalted butter, softened
4 eggs
1 cup granulated sugar
1 cup packed brown sugar
1 teaspoon salt
1 teaspoon vanilla extract
1/4 teaspoon ground nutmeg
Miniature marshmallows (optional)

For the topping, melt the butter in a skillet and stir in the pecans and brown sugar.

For the sweet potatoes, combine the sweet potatoes with enough water to cover in a large saucepan and bring to a boil. Boil for 20 to 30 minutes or until the pulp is soft and the skins are easily removed. Drain and cool. Discard the skins.

Preheat the oven to 350 degrees. Combine the sweet potatoes and butter in a mixing bowl and beat until smooth. (If the sweet potatoes are stringy, the blades of the mixer will catch the strings. Discard the strings.) Beat the eggs in a mixing bowl until light and frothy and add to the sweet potato mixture. Beat until smooth and fluffy. Add the granulated sugar, brown sugar, salt, vanilla and nutmeg and beat until blended.

Spoon the sweet potato mixture into a 2-quart soufflé dish or baking dish, allowing room for the soufflé to rise and for the toppings. Bake for 1 1/2 hours or until the center is set, sprinkling with the topping and marshmallows 10 to 15 minutes before the end of the baking process.

MARY SPOTSWOOD BOX

Photograph for this recipe on page 250.

SPINACH AND ARTICHOKE CASSEROLE

My sister-in-law, Mary Harmon Moman, makes this casserole every Christmas.
It is a favorite with my family, and children love it too.

SERVES 6 TO 8

2 (10-ounce) packages frozen chopped spinach
8 ounces light cream cheese
1/2 cup (1 stick) butter
1 teaspoon fresh lemon juice
1/2 teaspoon salt
1/4 teaspoon pepper
1 (14-ounce) can artichoke hearts, drained and
    cut into quarters
1/3 cup dry bread crumbs
3 tablespoons butter, softened

Preheat the oven to 350 degrees. Cook the spinach using the package directions. Drain and press any excess moisture from the spinach. Heat the cream cheese and 1/2 cup butter in a saucepan until blended, stirring constantly. Add the spinach, lemon juice, salt and pepper and mix well.

Arrange the artichokes in the bottom of a greased 2-quart baking dish and spoon the spinach mixture over the top. Sprinkle with the bread crumbs and dot with 3 tablespoons butter. Bake for 20 to 30 minutes or until heated through.

ELISSA HANDLEY TYSON

In 2006 the JLB, in partnership with Children's Hospital and Project Fit, built its first-ever Fitness Zone at Minor Elementary. This playground encourages exercise techniques that improve fitness levels.

Over the past six years JLB members have given more than twenty-five thousand pounds of nonperishable food items to the hungry.

NORMAN'S CREAMED SPINACH

SERVES 6 TO 8

2 (10-ounce) packages frozen
    chopped spinach
1/4 cup (1/2 stick) butter
3 tablespoons all-purpose flour
1/4 cup chopped onion
1 teaspoon minced garlic
1/2 teaspoon salt
1/2 teaspoon pepper
1/8 teaspoon nutmeg
1/2 cup (2 ounces) grated Parmesan cheese
1/2 cup (2 ounces) shredded Pepper
    Jack cheese
1 cup half-and-half
1/2 cup (2 ounces) grated Parmesan cheese
2 slices bacon, crisp-cooked and crumbled

Cook the spinach using the package directions. Drain the spinach in a strainer over a bowl. Press any remaining moisture from the spinach into the bowl, reserving 1/2 cup of the spinach liquid. Melt the butter in a large saucepan and stir in the flour.

Cook until smooth, stirring constantly. Add the onion and the reserved spinach liquid and cook for 5 minutes or until the onion is tender, stirring occasionally. Stir in the garlic, salt, pepper and nutmeg. Add 1/2 cup Parmesan cheese and the Pepper Jack cheese and cook until the cheeses melt, stirring constantly. Stir in the half-and-half and fold in the spinach. Cook just until heated through, stirring frequently. Spoon the spinach mixture into a serving bowl and sprinkle with 1/2 cup Parmesan cheese and the bacon and serve immediately.

You may bake in the oven if desired. Spoon the spinach mixture into a 2-quart baking dish and sprinkle with 1/2 cup Parmesan cheese and the bacon. Bake in a 300-degree oven for 15 minutes or until bubbly.

KELLI NELSON JETMUNDSEN

Photograph for this recipe on page 250.

The Alabama Foundation for Oncology created Camp Newsong in 1995 for children grieving the loss of a loved one. Counselors, along with JLB volunteers, lead children in art therapy and activities that bring them closer to healing.

BEST SQUASH CASSEROLE

This casserole makes a great side dish with anything. It is fancy enough for a special occasion, such as Thanksgiving or Christmas.

SERVES 6 TO 8

10 yellow squash
2 eggs
1/2 cup mayonnaise
1 envelope ranch salad dressing mix
1 cup (4 ounces) shredded mild Cheddar cheese
1/3 cup chopped green onions (optional)
12 butter crackers, finely crushed
1/2 teaspoon garlic salt
1/2 teaspoon freshly ground pepper
Shredded mild Cheddar cheese to taste (optional)
8 butter crackers, finely crushed

Preheat the oven to 325 degrees. Combine the squash with enough water to generously cover in a saucepan and bring to a boil. Boil for 10 minutes or until tender and drain. Let stand until cool and slice. Drain the sliced squash in a colander, pressing with the back of a spoon to extract any remaining moisture. The cooked squash should measure 5 cups.

Beat the eggs in a bowl until blended. Stir in the mayonnaise and salad dressing mix. Fold in the squash, 1 cup cheese, the green onions, 12 crushed crackers, the garlic salt and pepper. Spoon the squash mixture into a 2-quart baking dish and sprinkle with additional cheese and 8 crushed crackers. Bake for 30 minutes.

NANCY BEDSOLE BYNON

Photograph for this recipe on page 250.

BUTTERNUT SQUASH WITH APPLES AND BOURBON

This is a nice alternative to mashed potatoes. Serve with ham, pork tenderloin, or steak. You may substitute equal amounts of sweet potatoes for the butternut squash.

SERVES 6

2 small butternut squash (about 2 pounds)
3 small Rome apples
1/4 cup (1/2 stick) butter
1/4 cup packed brown sugar
1/4 cup bourbon
1/2 teaspoon salt
1/4 teaspoon chili powder
1/4 teaspoon pepper
3 tablespoons sour cream

Preheat the oven to 425 degrees. Cut the squash and apples lengthwise into halves and remove the seeds. Arrange the halves in a single layer on a lightly greased foil-lined baking sheet and bake for 45 minutes or until the squash is fork tender, removing the apples after 20 minutes. Let stand until cool.

Peel the squash and apples and place in a 3 1/2-quart saucepan. Stir in the butter, brown sugar, bourbon, salt, chili powder and pepper and cook over low heat until heated through, stirring occasionally. Mash the squash mixture with a potato masher until smooth and creamy. Remove from the heat and stir in the sour cream. Serve immediately.

KRISTIN DENSON SARTELLE

The number one killer of children in the United States is motor vehicle accidents. Project S.O.S. at Children's Hospital teaches parents the proper way to install child safety seats, which can reduce the likelihood of injury and death in an accident by 77 percent. JLB volunteers have worked tirelessly to educate thousands of parents.

Residential fire is the third leading cause of death for Alabama children. Over the years, JLB volunteers have helped Children's Hospital maintain Smokehouse, a twenty-five-foot interactive replica of a two-story house that travels to teach fire safety to children.

SQUASH TOMATO PIE WITH FETA CHEESE

This is an easy and savory squash dish. Serve as a side dish or as a light summer supper accompanied with fruit and salad.

SERVES 6

2 cups chopped peeled yellow squash
   (3 squash)
1/3 cup plain fat-free yogurt
2 eggs
1 cup herb-seasoned stuffing mix
1/2 cup chopped yellow onion
1/2 cup chopped green bell pepper
1/4 cup (1 ounce) grated Parmesan cheese
1 teaspoon salt
1/2 teaspoon cracked black pepper
2 or 3 yellow and/or red tomatoes, peeled
   and thinly sliced
1/4 cup crumbled sun-dried tomato and
   herb feta cheese or plain feta cheese
Black pepper to taste
Sprig of rosemary for garnish

Preheat the oven to 350 degrees. Steam the squash in a steamer basket over boiling water for 10 minutes or until tender. Drain in a colander and mash with a fork. Mix the yogurt and eggs in a bowl and stir in the squash, stuffing mix, onion, bell pepper, Parmesan cheese, salt and cracked pepper.

Spoon the squash mixture into a lightly greased medium baking dish or 9-inch pie plate. Layer with the tomatoes slightly overlapping and sprinkle with the feta cheese and black pepper to taste. Press the sprig of rosemary into the top and bake for 45 to 60 minutes. Broil for a few minutes if desired to brown the top.

LYNN COMPTON CHAPMAN

TOMATOES ROCKEFELLER

SERVES 12

1 (10-ounce) package frozen chopped
    spinach, thawed
6 tomatoes, cut into halves
2/3 cup dry bread crumbs
1/2 cup (1 stick) butter, melted
1/4 cup chopped green onions
1/4 cup crumbled crisp-cooked bacon
    (7 slices)
1/4 cup (1 ounce) grated Parmesan cheese
1 teaspoon fresh lemon juice
1/2 teaspoon salt
1/4 teaspoon garlic powder
3 drops of Tabasco sauce

Preheat the oven to 350 degrees. Drain the spinach on paper towels and press to remove any excess moisture. Arrange the tomato halves cut side up in an 11×15-inch baking pan sprayed with nonstick cooking spray. Combine the spinach, bread crumbs, butter, green onions, bacon and cheese in a bowl and mix well. Stir in the lemon juice, salt, garlic powder and Tabasco sauce.

Mound the spinach mixture evenly on the tomato halves and bake for 30 to 45 minutes or until heated through.

EVELYN BRITTON STUTTS

To drain spinach, thaw the spinach and spread on several layers of paper towels to drain. Press until barely moist.

BASIL AND TOMATO PIE

A great summer dish.

SERVES 8

2 or 3 tomatoes
1 (9-inch) refrigerator pie pastry
1 cup (4 ounces) grated provolone cheese
3/4 cup (3 ounces) grated Parmesan cheese
1 tablespoon vegetable oil
1/2 cup finely chopped Vidalia onion
2 tablespoons all-purpose flour
1/2 cup chopped fresh basil
1/2 teaspoon salt
1/2 teaspoon pepper
3/4 cup mayonnaise
2 tablespoons Dijon mustard

Preheat the oven to 350 degrees. Peel and thinly slice the tomatoes. Place on a paper towel to drain. Fit the pie pastry into a 9-inch pie plate and flute the edge. Bake for 5 to 7 minutes or until light brown. Mix the provolone cheese and Parmesan cheese in a bowl.

Heat the oil in a medium saucepan and add the onion. Sauté until tender. Sprinkle the bottom of the baked pie crust with 1/4 cup of the cheese mixture and top with 1/2 of the tomato slices. Sprinkle with 1 tablespoon of the flour. Spoon 1/2 of the sautéed onion and 1/4 cup of the basil over the prepared layers. Sprinkle with 1/4 teaspoon of the salt, 1/4 teaspoon of the pepper and 1/4 cup of the remaining cheese mixture.

Top with the remaining tomato slices, remaining 1 tablespoon flour, remaining sautéed onion, remaining 1/4 cup basil, remaining 1/4 teaspoon salt, remaining 1/4 teaspoon pepper and 1/4 cup of the remaining cheese mixture. Mix the mayonnaise, Dijon mustard and remaining 1 cup cheese mixture in a bowl and spread over the prepared layers. Bake for 20 to 30 minutes or until golden brown.

FRANCES SULLIVAN MAYHALL

FRIED GREEN TOMATOES

*Serve the tomatoes on a bed of salad greens topped with Caribbean Salsa on page 59,
or your favorite fruit salsa. Sprinkle with goat cheese or feta cheese.*

SERVES 12 TO 15

1/2 cup self-rising white cornmeal mix	2 eggs
1/2 cup all-purpose flour	2 tablespoons water
1/2 teaspoon salt	1/3 cup vegetable oil for frying
1/4 teaspoon garlic powder	3 large green tomatoes, thickly sliced
1/8 teaspoon ground red pepper	3/4 cup buttermilk
	Salt to taste

Mix the cornmeal mix, flour, 1/2 teaspoon salt, the garlic powder and red pepper in a shallow dish. Whisk the eggs and water in a bowl until blended. Heat the oil in a large skillet to about 350 degrees or until the oil sizzles when sprinkled with a small amount of cornmeal.

Dip the tomatoes in the buttermilk until coated on both sides and coat with the cornmeal mixture. Dip in the egg mixture and coat the tomatoes again with the cornmeal mixture. Fry the coated tomatoes in batches in the hot oil for 3 to 4 minutes per side or until crisp and golden brown. Drain and sprinkle with salt to taste. Serve immediately, or arrange on a foil-lined baking sheet and keep warm in a 225-degree oven.

KRISTIN DENSON SARTELLE

ITALIAN ZUCCHINI

SERVES 6 TO 8

8 small zucchini	1/2 teaspoon minced garlic
1 (8-ounce) can tomato sauce	1/4 teaspoon basil
1/4 cup water	1/2 cup (2 ounces) shredded mozzarella cheese
2 tablespoons olive oil	

Cut the zucchini into 1/4-inch slices and cut each slice into halves for bite-size pieces. This should measure about 4 cups. Combine the zucchini, tomato sauce, water, olive oil, garlic and basil in a saucepan and bring to a gentle boil. Reduce the heat. Cook for 10 to 15 minutes or until the zucchini is tender, stirring occasionally. Do not overcook the zucchini as it will become mushy. Spoon the zucchini mixture into a serving bowl and sprinkle with the mozzarella cheese. Serve immediately.

KAY IVEY WEST

Health Fare

FLAVOR BOOST

The following accompaniments represent a collection of quick sauces and compound butters that are very versatile. This is a great way to breathe new life into steamed vegetables, but they also work well paired with meats and poultry.

- Toss steamed asparagus or zucchini with Chimichurri on page 242.
- Prepare **Blue Cheese Butter** by mixing 6 tablespoons softened unsalted butter, 1/4 cup crumbled blue cheese, 1/4 teaspoon kosher salt and 1 minced garlic clove.

Shape the butter mixture into a cylinder on a sheet of plastic wrap and enclose with the plastic wrap. Chill until firm. Toss with roasted potatoes or spread over grilled steaks.

- Prepare **Walnut Pesto** by combining 1/2 cup toasted walnuts, 1/2 cup fresh flat-leaf parsley leaves, 2 tablespoons fresh sage leaves, 2 tablespoons fresh lemon juice, 1 teaspoon kosher salt and 1 garlic clove in a food processor. Process until smooth, scraping the side. Add 1/2 cup extra-virgin olive oil gradually, processing constantly until the oil is incorporated. Toss with cooked fresh green beans or cooked pasta.

276

HOLIDAY FARE

MENU

SUGGESTED WINES:
- *Lagaria Pinot Grigio 2004*
- *Alois Lageder Pinot Blanco 2004*
- *Keltie Brook Pinot Noir 2004*
- *Zenato Valpolicella 2002*
- *Domaine Chandon Extra Dry Riche*

Asparagus Tart

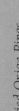

Fried Onion Rings

Company Corn Pudding

Works of Art

DESSERTS

What's your response to art? The delicacy of the vibrant and colorful Dale Chihuly glass sculpture at the Birmingham Museum of Art begs for a closer look from children as well as sophisticated collectors. The superb craftsmanship of the magnificent Wedgwood pottery in the Beeson Collection draws in even the casual visitor. However, the culinary craftsmanship and sweet delicacy of the recipes in this chapter require only one response—the taste test.

The Birmingham Museum of Art has experienced an astounding history of growth during the past fifty years and is billed as one of the finest regional museums in the country. From a modest start as four rooms in City Hall, the museum now boasts thirty-seven galleries and is one of the largest municipal museums in the Southeast.

This museum offers a nationally recognized permanent collection of over 21,000 works of art from around the globe, dating from ancient eras to present day. These delightful collections include: the Kress Collection of Renaissance Art, the Beeson Collection of Wedgwood (the finest outside England), the Lamprecht Collection of Decorative Cast-Iron, and the Asian Art Collection, the most comprehensive collection in the region.

Warm Chocolate Lava Cakes on page 284 are for baking and chocolate art connoisseurs. Chocolate Mascarpone Cheesecake with Truffle Glaze on page 282 will delight the eye as well as the palate. Go ahead—indulge and enjoy!

Visit the Birmingham Museum of Art at www.artsbma.org.

Birmingham Museum of Art

Top: Cho Cho Chewy Bars
Bottom: Rocky Road Fudge Bars

Desserts

CONTENTS

CHOCOLATE MASCARPONE CHEESECAKE WITH TRUFFLE GLAZE

MAKES 12 (1-SLICE) SERVINGS

Chocolate Chip Crust
28 medium chocolate chip cookies
1/4 cup (1/2 stick) butter
1/4 cup all-purpose flour

Chocolate Mascarpone Filling
2 cups (12 ounces) semisweet chocolate morsels
24 ounces cream cheese, softened
8 ounces mascarpone cheese, softened
1 3/4 cups sugar
5 eggs
1 teaspoon vanilla extract

Truffle Glaze and Assembly
1 cup (6 ounces) semisweet chocolate morsels
1/4 cup light corn syrup
1/3 cup heavy cream or whipping cream
1/2 teaspoon vanilla extract

For the crust, preheat the oven to 300 degrees. Pulse the cookies in a food processor until the consistency of coarse bread crumbs. The cookie crumbs should measure 1 1/2 cups. Add the butter and enough of the flour to the cookie crumbs until the mixture adheres, processing constantly. Pat over the bottom of a 9-inch springform pan and bake for 7 minutes. Maintain the oven temperature.

For the filling, melt the chocolate in a double boiler over simmering water, stirring occasionally. Beat the cream cheese and mascarpone cheese in a mixing bowl until smooth. Add the sugar and beat until fluffy, scraping the bowl occasionally. Add the eggs 1 at a time, beating until blended after each addition. Stir in the melted chocolate and vanilla and scrape the side and bottom of the bowl to ensure the ingredients are blended well. The mixture will be thick. Spread the filling over the baked crust and bake for 1 hour and 40 minutes. Cool in the pan on a wire rack for 1 hour.

For the glaze, combine the chocolate, corn syrup, cream and vanilla in a saucepan and cook over medium heat until thickened, stirring frequently. Spread the glaze over the top of the cooled cheesecake. Remove the side of the pan and wrap the cheesecake in waxed paper and then in foil. Chill for 8 hours before slicing for enhanced flavor.

SUSAN MEADOWS LEACH

FIG CROSTADA

SERVES 8 TO 10

2 cups all-purpose flour
1/4 cup sugar
1/8 teaspoon salt
1/3 cup butter, chilled and cubed
1/3 cup ice water
1 cup hazelnuts, toasted
1 cup sugar
1 cup (2 sticks) butter, softened
2 eggs
10 fresh figs, quartered
1/4 cup honey
1/4 cup sugar
1/8 teaspoon salt
2 egg yolks
1/4 cup heavy cream or whipping cream
1/4 cup sugar

Combine the flour, 1/4 cup sugar and 1/8 teaspoon salt in a food processor and pulse to combine. Add 1/3 cup butter and pulse 6 to 8 times or until the butter is the size of small peas. Gradually add the ice water, pulsing constantly until the dough just begins to adhere. Place the dough on a piece of plastic wrap and shape into a disc. Wrap with the plastic wrap and chill for 2 hours or longer.

Combine the hazelnuts and 1 cup sugar in a food processor and pulse until finely ground. Add 1 cup butter and pulse until combined. Add the eggs 1 at a time, processing until combined after each addition. Chill for 2 hours or longer.

Let the dough stand at room temperature for 5 to 10 minutes. Roll the dough 1/2 inch thick on a lightly floured surface and cut into 8 to 10 rounds with a 5-inch cutter. Chill the rounds for 20 minutes. Roll the rounds into 6-inch circles on a lightly floured surface. Toss the figs, honey, 1/4 cup sugar and 1/8 teaspoon salt in a bowl and let stand at room temperature for 20 minutes.

Preheat the oven to 325 degrees. Place the chilled rounds on 1 or 2 baking sheets and spoon 1 tablespoon of the hazelnut mixture in the center of each of the chilled circles. Evenly divide the fig mixture among the rounds. Beginning at the top, fold the dough over itself toward the center, working all the way around the circle. You should have an 1 1/2-inch rolled edge enclosing the figs. Whisk the egg yolks and cream in a bowl until blended and brush over the dough. Sprinkle with 1/4 cup sugar and bake for 20 to 30 minutes or until golden brown.

FRANK STITT, HIGHLAND'S BAR AND GRILL IN SOUTHSIDE

WARM CHOCOLATE LAVA CAKES

To make in advance, prepare through the second step and then cover and chill. This recipe can easily be doubled.

SERVES 6

6 ounces bittersweet chocolate
3/4 cup (1 1/2 sticks) unsalted butter
3 eggs
3 egg yolks
6 tablespoons sugar
1 tablespoon vanilla extract
1/2 teaspoon salt
5 tablespoons all-purpose flour
Ice cream, whipped cream, berries, and/or mint leaves
    for garnish

Preheat the oven to 375 degrees. Melt the bittersweet chocolate and 3/4 cup butter in a medium saucepan over low heat, stirring occasionally. Remove from the heat and cool slightly. Beat the eggs, egg yolks and sugar in a mixing bowl until light and fluffy. Add the vanilla and salt and beat until blended. Mix in the flour. Add the chocolate mixture to the egg mixture and beat for 5 minutes or until thick and glossy, scraping the bowl occasionally.

Coat 6 custard cups or ramekins with butter and sprinkle lightly with baking cocoa. Spoon the chocolate mixture into the prepared custard cups and arrange on a baking sheet. Bake for 10 minutes or until the cakes are set around the edges and the centers move slightly. Cool slightly and run a knife around the edges of the custard cups and invert onto individual dessert plates. Garnish with ice cream, whipped cream, berries and/or mint leaves. Serve immediately.

TOOKIE DAUGHERTY HAZELRIG

CRANBERRY COBBLER

Add color to your holiday table with this festive berry dessert.

SERVES 6 TO 8

2 cups fresh or thawed frozen
   cranberries or blueberries
1 cup chopped walnuts or pecans
1/2 cup sugar
1 cup all-purpose flour

3/4 cup (1 1/2 sticks) unsalted
   butter, melted
3/4 cup sugar
1 teaspoon almond extract
2 eggs, beaten

Preheat the oven to 350 degrees. Mix the cranberries, walnuts and 1/2 cup sugar in a bowl and spoon into a 9×9-inch baking pan sprayed with nonstick cooking spray. Combine the flour, butter, 3/4 cup sugar and flavoring in a bowl and mix until blended. Stir in the eggs and spoon the batter over the prepared layer. Bake for 35 to 40 minutes or until golden brown.

LISA BELL LEWIS

SIMPLE BLACKBERRY COBBLER

Substitute fresh peaches, blueberries or raspberries for the blackberries, if desired.

SERVES 6

5 cups fresh blackberries
1 cup all-purpose flour
1 cup sugar
1 teaspoon baking powder

3/4 teaspoon salt
1 egg, beaten
1/2 cup (1 stick) butter, melted
1/4 teaspoon ground cinnamon

Preheat the oven to 350 degrees. Spread the blackberries in a 2-quart baking dish. Combine the flour, sugar, baking powder and salt in a bowl and mix well. Stir in the egg and crumble the mixture over the berries. Drizzle with the butter and sprinkle with the cinnamon. Bake for 45 minutes. Serve warm in dessert bowls topped with vanilla ice cream.

SUSAN HENAGAN LOGAN

Photograph for this recipe on page 318.

ARLINGTON'S MINT JULEP ICE CREAM

This unique twist on a mint julep is served for lunch every Thursday at the Arlington Historic House. If you enjoy bourbon, you are sure to love this ice cream.

SERVES 12

1 quart milk
6 egg yolks, slightly beaten
1 cup sugar
2 cups half-and-half
1 cup water
1/4 cup dried mint
1/4 cup sugar
1/4 cup bourbon
12 sprigs of mint for garnish

Heat the milk in a double boiler over simmering water. Whisk the egg yolks and sugar in a bowl until blended and stir into the hot milk. Cook until the mixture coats the back of a spoon, stirring frequently. Chill, covered, for 1 hour. Stir in the half-and-half and pour the custard mixture into a 3-quart ice cream freezer container. Freeze using the manufacturer's directions.

Combine the water, dried mint and sugar in a medium saucepan and bring to a boil. Reduce the heat and simmer for 7 minutes. Remove from the heat and let stand until cool. Strain the syrup into a jar with a tight-fitting lid, discarding the solids. Chill in the refrigerator.

Spoon the frozen custard into a bowl and stir in the mint syrup and bourbon. Pour into a freezer container and freeze, tightly covered, for 8 to 10 hours. Spoon the ice cream into silver mint julep cups or stemmed dessert goblets and garnish each with a sprig of mint.

DANIEL BROOKS AND BLANCH DANSBY, ARLINGTON HISTORIC HOUSE

Photograph for this recipe on page 320.

The League Cares committee offers JLB members a little "TLC," welcoming new babies and acknowledging special thanks to members going above and beyond. The committee also delivers casseroles to members in need, whether there is a death in the family or someone has an illness.

MARGARITA ICE CREAM

*This festive, tangy ice cream is the perfect way to end a
Mexican-themed dinner party or a warm summer night. Serve
in margarita glasses with rims that have been moistened with
lime juice and dipped in a sugar/salt mixture.*

SERVES 10 TO 12

1½ cups plus 3 tablespoons heavy cream or
    whipping cream
6 egg yolks, beaten
1¾ cups sweetened condensed milk
1 cup fresh lime juice (about 7 limes)
½ cup tequila
3 tablespoons orange liqueur
2 to 3 teaspoons grated lime zest
    (about 1 lime)

Heat the cream in a small saucepan over medium heat until simmering. Gradually
add the warm cream to the egg yolks in a heatproof bowl, whisking constantly to
prevent the eggs from curdling. Pour the egg mixture into a clean saucepan and
cook over medium heat until thickened, whisking constantly. Pour into a bowl
and cool slightly.

Stir the condensed milk, lime juice, tequila, liqueur and lime zest into the cream
mixture. Cool the custard mixture completely before freezing in an electric ice
cream maker. Follow the manufacturer's directions. Spoon the ice cream into a
freezer container and freeze, covered, for 1 hour or until firm. For testing purposes,
Triple Sec was used.

KATE GILMER PHILLIPS

*Before juicing, roll limes or
lemons on the countertop or
microwave for thirty seconds
to break the membranes and
release more juice.*

HOMEMADE CHOCOLATE ICE CREAM

Create your own chocolate-based ice cream by adding chopped nuts,
miniature chocolate morsels, or peppermint extract.

MAKES 1 GALLON

2 cups sugar
1/2 cup milk
5 eggs
2 tablespoons all-purpose flour
1 tablespoon vanilla extract

2 cups (12 ounces) semisweet
chocolate morsels
1 quart half-and-half
1 quart heavy cream or whipping cream
3/4 cup (about) milk

Whisk the sugar, 1/2 cup milk, eggs and flour in a double boiler until blended. Cook over simmering water until thickened, whisking frequently. Remove from the heat and add the vanilla and chocolate, stirring until the chocolate melts. Cool for 5 minutes. Pour the chocolate mixture into 1-gallon ice cream freezer container and add the half-and-half and cream. Add just enough of 3/4 cup milk to reach the fill line and freeze using the manufacturer's directions.

STEPHANIE STEVENS CAROTHERS

BLACKBERRY MASCARPONE ICE CREAM

Pair a scoop of this rich fruity ice cream with gingersnaps for an impressive presentation. Serve in martini glasses.

MAKES 12 (1-CUP) SERVINGS

1 quart 2% milk
1 cup half-and-half
1/2 cup pure maple syrup
6 ounces mascarpone cheese

3 eggs
2 cups sugar
2 pints fresh blackberries

Heat the 2% milk and half-and-half in a heavy saucepan until hot; do not boil. Combine the syrup, cheese and eggs in a bowl and whisk until combined. Add the sugar and mix well. Stir the cheese mixture into the hot milk mixture and cook over medium-low heat for 12 minutes or until a thermometer registers 160 degrees, stirring constantly. Cool completely. Pour the custard mixture into an ice cream freezer container and add 2 1/2 cups of the blackberries. Freeze using the manufacturer's directions. Spoon the ice cream into a freezer container and freeze, covered, for 1 hour or until firm. Garnish with the remaining blackberries.

LAURA GRAY BARRON

Nutritional Profile for this recipe on page 327.

GRANDMOTHER'S GRAPE SHERBET

MAKES 1 GALLON

1 quart white or purple grape juice
3 cups sugar
1 cup fresh lemon juice (about 7 lemons)
2 cups heavy cream or whipping cream
1 quart milk

Combine the grape juice, sugar and lemon juice in a blender and process until the sugar dissolves. Pour the grape juice mixture into an ice cream freezer container and gradually add the cream, stirring constantly. Stir in the milk and freeze using the manufacturer's directions.

LESLIE BERRY MCLEOD

TOO-EASY RASPBERRY SORBET

For a lower calorie variation, use low-fat sour cream and artificial sweetener, such as Splenda or Equal.

MAKES 3 CUPS

1 cup sour cream
1 cup sugar
1 (12-ounce) package frozen unsweetened raspberries
1 teaspoon vanilla extract

Process the sour cream, sugar, raspberries and vanilla in a blender or food processor until smooth. Pour the raspberry mixture into sorbet cups and freeze until firm.

KATE GILMER PHILLIPS

OLD-FASHIONED BANANA PUDDING

SERVES 8 TO 10

1/2 cup sugar
3 tablespoons all-purpose flour
1/8 teaspoon salt
2 cups milk
1 egg, lightly beaten
3 egg yolks, lightly beaten

1 teaspoon vanilla extract
1/2 (12-ounce) package vanilla wafers
3 ripe bananas, sliced
3 egg whites
1/4 cup sugar

Preheat the oven to 350 degrees. Mix 1/2 cup sugar, the flour and salt in a 3 1/2-quart saucepan and stir in the milk, egg and egg yolks. Cook over medium heat until the mixture thickens and coats the back of a spoon, stirring constantly. Remove from the heat and stir in the vanilla. Alternate layers of the pudding, vanilla wafers and bananas in a 2-quart baking dish until all of these ingredients are used, ending with the pudding. Beat the egg whites in a mixing bowl until frothy. Add 1/4 cup sugar gradually, beating until stiff peaks form. Spread the meringue over the top and bake for 10 to 13 minutes or until light brown.

LORI HELBERT PHILLIPS

WHITE CHOCOLATE BREAD PUDDING

SERVES 8 TO 12

3 cups heavy cream or whipping cream
10 ounces white chocolate, chopped
1 cup milk
1/2 cup sugar
8 egg yolks
2 eggs

1 (1-pound) baguette, cut into
    1-inch slices
8 ounces white chocolate, chopped
6 tablespoons heavy cream or
    whipping cream
2 tablespoons white chocolate shavings

Preheat the oven to 350 degrees. Heat 3 cups cream and 10 ounces white chocolate in a double boiler over simmering water until the white chocolate melts, stirring frequently. Remove from the heat. Whisk the milk, sugar, egg yolks and eggs in a saucepan until blended. Cook over low heat until warm, stirring occasionally. Gradually add the egg mixture to the chocolate mixture, stirring constantly until blended. Arrange the baguette slices over the bottom of a greased 9×13-inch baking dish and pour 1/2 of the egg mixture over the top. Let settle and top with the remaining egg mixture. Bake, covered with foil, for 1 hour. Remove the foil and bake for 15 minutes longer or until golden brown. Melt 8 ounces white chocolate in a saucepan over low heat. Remove from the heat and stir in 6 tablespoons cream. Drizzle over the warm bread pudding and sprinkle with the white chocolate shavings. Serve immediately.

LENA CLARK BLAKENEY

ORANGE GRAND MARNIER SOUFFLÉ

SERVES 6

1 1/2 cups milk
2 teaspoons grated orange zest
3 egg yolks
1/3 cup granulated sugar
1/2 cup all-purpose flour
1/8 teaspoon salt
1/3 cup Grand Marnier, or any orange liqueur
8 egg whites
1/2 teaspoon cream of tartar
1 tablespoon confectioners' sugar

Scald the milk and orange zest in a medium heavy saucepan over medium-high heat. Remove from the heat and steep, covered, for 10 minutes. Whisk the egg yolks and granulated sugar in a bowl. Add the flour and salt and whisk until blended. Stir in the liqueur.

Stir the egg mixture into the scalded milk mixture and cook over medium heat for 2 to 3 minutes or until thickened, whisking constantly. Spoon the thickened mixture into a bowl and press plastic wrap directly on the surface. Chill in the refrigerator until cold.

Preheat the oven to 350 degrees. Beat the egg whites in a mixing bowl at medium speed until frothy. Add the cream of tartar and beat at high speed until stiff peaks form. Fold the meringue 1/2 at a time into the chilled liqueur mixture.

Spread the batter in a buttered and sugared 2-quart soufflé dish. Gently tap the soufflé dish on the work surface to remove any bubbles and bake for 30 to 35 minutes or until golden brown and the edge and top feel firm when lightly touched. Dust the soufflé with the confectioners' sugar and serve immediately with caramel or chocolate sauce on the side.

BECKY SATTERFIELD, SATTERFIELD'S IN CAHABA HEIGHTS

CHOCOLATE CARAMEL PARFAITS WITH SHORTBREAD

We dressed up a basic pudding mix by adding half-and-half, chocolate morsels, and butter to achieve the ultimate creamy texture. To save even more time, use a commercial caramel sauce instead of making your own.

SERVES 6

1 (3-ounce) package chocolate cook-and-serve
    pudding mix
2 cups half-and-half
1/2 cup bittersweet chocolate morsels
1 1/2 tablespoons butter
1/2 cup packed light brown sugar
1/2 cup (1 stick) butter
1/2 cup heavy cream or whipping cream
12 shortbread cookies
6 tablespoons frozen whipped topping, thawed

Prepare the pudding using the package directions, substituting the half-and-half for the milk. Add the chocolate and 1 1/2 tablespoons butter and stir until blended. Spoon the pudding into a bowl and press plastic wrap directly on the surface. Chill in the refrigerator.

Combine the brown sugar and 1/2 cup butter in a small saucepan. Bring to a boil over medium heat and cook for 5 minutes or until a thermometer registers 238 degrees. Remove from the heat and stir in the cream. Let stand until cool.

Spoon about 1/4 cup of the chocolate pudding into each of 6 stemmed glasses and crumble 1 cookie in each glass. Drizzle each with 2 tablespoons of the caramel sauce. Repeat the process with the remaining pudding, remaining cookies and remaining caramel sauce. Top each with 1 tablespoon of the whipped topping and serve immediately.

LAURA GRAY BARRON

A Sustainer Art Show is held each spring to feature the work of former JLB active members. One year, a percentage of the proceeds was given to Glenn Middle School to replace musical instruments lost in a fire. Another benefited the Birmingham Museum of Art's "Start with Art" program.

APRICOT AND ALMOND TORTE

SERVES 8

1¹/2 cups finely crushed vanilla wafers
¹/3 cup chopped almonds, toasted
3 tablespoons butter, melted
1 tablespoon almond extract
6 cups vanilla ice cream, softened (3 pints)
1 (10-ounce) jar apricot preserves
¹/2 cup frozen whipped topping, thawed

Mix the wafer crumbs, almonds, butter and flavoring in a bowl. Press ¹/3 of the crumb mixture over the bottom of a buttered 9×9-inch dish. Spread with ¹/2 of the ice cream and ¹/2 of the preserves. Top with ¹/2 of the remaining crumb mixture, the remaining ice cream and the remaining preserves. Sprinkle with the remaining crumb mixture and freeze, covered, for 4 hours or until firm. Cut into squares and top each serving with a dollop of the whipped topping.

JULIE VASCOCU STEWART

CHOCOLATE TOFFEE TRIFLE

Chocolate liqueur may be purchased at a liquor store or specialty baking store.

SERVES 8 TO 12

1 (2-layer) package German chocolate
    cake mix
1 (3-ounce) package chocolate instant
    pudding mix
¹/4 cup chocolate liqueur (optional)
12 ounces frozen whipped topping, thawed
1 (8-ounce) package crushed toffee bits

Prepare the cake using the package directions. Let stand until cool. Prepare the pudding mix using the package directions. Cut the cake into cubes.

Layer the cake cubes, liqueur, pudding, whipped topping and toffee bits ¹/2 at a time in a trifle dish. Chill, covered, until serving time.

PAT SANDLIN JOHNSON

To finely crush vanilla wafers, place the wafers in a large sealable plastic bag and crush with a meat mallet or rolling pin.

APPLE CAKE

SERVES 12

3 cups all-purpose flour
2 cups granulated sugar
1 teaspoon salt
1 teaspoon baking soda
1½ cups vegetable oil
3 eggs
2 teaspoons vanilla extract

3 large apples, peeled and cut into
   bite-size pieces
1 cup chopped nuts
½ cup (1 stick) butter
½ cup packed light brown sugar
2 teaspoons milk

Preheat the oven to 325 degrees. Combine the flour, granulated sugar, salt and baking soda in a bowl and mix well. Mix the oil, eggs and vanilla in a bowl until combined and add to the flour mixture, stirring until blended. Fold in the apples and nuts. Spoon the batter evenly into two 9-inch loaf pans and bake for 1 hour. Bring the butter, brown sugar and milk to a boil in a small saucepan and boil for 5 minutes, stirring constantly. Pour the hot sauce over the hot loaves and cool in the pans on a wire rack.

DAWN GOTLIEB HOLLOWAY

CHOCOLATE CHIP SPICE CAKE

SERVES 8

1 cup dates, pitted and chopped
1 teaspoon baking soda
1 cup boiling water
½ cup (1 stick) butter, softened
1 cup sugar
2 eggs
1⅔ cups sifted all-purpose flour

¾ teaspoon baking soda
½ teaspoon salt
½ cup (3 ounces) semisweet
   chocolate morsels
½ cup chopped walnuts
½ cup sugar

Preheat the oven to 350 degrees. Mix the dates and 1 teaspoon baking soda in a heatproof bowl. Add the boiling water and mix well. Let stand until cool. Beat the butter, 1 cup sugar and the eggs in a mixing bowl at medium speed until light and fluffy, scraping the bowl occasionally. Stir in the undrained date mixture, flour, ¾ teaspoon baking soda and the salt. Spoon the batter into a greased and floured 9×13-inch cake pan and sprinkle with the chocolate morsels, walnuts and ½ cup sugar. Bake for 30 to 32 minutes or until a wooden pick inserted in the center comes out clean. Cool in the pan on a wire rack.

SHERRI STAMP PLEDGER

MOCHA CAKE

SERVES 12

1 teaspoon baking soda
1 cup strong coffee
2 cups sugar
2 cups cake flour
1/2 cup (1 stick) butter, softened
1/2 cup sour cream

2 eggs
3 ounces unsweetened chocolate,
    melted and cooled
1 (16-ounce) can chocolate sauce
Sliced fresh strawberries for garnish

Preheat the oven to 350 degrees. Stir the baking soda into the coffee in a mixing bowl. Add the sugar, cake flour, butter, sour cream, eggs and chocolate and beat until blended, scraping the bowl occasionally.

Spoon the batter evenly into two 8-inch cake pans sprayed with nonstick cooking spray and bake for 27 to 30 minutes or until wooden picks inserted in the centers come out clean. Cool in the pans for 10 minutes and remove to a wire rack to cool completely. Drizzle each layer with 1/2 of the chocolate sauce and garnish with sliced strawberries. You may also bake in a bundt pan sprayed with nonstick cooking spray for 30 minutes or until a wooden pick inserted in the center comes out clean.

DAWN GOTLIEB HOLLOWAY

PUMPKIN CRUNCH CAKE

This dessert is more like a cobbler than a cake. Serve warm with vanilla ice cream

SERVES 10 TO 12

1 (15-ounce) can pumpkin
1 (12-ounce) can evaporated milk
1 1/2 cups sugar
4 eggs
1 teaspoon pumpkin pie spice

1 teaspoon salt
1 (2-layer) package yellow cake mix
1 cup chopped pecans
3/4 cup (1 1/2 sticks) butter,
    thinly sliced

Preheat the oven to 350 degrees. Beat the pumpkin, evaporated milk, sugar, eggs, pumpkin pie spice and salt in a mixing bowl at medium speed until blended. Spoon the batter into a greased 9×13-inch cake pan. Sprinkle the cake mix over the prepared layer and then sprinkle with the pecans. Arrange the butter slices evenly over the top and bake for 50 minutes or until a wooden pick inserted in the center comes out clean. Cool in the pan on a wire rack.

ELLIE SMOTHERMAN TAYLOR

RED VELVET CAKE WITH CREAM CHEESE FROSTING

This cake may also be baked in a large bundt pan for 35 to 38 minutes.
When using a bundt pan only one-half of frosting is needed.

SERVES 12 TO 15

Red Velvet Cake
2¹/2 cups sifted cake flour, sifted
3 tablespoons baking cocoa
1 teaspoon salt
1 teaspoon baking soda
1¹/2 cups sugar
¹/2 cup (1 stick) butter, softened
2 eggs
2 teaspoons vanilla extract
³/4 teaspoon pumpkin pie spice
1 (¹/2-ounce) bottle red food coloring
1 cup buttermilk
1 tablespoon white vinegar

Cream Cheese Frosting and Assembly
¹/2 cup (1 stick) butter
8 ounces cream cheese
1 (1-pound) package
   confectioners' sugar
1 teaspoon vanilla extract
2 tablespoons milk

For the cake, preheat the oven to 350 degrees. Mix the cake flour, baking cocoa, salt and baking soda in a bowl. Beat the sugar and butter in a mixing bowl at medium speed until light and fluffy. Add the eggs 1 at a time and beat at low speed until smooth after each addition. Add the vanilla, pumpkin pie spice and food coloring and beat until blended. Add the buttermilk and cake flour mixture alternately to the creamed mixture, beginning and ending with the buttermilk and mixing well after each addition. Stir in the vinegar. The batter will be thick and shiny. Spoon the batter into 3 greased and floured 9-inch cake pans and bake for 23 to 25 minutes or until wooden picks inserted in the centers come out clean. Cool in the pans for 10 minutes and remove to a wire rack to cool completely.

For the frosting, beat the butter and cream cheese in a mixing bowl until smooth. Add the confectioners' sugar and vanilla and beat until creamy, scraping the bowl occasionally and adding the milk if needed for the desired spreading consistency.

Arrange 1 cake layer on a cake plate and spread with ¹/4 of the frosting. Layer with another cake layer and spread with ¹/3 of the remaining frosting. Top with the remaining cake layer and spread the remaining frosting over the top and side of the cake. Store, loosely covered, in the refrigerator.

Photograph for this recipe on page 319.

BLUEBERRY POUND CAKE

Two cups of rinsed drained canned blueberries may be substituted for the fresh blueberries.

SERVES 10

2 cups all-purpose flour
1 teaspoon baking powder
1/2 teaspoon salt
2 cups sugar
1 cup (2 sticks) butter, softened

4 eggs
1 teaspoon vanilla extract
1 pint fresh blueberries
1 cup all-purpose flour

Preheat the oven to 325 degrees. Sift 2 cups flour, the baking powder and salt together. Beat the sugar and butter in a mixing bowl until light and fluffy. Add the eggs 1 at a time, beating until light and fluffy after each addition. Blend in the vanilla. Add the flour mixture to the creamed mixture and beat until smooth.

Toss the blueberries with 1 cup flour in a bowl and fold the blueberry mixture into the batter. Spoon the batter into a buttered and sugared tube pan and bake for 1 1/4 hours or until golden brown. Cool in the pan for 10 minutes and remove to a wire rack to cool completely.

BETH PULLIAM WELDEN

BUTTER POUND CAKE

SERVES 10

3 cups all-purpose flour, sifted
1/4 teaspoon baking powder
1/4 teaspoon salt
3 cups sugar
1 cup (2 sticks) butter, softened

1/4 cup shortening
5 eggs
1 teaspoon vanilla extract
1 cup milk

Preheat the oven to 350 degrees. Sift the flour, baking powder and salt together. Beat the sugar, butter and shortening in a mixing bowl at medium speed until light and fluffy. Add the eggs 1 at a time, beating until blended after each addition. Mix in the vanilla. Add the flour mixture alternately with the milk, beginning and ending with the flour mixture and beating well after each addition.

Spoon the batter into a greased and floured bundt pan or tube pan and bake for 1 hour and 20 minutes or until the cake pulls from the side of the pan. Cool in the pan for 10 minutes and remove to a wire rack to cool completely.

JENNIFER RUBY McCAIN

LEMON SOUR CREAM POUND CAKE

*One tablespoon of fresh lemon juice and 1 teaspoon of lemon zest
may be substituted for the lemon extract in the pound cake.*

SERVES 10

Pound Cake
3 cups all-purpose flour
1/2 teaspoon baking powder
1 cup (2 sticks) butter, softened
1/2 cup shortening
3 cups sugar
5 eggs
1 cup sour cream
1/4 cup buttermilk
2 teaspoons lemon extract
1 teaspoon vanilla extract
1/2 teaspoon grated lemon zest

Lemon Glaze and Assembly
2 cups confectioners' sugar
1/4 cup fresh lemon juice (about 3 small lemons)
1/2 teaspoon vanilla extract
Lemon zest for garnish

For the cake, preheat the oven to 325 degrees. Mix the flour and baking powder in a bowl. Beat the butter and shortening in a mixing bowl at medium speed until light and fluffy. Gradually add the sugar and beat until blended. Add the eggs and beat until smooth. Mix the sour cream and buttermilk in a bowl. Add the flour mixture and sour cream mixture alternately to the creamed mixture, beginning and ending with the flour mixture and beating just until blended after each addition. Stir in the flavorings and lemon zest.

Spoon the batter into a greased and floured bundt pan and bake for 1 hour and 40 minutes to 1 hour and 45 minutes or until a wooden pick inserted in the center comes out clean. Cool in the pan for 10 to 15 minutes. Remove to a wire rack to cool completely.

For the glaze, mix the confectioners' sugar, lemon juice and vanilla in a bowl until of a glaze consistency. Drizzle over the cooled cake and garnish with lemon zest.

ELISSA HANDLEY TYSON

For a quick and easy dessert, serve store-bought cake or pound cake with a dusting of confectioners' sugar or baking cocoa. Pour a small amount of the confectioners' sugar or baking cocoa in a fine-mesh sieve, and tap it over the plate.

CHOCOLATE CHIP CREAM CHEESE CUPCAKES

MAKES 18 TO 22 CUPCAKES

1¹/2 cups all-purpose flour

1 cup sugar

¹/4 cup baking cocoa

1 teaspoon baking soda

1 cup water

¹/3 cup vegetables oil

1 tablespoon vinegar

1 teaspoon vanilla extract

8 ounces cream cheese, softened

1 cup (6 ounces) semisweet
   chocolate morsels

¹/3 cup sugar

1 egg

Preheat the oven to 350 degrees. Mix the flour, 1 cup sugar, the baking cocoa and baking soda in a mixing bowl. Add the water, oil, vinegar and vanilla and beat until blended. Fill paper-lined muffin cups ¹/2 full.

Beat the cream cheese, chocolate morsels, ¹/3 cup sugar and egg in a mixing bowl until combined and spoon enough of the cream cheese mixture into each prepared muffin cup to fill ³/4 full. Bake for 21 to 24 minutes or until the cupcakes test done.

DAWN GOTLIEB HOLLOWAY

CHEWY FUDGE MUFFINS

MAKES 16 MUFFINS

1³/4 cups sugar

1 cup all-purpose flour

1 cup (2 sticks) butter

4 ounces semisweet chocolate

4 eggs, beaten

1 teaspoon salt

1 teaspoon vanilla extract

1 cup (6 ounces) semisweet
   chocolate morsels

1 cup chopped pecans (optional)

Preheat the oven to 300 degrees. Mix the sugar and flour in a bowl. Heat the butter and chocolate in a 2-quart saucepan over low heat until blended, stirring occasionally. Add the chocolate mixture and eggs to the flour mixture and mix well. Stir in the salt and vanilla. Mix in the chocolate morsels and pecans.

Fill greased muffin cups ²/3 full and bake for 43 to 45 minutes or until wooden picks inserted in the centers come out clean.

KATHY COUVILLON SKINNER

COCONUT PECAN BALLS

Bring your children into the kitchen and encourage them to help you roll the pecan balls in the coconut.

MAKES 2 DOZEN

1¹/2 cups chopped dates
1 cup sugar
¹/2 cup (1 stick) butter
1 egg, beaten

4 cups crisp rice cereal
1 cup chopped pecans
1 teaspoon vanilla extract
1 cup shredded coconut

Combine the dates, sugar, butter and egg in a saucepan and cook over low heat for 10 minutes until combined, stirring frequently. Remove from the heat and stir in the cereal, pecans and vanilla. Cool for 20 minutes. Shape the date mixture into bite-size balls and roll in the coconut. Store in an airtight container.

LeAnn Holifield Cox

IRISH CREAM FUDGE

This recipe can easily be doubled and given as gifts.

MAKES 2¹/2 POUNDS

2 cups (12 ounces) milk
   chocolate morsels
1 cup (6 ounces) semisweet chocolate
   morsels
1 (7-ounce) jar marshmallow creme
1 cup chopped nuts (optional)

¹/3 cup Irish cream liqueur
1 teaspoon vanilla extract
2¹/4 cups sugar
1 cup evaporated milk
¹/2 cup (1 stick) butter

Line a 9×13-inch pan with foil and lightly coat with butter. Combine the milk chocolate morsels, semisweet chocolate morsels, marshmallow creme, nuts, liqueur and vanilla in a heatproof bowl.

Bring the sugar, evaporated milk and ¹/2 cup butter to a boil in a saucepan. Reduce the heat to low and cook for 11 minutes, stirring constantly. Pour the evaporated milk mixture over the chocolate mixture and stir by hand until combined. Pour the chocolate mixture into the prepared pan and chill until set. Cut into squares. For testing purposes, Bailey's Irish Cream was used.

Amber Lynne McKinstry

NANA'S PRALINES

*This is truly a family recipe that has been passed down from my Great Aunt Nana.
My cousin prepared this recipe at the 1986 Gourmet Gala judged by Pierre Franey, food editor
of* The New York Times, *and Joseph Amendola of the Culinary Institute of America,
Hyde Park, New York. This recipe won first place at the Gala.*

MAKES 12 TO 20 PRALINES

1 cup granulated sugar
1 cup packed light brown sugar
1/2 cup half-and-half
1/4 teaspoon cream of tartar
1/4 teaspoon salt
1 1/2 cups pecan halves
3 tablespoons unsalted butter

Bring the granulated sugar, brown sugar, half-and-half, cream of tartar and salt to a boil in a small saucepan over medium heat, stirring occasionally with a wooden spoon. Boil until a candy thermometer registers 228 degrees. Stir in the pecans and butter and cook over medium heat until a candy thermometer registers 236 degrees, soft-ball stage.

Remove from the heat and cool in the saucepan on a wire rack for 8 minutes or until a candy thermometer registers 200 degrees. Stir with a wooden spoon until thick and glossy.

Drop by rounded tablespoonfuls onto a sheet of foil, working quickly with 2 spoons. If the mixture begins to harden, add water 1 drop at a time until the desired consistency. Let stand until firm.

HALLIE TRIMMIER GIBBS

PAULA'S SPICED PECANS

MAKES 4 CUPS

1 cup sugar
1 tablespoon pumpkin pie spice
1 egg white
1 teaspoon water
4 cups pecan halves

Preheat the oven to 300 degrees. Combine the sugar and pumpkin pie spice in a deep bowl and mix well. Lightly beat the egg white in a large bowl and mix in the water. Add the pecans to the egg white mixture and stir to coat. Stir the pecans into the sugar mixture and toss to coat. Spread the pecan mixture on a baking sheet sprayed with nonstick cooking spray and bake for 25 minutes. Let stand until cool and break into bite-size pieces. Store in an airtight container.

SHERYL WILLIAMS KIMERLING

OUR FAVORITE TOFFEE

*Buttering the sides of your bowl prevents the mixture from sticking
when it bubbles up in the microwave.*

MAKES 1 POUND

3/4 cup finely chopped pecans
1/2 cup (1 stick) butter
1 cup sugar
1/4 cup water
1 teaspoon salt
1 cup (6 ounces) semisweet chocolate morsels
1/2 cup finely chopped pecans

Sprinkle 3/4 cup pecans over the bottom of a greased 9-inch round baking dish. Coat 2 inches of the side of a microwave-safe 2 1/2-quart glass bowl with some of the butter and place the remaining butter in the bowl. Add the sugar, water and salt; do not stir. Microwave on High for 9 to 11 minutes or until the mixture just begins to turn light brown and pour over the pecans. Sprinkle with the chocolate morsels and spread evenly with a knife. Top with 1/2 cup pecans and press lightly if needed. Chill until firm. Break into bite-size pieces and store in an airtight container.

CORA BRASFIELD CAUSEY

ALMOND TOFFEE BUTTERCRUNCH

A great gift for the holidays, this buttery crunchy candy makes a delicious treat. Eat it out of your hand, or pulse the toffee in a food processor until crumbly and use for an ice cream topping.

MAKES 25 TO 30 (2- TO 3-INCH) PIECES

1$1/2$ cups sugar
$1/4$ cup light corn syrup
3 tablespoons water
6 tablespoons unsalted butter, softened
$1/4$ teaspoon salt
2 cups sliced almonds
Melted chocolate (optional)

Line a baking sheet with 2-inch sides with baking parchment. Bring the sugar, corn syrup and water to a boil in a small heavy saucepan over medium-high heat, stirring occasionally until the sugar dissolves. Cook for 12 minutes or until a candy thermometer registers 260 degrees. Stir in the butter and salt. Add the almonds and mix well. Remove from the heat.

Pour the toffee mixture on the prepared baking sheet, spreading in an even layer about $1/4$ inch thick. Cool completely and break into 2- to 3-inch pieces. Dip in chocolate and let stand until set. Store in an airtight container.

KIMBERLY WOOD GEISLER

WHITE CHOCOLATE PEANUT BUTTER BITES

Melt the white chocolate morsels in a saucepan over low heat, stirring constantly, or in the microwave on High for two minutes.

MAKES 75 TO 100 PIECES

4 cups crisp rice cereal
3 cups miniature marshmallows
1 cup crunchy peanut butter
1 cup dry roasted peanuts
4 cups (24 ounces) white chocolate morsels, melted

Mix the cereal, marshmallows, peanut butter and peanuts in a large bowl with a spatula. Pour the white chocolate over the cereal mixture and quickly mix to coat. Spread the cereal mixture on a sheet of waxed paper and let stand until cool and firm. Break into small pieces and store in an airtight container.

CHRISTINE McGRATH VELEZIS

CHO CHO CHEWY BARS

An all-time family favorite. My grandmother offers these bars the minute you walk in her home.

MAKES 150 (1×1-INCH) BARS

2 cups (12 ounces) chocolate morsels
1 (14-ounce) can sweetened
    condensed milk
2 tablespoons butter
1 (1 pound) package light brown sugar
1 cup (2 sticks) butter, melted

2 eggs
1 teaspoon vanilla extract
1 cup all-purpose flour
1 cup chopped pecans
1/2 cup flaked coconut
1/2 teaspoon salt

Preheat the oven to 350 degrees. Line a 10×15-inch baking sheet with sides with foil and grease lightly. Heat the chocolate morsels, condensed milk and 2 tablespoons butter in a double boiler over boiling water until smooth, stirring occasionally. Beat the brown sugar, 1 cup butter, the eggs and vanilla in a mixing bowl until creamy, scraping the bowl occasionally. Stir in the flour, pecans, coconut and salt. Spread 1/2 of the coconut mixture on the prepared baking sheet and drizzle with the chocolate mixture. Dot with the remaining coconut mixture and swirl lightly with the tip of a knife. Bake for 30 to 35 minutes or until golden brown. Cool slightly and lift the foil carefully to a work surface. Cool completely and cut into bars.

SUSANNAH TIMS WESSEL

Photograph for this recipe on page 280.

NO-BAKE CHOCOLATE BARS

MAKES 7 TO 8 DOZEN BARS

2 cups fine graham cracker crumbs
2 1/4 cups confectioners' sugar
1 cup (2 sticks) butter, melted
1 (18-ounce) jar extra-crunchy
    peanut butter

1 1/2 cups (9 ounces) semisweet
    chocolate morsels
1 1/2 cups (9 ounces) white
    chocolate morsels
1/2 cup (1 stick) butter

Mix the graham cracker crumbs and confectioners' sugar in a bowl. Combine 1 cup melted butter and the peanut butter in a bowl and mix until creamy. Add the crumb mixture and mix well. Press the crumb mixture over the bottom of a greased 11×17-inch baking sheet with sides. Heat the chocolate morsels, white chocolate morsels and 1/2 cup butter in a saucepan over low heat until blended, stirring occasionally. Pour the chocolate mixture over the prepared layer and chill for 1 hour or until set. Cut into bars.

JEANIE PARKER CENTENO

ROCKY ROAD FUDGE BARS

This recipe was given to me by my daughter, Mary.

MAKES 4 DOZEN BARS

Chocolate Nutty Crust
1 cup all-purpose flour
1 cup sugar
1 teaspoon baking powder
1/2 cup (1 stick) butter
1 ounce unsweetened
    chocolate, chopped
3/4 cup chopped pecans
2 eggs, lightly beaten
11/2 teaspoons vanilla extract

Creamy Chocolate Filling
8 ounces cream cheese, softened
1/2 cup sugar
1/4 cup (1/2 stick) butter, softened

1 egg
2 tablespoons all-purpose flour
1/2 teaspoon vanilla extract
1/4 cup chopped pecans
1 cup semisweet chocolate morsels
2 cups miniature marshmallows

Chocolate Frosting (optional)
1/4 cup (1/2 stick) butter
1/4 cup milk
1 ounce unsweetened
    chocolate, chopped
2 ounces cream cheese
3 cups confectioners' sugar
1 teaspoon vanilla extract

For the crust, mix the flour, sugar and baking powder in a bowl. Melt the butter and chocolate in a large saucepan over low heat, stirring frequently. Stir in the flour mixture, pecans, eggs and vanilla. Spread in a greased and floured 9×13-inch baking pan.

For the filling, preheat the oven to 350 degrees. Combine the cream cheese, sugar, butter, egg, flour and vanilla in a mixing bowl and beat at medium speed for 1 minute or until smooth and fluffy. Stir in the pecans and spread over the prepared layer. Sprinkle evenly with the chocolate morsels. Bake for 25 to 35 minutes or until the edges pull from the sides of the pan. Remove from the oven and immediately sprinkle with the marshmallows. Bake for 2 minutes longer.

For the frosting, combine the butter, milk, chocolate and cream cheese in a large saucepan and cook over low heat until blended, stirring constantly. Remove from the heat and add the confectioners' sugar and vanilla, stirring until smooth. Immediately pour the hot frosting over the warm baked layers and swirl with a knife to marbleize. Chill for 1 hour or until set. Cut into bars and store, covered, in the refrigerator.

PAT MCCABE FORMAN

Photograph for this recipe on page 280.

OATMEAL BROWNIES

MAKES 16 BROWNIES

Oat Crust
1 cup quick-cooking oats
1/2 cup all-purpose flour
1/2 cup packed brown sugar
1/4 teaspoon baking soda
1/4 teaspoon salt
1/2 cup (1 stick) butter, melted

Brownies
1 cup sugar
3/4 cup all-purpose flour
1/3 cup butter, melted

2 ounces unsweetened chocolate,
    melted
2 eggs
1 teaspoon vanilla extract

Cocoa Icing
13/4 cups confectioners' sugar
1/4 cup (1/2 stick) butter, softened
1/4 cup baking cocoa
2 tablespoons milk
1 teaspoon vanilla extract

For the crust, preheat the oven to 350 degrees. Combine the oats, flour, brown sugar, baking soda and salt in a bowl and mix well. Stir in the butter. Spread the oat mixture over the bottom of a greased 9×9-inch baking pan and bake for 10 minutes. Maintain the oven temperature.

For the brownies, combine the sugar, flour, butter, chocolate, eggs and vanilla in a mixing bowl and beat until blended. Spread the chocolate mixture over the baked layer and bake for 25 minutes. Cool in the pan on a wire rack.

For the icing, combine the confectioners' sugar, butter, baking cocoa, milk and vanilla in a bowl and stir until of a spreading consistency. Spread over the top of the cooled brownies. Let stand until set and cut into bars.

PAT McCABE FORMAN

SAUCEPAN BROWNIES

This made-from-scratch brownie is so simple you will never want to use a brownie mix again.

MAKES 16 BROWNIES

1/2 cup all-purpose flour
1 teaspoon baking powder
1/8 teaspoon salt
2 ounces unsweetened
    chocolate, chopped

1/2 cup (1 stick) butter
1 cup sugar
2 eggs, lightly beaten
1/2 teaspoon vanilla extract
1/2 cup chopped pecans (optional)

Preheat the oven to 350 degrees. Mix the flour, baking powder and salt together. Melt the chocolate and butter in a saucepan over medium-low heat, stirring occasionally. Remove from the heat and stir in the flour mixture, sugar, eggs, vanilla and pecans. Spoon the batter into a greased and floured 8×8-inch baking pan and bake for 25 minutes. Cool in the pan on a wire rack and cut into bars.

CHARLANN POTTER ANDERSON

CHOCOLATE BROWNIE COOKIES

MAKES 5 DOZEN COOKIES

4 ounces unsweetened chocolate
1 cup (6 ounces) semisweet
    chocolate morsels
1/4 cup (1/2 stick) unsalted butter
1/2 cup sifted all-purpose flour
1/2 teaspoon baking powder
1/4 teaspoon salt

1 1/2 cups sugar
4 eggs
1 teaspoon vanilla extract
2 cups (12 ounces) semisweet
    chocolate morsels
4 1/2 cups coarsely chopped walnuts

Preheat the oven to 350 degrees. Melt the unsweetened chocolate, 1 cup semisweet chocolate morsels and the butter in a 2-quart saucepan over low heat. Remove from the heat and let stand until cool. Sift the flour, baking powder and salt together. Beat the sugar, eggs and vanilla in a mixing bowl at medium speed until light and fluffy. Add the cooled chocolate mixture and mix well. Add the flour mixture and beat just until blended, scraping the bowl occasionally. Fold in 2 cups chocolate morsels and the walnuts. Drop by heaping tablespoonfuls onto a foil-lined cookie sheet and bake for 10 to 12 minutes or until the edges are crisp. Cool on the cookie sheet for 2 minutes and remove to a wire rack to cool completely.

JENNIFER RUBY McCAIN

Photograph for this recipe on page 318.

"Start with Art" is a partnership with the Birmingham Museum of Art and the JLB that introduces students in the city of Birmingham and Jefferson County to fine art. Each year, more than five thousand students complete an art project that relates to a work in the Museum's collection, and JLB volunteers give over five hundred hours serving as classroom assistants.

CRANBERRY WHITE CHOCOLATE BISCOTTI

MAKES 2¹/₂ DOZEN COOKIES

2³/4 cups all-purpose flour
1 cup sugar
1 teaspoon baking soda
¹/4 teaspoon salt
3 eggs
1 egg white
³/4 teaspoon almond extract
³/4 teaspoon vanilla extract
¹/2 cup dried cranberries, chopped
¹/2 cup white chocolate morsels
¹/3 cup slivered almonds, toasted

Preheat the oven to 350 degrees. Combine the flour, sugar, baking soda and salt in a large bowl and mix well. Whisk the eggs, egg white and flavorings in a bowl until blended and stir into the flour mixture. Add the cranberries, white chocolate morsels and almonds and mix well. Add 2 additional tablespoons flour if the dough is not dry and crumbly.

Knead the dough 5 or 6 times on a lightly floured surface. Divide the dough into 2 equal portions and shape each portion into a roll 8 inches long. Arrange the rolls 4 to 5 inches apart on a cookie sheet coated with nonstick cooking spray. Flatten each roll until 1 inch thick. Bake for 25 to 28 minutes or until light brown. Remove the rolls to a wire rack and cool for 10 minutes. Reduce the oven temperature to 325 degrees.

Cut each roll diagonally into ¹/2-inch slices. Arrange the slices cut side down on a cookie sheet coated with nonstick cooking spray. Bake for 10 minutes and turn. Bake for 10 minutes longer. Cool on the cookie sheet for 2 minutes. Remove to a wire rack to cool completely. Store in an airtight container.

LORI JOHNSON GOODSON

Photograph for this recipe on page 318.

CHOCOLATE CHIP TOFFEE COOKIES

Use kitchen shears to quickly chop the chocolate bar.

MAKES 5 TO 6 DOZEN COOKIES

3¼ cups all-purpose flour
1 teaspoon baking soda
1 teaspoon salt
1 cup (2 sticks) butter, softened
1 cup granulated sugar
1 cup packed brown sugar
⅓ cup shortening
2 eggs
1 tablespoon vanilla extract
1 (5-ounce) chocolate bar, finely chopped
2 cups (12 ounces) semisweet
    chocolate morsels
1 cup toffee morsels
1 cup chopped pecans (optional)

Mix the flour, baking soda and salt together. Beat the butter, granulated sugar, brown sugar and shortening in a bowl until light and fluffy. Add the eggs 1 at a time, beating well after each addition. Stir in the vanilla and flour mixture. Add the chocolate bar, chocolate morsels, toffee morsels and pecans and mix well. Shape the dough into rolls on baking parchment or waxed paper and wrap to enclose. Freeze until firm.

Preheat the oven to 350 degrees. Cut the rolls into thick slices and arrange on a baking parchment-lined or lightly greased cookie sheet. Bake for 10 to 12 minutes or until light brown and the centers are set. Cool on the cookie sheet for 2 minutes. Remove to a wire rack to cool completely. Store in an airtight container.

PENNEY PARKER HARTLINE

Photograph for this recipe on page 318.

The JLB Choral Group is the longest running choir in Junior League history. Performing for a variety of people, such as those with long-term illnesses or nursing home residents, they specialize in musical outreach therapy. In 2000 the group was named "Outstanding Community Project" for best demonstrating the League's mission for community service.

CREAM CHEESE COOKIES

MAKES 4 DOZEN COOKIES

1^1/4 cups all-purpose flour
^{1}/2 cup self-rising flour
8 ounces cream cheese, softened
^{1}/2 cup (1 stick) butter, softened
2 cups granulated sugar
1 teaspoon vanilla extract
1 cup pecans or walnuts, finely chopped
^{1}/2 cup rolled oats (optional)
Confectioners' sugar

Mix the all-purpose flour and self-rising flour together. Beat the cream cheese and butter in a mixing bowl until light and fluffy. Gradually add the granulated sugar and vanilla to the creamed mixture, beating constantly until blended. Mix in the flour mixture and fold in the pecans and oats. Chill, covered, until the dough becomes easy to shape into balls.

Preheat the oven to 350 degrees. Shape the dough into 1-inch balls and arrange 1 inch apart on a cookie sheet lined with baking parchment. Bake for 10 to 12 minutes or until light brown. Remove from the oven and immediately dust the hot cookies with confectioners' sugar. Cool on the cookie sheet for 2 minutes and remove to a wire rack to cool completely.

ELISSA HANDLEY TYSON

MASTERING MEASURING

Properly measured flour can be the difference between a fabulous baked goodie and a dry disappointment. To make sure your baking measures up, follow these easy steps.

1. Lightly spoon flour into a dry measuring cup. Don't use a glass measuring cup with a pour spout—these should be used to measure liquids only.

2. Don't pack the flour into the measuring cup, but do fill it over the rim.

3. Level gently with a knife.

4. When a recipe calls for sifted flour, sift first and then measure according to the steps above.

LEMON GINGERSNAPS

MAKES 5 DOZEN COOKIES

Cookies

4 cups all-purpose flour
2 teaspoons baking soda
1 teaspoon ground cinnamon
1 teaspoon ground cloves
1 teaspoon ground ginger
1½ cups shortening or butter, softened
2 cups sugar
½ cup molasses
2 eggs, beaten
½ cup sugar

Lemon Glaze

1 (1-pound) package confectioners' sugar
⅓ cup fresh lemon juice
2 teaspoons grated lemon zest (about 1 large lemon)

For the cookies, preheat the oven to 375 degrees. Mix the flour, baking soda, cinnamon, cloves and ginger together. Beat the shortening and 2 cups sugar in a mixing bowl at medium speed until light and fluffy. Add the molasses and eggs to the creamed mixture and beat until smooth. Add the flour mixture and beat until blended.

Shape the dough into 1-inch balls and coat with ½ cup sugar. Arrange the balls on a greased cookie sheet and flatten slightly with the bottom of a glass. Bake for 8 to 10 minutes or until golden brown. Cool on the cookie sheet for 2 minutes and remove to a wire rack.

For the glaze, combine the confectioners' sugar, lemon juice and lemon zest in a bowl and mix until smooth. Spread the glaze over the slightly warm cookies. Let stand until cool and store in an airtight container.

MARGARET REYNOLDS OPOLKA

Photograph for this recipe on page 318.

SOUTHERN PECAN COINS

MAKES 5 TO 6 DOZEN COOKIES

3¹/2 cups self-rising flour
1 teaspoon baking soda
1/4 teaspoon salt
2 cups packed light brown sugar
1 cup (2 sticks) butter, softened

2 eggs
1 teaspoon vanilla extract
2 cups pecans halves, toasted and
    finely chopped

Mix the self-rising flour, baking soda and salt together. Beat the brown sugar and butter in a mixing bowl until light and fluffy. Beat in the eggs and vanilla until blended. Gradually add the flour mixture and beat until smooth. Divide the dough into 6 equal portions. Roll each portion in the pecans and work the dough to ensure even distribution of the pecans. Chill, covered, for 1 hour or until firm. Shape the dough into 1-inch logs. Wrap the logs tightly in waxed paper and freeze for 3 hours or longer. Preheat the oven to 350 degrees. Cut the logs into thin slices and arrange on a lightly greased cookie sheet. Bake for 8 minutes. Cool on the cookie sheet for 2 minutes and remove to a wire rack to cool completely.

VALERIE YOUNG LIGHTFOOT

Photograph for this recipe on page 318.

PEANUT BUTTER AND CHOCOLATE CHIP COOKIES

MAKES 3 DOZEN COOKIES

1²/3 cups all-purpose flour
1¹/2 tablespoons cornstarch
1³/4 teaspoons baking powder
1/2 teaspoon baking soda
3/4 cup packed brown sugar
1/2 cup creamy peanut butter
1/4 cup (1/2 stick) butter, softened

1/4 cup granulated sugar
1¹/2 tablespoons light corn syrup
2¹/2 teaspoons vanilla extract
1 egg
2 cups (12 ounces) milk
    chocolate morsels
1 cup coarsely chopped pecans, toasted

Preheat the oven to 375 degrees. Mix the flour, cornstarch, baking powder and baking soda together. Beat the brown sugar, peanut butter, butter and granulated sugar in a mixing bowl at medium speed until blended. Beat in the corn syrup, vanilla and egg. Stir in the flour mixture, chocolate morsels and pecans. Coat hands lightly with nonstick cooking spray and shape the dough into 1¹/2-inch balls. Arrange the balls 2 inches apart on a cookie sheet coated with nonstick cooking spray. Bake for 9 minutes or until light brown. Cool on the cookie sheet for 2 minutes and remove to a wire rack to cool completely.

HOLLEY CONTRI JOHNSON

RASPBERRY ALMOND SHORTBREAD

MAKES 3½ DOZEN COOKIES

1 cup (2 sticks) butter, softened
2/3 cup granulated sugar
1/2 teaspoon almond extract
2 cups all-purpose flour

1/2 cup raspberry jam
1 cup confectioners' sugar
2 tablespoons water
1 teaspoons almond extract

Combine the butter, granulated sugar and ½ teaspoon flavoring in a mixing bowl and beat at medium speed for 2 to 3 minutes or until creamy. Reduce the speed to low and add the flour. Beat for 2 to 3 minutes or until blended. Shape the dough into a ball and chill, covered, for 1 hour or longer.

Preheat the oven to 350 degrees. Shape the chilled dough into 1-inch balls and arrange the balls 2 inches apart on a cookie sheet. Smaller balls are better as the almond flavor can be overpowering if the cookie is too large. Make an indentation with your thumb in the center of each ball and fill each indentation with about ¼ teaspoon of the jam. Bake for 14 to 18 minutes or until golden brown. Cool on the cookie sheet for 2 minutes and remove to a wire rack to cool completely. Mix the confectioners' sugar, water and 1 teaspoon flavoring in a bowl and drizzle over the cooled cookies. Let stand until set and store in an airtight container.

CHRISTINE McGRATH VELEZIS

Photograph for this recipe on page 318.

ROSEMARY SHORTBREAD

MAKES 5 DOZEN COOKIES

1 cup (2 sticks) butter, softened
2/3 cup confectioners' sugar, sifted

3 cups all-purpose flour
3 tablespoons chopped fresh rosemary

Preheat the oven to 325 degrees. Beat the butter in a mixing bowl until creamy. Gradually add the confectioners' sugar, beating constantly until blended. Beat in the flour until smooth and stir in the rosemary.

Roll the dough ¼ inch thick on a lightly floured surface and cut into rounds using a small round cutter. Arrange the rounds on a lightly greased cookie sheet and bake for 16 to 18 minutes or until light brown around the edges. Cool on the cookie sheet for 2 minutes and remove to a wire rack to cool completely. Store in an airtight container. Omit the rosemary for a basic shortbread.

AMY LYN TOOTHAKER

FROZEN CHOCOLATE PEANUT BUTTER PIE

Serve this simple five-ingredient frozen pie at your next dinner party.

SERVES 8

1 1/2 cups chocolate wafer crumbs
1/4 cup (1/2 stick) butter, softened
3/4 cup chunky or creamy peanut butter
1 cup frozen whipped topping, thawed
1 quart chocolate ice cream, softened

Mix the wafer crumbs and butter in a bowl and press the crumb mixture over the bottom of a buttered 9-inch pie plate. Fold the peanut butter and whipped topping into the ice cream in a bowl and spread the peanut butter mixture over the prepared layer. Freeze, covered, for 8 hours.

ELISSA HANDLEY TYSON

FROZEN COCONUT CARAMEL PIE

This pie is a big hit with coconut lovers.

SERVES 16

2 unbaked (9-inch) deep-dish pie shells
1/4 cup (1/2 stick) butter
1 (7-ounce) package flaked coconut
1/2 cup chopped pecans
8 ounces cream cheese, softened
1 (14-ounce) can sweetened condensed milk
16 ounces frozen whipped topping, thawed
1 (12-ounce) jar caramel ice cream topping

Bake the pie shells using the package directions and let stand until cool. Melt the butter in a large skillet over medium heat and add the coconut and pecans. Cook until golden brown, stirring frequently.

Beat the cream cheese in a mixing bowl until smooth. Add the condensed milk and beat until blended. Fold in the whipped topping. Spread 1/4 of the cream cheese mixture in each pie shell and drizzle with 1/4 of the caramel topping. Sprinkle each with 1/4 of the coconut mixture. Repeat the process with the remaining ingredients. Freeze, covered, for 4 hours or until firm. Let stand at room temperature for 5 to 10 minutes before slicing.

MARILYN CROWELL INGRAM

SOUTHERN PECAN PIE

Baking this pie in a springform pan makes for an impressive presentation, but the recipe works in a ten-inch deep-dish pie plate as well. In a rush, purchase a refrigerator pie pastry from the supermarket and roll to fit the springform pan or pie plate. My children help me prepare these pies, and we give them as Christmas gifts.

SERVES 10

Pie Pastry
1¼ cups all-purpose flour
⅛ teaspoon salt
⅓ cup sugar
½ cup (1 stick) unsalted butter, softened
1 egg yolk
1 teaspoon vanilla extract

Pecan Filling
1½ cups sugar
1 cup light corn syrup
5 eggs, lightly beaten
6 tablespoons butter, melted
1½ teaspoons vanilla extract
1½ cups pecan halves

For the pastry, combine the flour and salt in a bowl and whisk to combine. Combine the sugar and butter in a mixing bowl and beat at high speed until light and fluffy. Add the egg yolk and vanilla and beat until blended. Reduce the speed to low and add the flour mixture, beating just until a soft dough forms. Chill, covered, for 30 minutes. Press the pastry over the bottom and halfway up the side of a lightly greased 9-inch springform pan and freeze for 25 minutes or until firm.

Preheat the oven to 350 degrees. Line the prepared pastry with baking parchment and top with pie weights or dried beans. Arrange the pan on a baking sheet and bake for 25 to 30 minutes or until golden brown. Remove the weights and baking parchment. Maintain the oven temperature.

For the filling, combine the sugar, corn syrup, eggs, butter and vanilla in a bowl and whisk until blended. Pour the filling into the baked pastry. Arrange the pecans over the filling in a circular pattern by lining the outside edge and working toward the center. Bake for 1 hour or until set.

KELLY ROBERTS SORRELLS

Photograph for this recipe on page 319.

WALNUT CHOCOLATE CHIP PIE

One recipe tester recalls that this recipe is similar to one from her hometown titled Kentucky Derby Pie®.

SERVES 8

1/2 cup all-purpose flour
1/2 cup granulated sugar
1/2 cup packed brown sugar
3/4 cup (11/2 sticks) butter, melted and cooled
2 eggs, lightly beaten
2 tablespoons bourbon or vanilla extract
1 cup (6 ounces) semisweet chocolate morsels
3/4 cup chopped walnuts, toasted
1 unbaked (9-inch) frozen pie shell
Chocolate sauce (optional)

Preheat the oven to 325 degrees. Combine the flour, granulated sugar and brown sugar in a bowl and mix well. Stir in the butter, eggs and bourbon. Fold in the chocolate morsels and walnuts.

Pour the chocolate mixture into the frozen pie shell and arrange the pie on the lowest oven rack. Bake for 1 hour or until the center is set. Serve with a scoop of ice cream and drizzle with chocolate sauce.

Derby-Pie® is a registered trademark of Kern's Kitchen, Inc., Louisville, Kentucky.

HOLLY HOLMES WILLIAMS

SIMPLE BERRY SAUCE

You can use any combination of fresh berries to make this simple sauce.

SERVES 6

1/4 cup currant jelly
3 tablespoons orange liqueur
1 cup sliced fresh strawberries
1/2 cup fresh blueberries
1/2 cup fresh raspberries

Heat the jelly and liqueur in a small saucepan. Add the strawberries, blueberries and raspberries and cook until heated through and slightly thickened, stirring occasionally. Cool to room temperature and drizzle over ice cream, sherbet or pound cake. For testing purposes, Grand Marnier was used.

JEANNE REID SHEARER

RASPBERRY SAUCE

MAKES 3 CUPS

2 (10-ounce) packages frozen raspberries, thawed
4 to 6 tablespoons sugar
2 tablespoons cornstarch
1/4 cup raspberry liqueur

Process the undrained raspberries in a blender or food processor until puréed. Press the purée through a strainer, discarding the seeds. Mix the raspberry purée, desired amount of sugar and cornstarch in a saucepan and cook until thickened, stirring constantly. Let stand until cool and stir in the liqueur. Serve chilled. For testing purposes, Chambord was used.

ABBY CURRY FINNEY

FUDGE SAUCE

MAKES 4 CUPS

4 ounces unsweetened chocolate, chopped
1/2 cup (1 stick) butter
3 cups sugar
1 (12-ounce) can evaporated milk

Melt the chocolate and butter in a medium saucepan over low heat, stirring occasionally. Stir in the sugar and evaporated milk and cook until thickened, stirring occasionally. Let stand until cool and store, covered, in the refrigerator.

MANDY MCNAMES HOGAN

Simple Blackberry Cobbler

RUSH HOUR DESSERTS

No time for dessert? Think again! This collection of stress-free finales satisfies any sweet tooth, and as the cook, you will be in and out of the kitchen in a flash. Whether you need a standby for Wednesday night supper or something impressive enough for guests, you will find what you need. Many of these recipes may be prepared in advance, and they all have a preparation time of twenty minutes or less.

- **KEY LIME DESSERT SAUCE**

  Whisk $3/4$ cup sweetened condensed milk, $1/2$ cup fresh lime juice and $1/4$ cup water in a bowl until blended. Serve over pound cake or ice cream.

- **BUTTERMILK SAUCE**

  Mix $3/4$ cup buttermilk, $1/4$ cup sugar, 2 tablespoons all-purpose flour and 1 egg in a saucepan. Cook over medium-low heat for 10 minutes or until the sauce coats the back of a wooden spoon or a thermometer registers 160 degrees, whisking constantly. Serve chilled or warm drizzled over cake or pie.

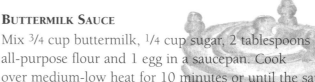

- **BLACKBERRY SWIRL**

  Process $3/4$ cup blackberries, $1/4$ cup confectioners' sugar and $1 1/2$ tablespoons fresh lemon juice in a blender until puréed. Strain if desired. Process 4 scoops of vanilla ice cream, 2 tablespoons milk and 2 tablespoons vanilla yogurt in a blender until smooth and divide evenly among 4 stemmed goblets. Divide the blackberry mixture evenly among the goblets and swirl with a straw or the tip of a knife and serve immediately.

- **RASPBERRY TIRAMISU**

  Beat $1/2$ cup whipping cream in a mixing bowl until soft peaks form. Gradually add $1/4$ cup confectioners' sugar, beating constantly until stiff peaks form. Beat 6 ounces softened mascarpone cheese and 2 tablespoons raspberry liqueur in a mixing bowl until blended. Reserve $1/2$ cup of the whipped cream and fold the remaining whipped cream into the cheese mixture. Brush 1 side of 24 ladyfingers with 2 tablespoons raspberry liqueur. Spread the cheese mixture evenly over the moistened side of 12 of the ladyfingers on a plate and top with the remaining ladyfingers moistened side down. Arrange 3 ladyfingers on each of 4 dessert plates and top each serving with 2 tablespoons fresh raspberries and 2 tablespoons of the reserved whipped cream.

- **LACE COOKIES**

  Preheat the oven to 325 degrees. Mix 1 cup rolled oats, 1 cup sugar, 1 1/2 teaspoons all-purpose flour and 1/4 teaspoon salt in a bowl. Whisk 1/2 cup (1 stick) melted unsalted butter, 2 eggs and 1/2 teaspoon vanilla extract in a bowl until blended and add to the oats mixture, mixing well. Drop the dough by 1/2 teaspoonfuls 2 inches apart onto a cookie sheet lined with baking parchment. Bake for 10 minutes or until light brown. Cool completely on the cookie sheet. Store in an airtight container.
  Pat McCabe Forman

- **PISTACHIO AND COCONUT TORTONI**

  Slightly soften 1 quart vanilla ice cream. Beat 1 cup whipping cream in a mixing bowl until stiff peaks form. Fold 2 tablespoons dark rum (optional), 1/2 cup coarsely chopped pistachios and 1/2 cup toasted sweetened flaked coconut into the whipped cream. Beat the softened ice cream and 2 tablespoons coconut liqueur or 1/2 teaspoon coconut extract in a mixing bowl until smooth. Fold the whipped cream mixture into the ice cream mixture and spoon into paper-lined muffin cups. Sprinkle with chopped pistachios and toasted coconut and freeze until firm.

Southern Pecan Pie

DESSERT BUFFET   MENU

SUGGESTED WINES:
- *Robert Mondavi Moscato d'Oro 2003*
- *Valckenberg Madonna Eiswein 2003*
- *Eroica Riesling 2004*
- *Banfi Rosa Regale 2003*

Red Velvet Cake with Cream Cheese Frosting

Arlington Historic House is the only antebellum mansion remaining in Birmingham. Originally called "The Grove," it was constructed in the 1840s for Judge William S. Mudd, one of the ten founders of Birmingham, in the farming community of Elyton. Notably, just one month before the Civil War's end in 1865, General James H. Wilson arrived in Alabama, headquartered at Arlington, and dispatched 13,500 troops known as Wilson's Raiders to destroy the Confederate iron furnaces in the area as well as the military school at the University of Alabama in Tuscaloosa.

The property was subsequently sold several times and eventually became a summer retreat, and then the permanent home, of the Munger family. Finally, in 1953, the Greek Revival mansion was acquired by the City of Birmingham to serve as a house museum and was carefully restored with a collection of nineteenth-century furniture and decorative arts. Today it features an annual Birmingham Belles celebration as well as a period Christmas holiday and other historical and cultural activities.

With Arlington Historic House, this cookbook has come full circle—from Rick Bragg's "stainless steel" to Arlington's silver service, from "seafoam green linoleum" to a white lace vintage tablecloth, from "barbecued pork chops with butter-laden mashed potatoes" to Arlington Mint Julep Ice Cream on page 286. Many of Birmingham's most notable settings have been sandwiched in between, along with menu ideas, our best recipes, cooking tips, and the history of The Junior League of Birmingham.

So the ending is the beginning—not just of Birmingham's history but of new *Tables of Content* created by each one of us. And whether modest or lavish, Old South or contemporary, using elaborate recipes or just a few ingredients, it will be the memories of the table—the food, the setting, and the conversation—that stay with us all.

For more information on Arlington Historic House as well as Birmingham's listings in the National Historic Register, visit The Birmingham Historical Society at www.bhistorical.org/things_to_do/historic _districts.html.

Arlington Historic House

COOKBOOK COMMITTEE RECIPE TESTERS

Jill DeWitt Acosta

Paige Dowdy Albright

Heather Bryant Anthony

Ashley Coleman Bates

Anne Carr Bethea

Mary McCutcheon Bolus

Heather Chandash Brock

Cheryl Croxford Brown

Cyndy Craig Cantley

Harriet Kennedy Cochrane

Cilie Collins Cowin

LeAnn Holifield Cox

Elizabeth Baird Crawford

Jane Huston Brown Crommelin

Nina Haas Daniels

Kathleen Sprouse Doss

Julie Mathis Freeland

Dawn Gotlieb Holloway

Mary Carson Baker LaRussa

Amy Hamilton Lewis

Mary Black Little

Michelle Marie Mathews

Adriana Wahl Morros

Karria Wren Myers

Margaret Reynolds Opolka

Amy Lyn Toothaker

Holly Holmes Williams

RECIPE TESTERS

Maria Adlercreutz Alexander

Elizabeth Little Allen

Sandy Bolen Ballard

Marylon Hand Barkan

Laura Gray Barron

Supreet Rangi Bauer

Nancy LeBey Baxley

Donna Scott Bishop

Joanne McCrary Brasseal

Alicia Frances Brown

Betsy Avant Burkhart

Mary Katherine Luckie Cabaniss

Stephanie Stevens Carothers

Cora Brasfield Causey

Jennifer Barnett Childs

Cheryl Amiel Collat

Christine Hughmark Denniston

Julia Gray Doster

Christina Ellis Elliott

Anna Armstrong Emblom

Betsy Orcutt French

Faith Garner Gardner

Sally Henderson Garner

Shaun Davidson Gray

Diane Stewart Griswold

Aimee Blake Hager

Kate Wood Hamilton

Leigh Hardin Hancock

Penney Parker Hartline

Nancy Holt Higginbotham

Michele Brewer Hill

Leslee Hopkins Hunter

Marilyn Crowell Ingram

Joanna Upchurch Jones

Sharon Hilyer Jones

Laura Watkins Jordan

Lindsay Rogers Keith

Sara Lynne Jackson Keith

Loretta Gleason Keller

Sheryl Williams Kimerling

Melanie Remmert Kohn

Beth Shelfer Little

Stephanie Zohar Lynton

Rhanya Malki

Molly Cameron Martin

Andrea Garrett McCaskey

Libba Paulk McKinney

Kate Adams McKnight

Stephanie Gibson Mims

Dianna Jill Mize

Carrie Boyd Morrow

Rhonda Tamblyn Moss

Traci Manning Parker

Kimberly Till Powell

Leigh Rumbley

Teresa Chamblee Shufflebarger

Dorothy Klip Smith

Sara Arellano Smith

Kay Teas Teschner

Renae Hilyer Thigpen

Elissa Handley Tyson

Elizabeth Dunn Yielding

OTHER ACKNOWLEDGMENTS

We would like to extend our appreciation to our families and friends, whose commitment and generosity of time, patience, and support made the production of this cookbook possible.

Heather H. Chadduck
Mitzi Munger Ireland
Denise Calderaro Modling
Ann Lowe Moore
Patricia O' Bannon Muse
Elizabeth Anne Skinner
Nancy Lowe Wilson

We would also like to thank the many community members and businesses who have helped to make *Tables of Content* what it is. Their support, advice, and generous contributions have been extremely valuable to us during this project.

AmSouth Bank
Balch & Bingham, LLP
Southern Progress

COMMUNITY ADVISORS

Clyde Anderson, Books-A-Million
Hunter George, *The Birmingham News*
Dennis Leonard, WBRC-TV Fox 6
Maloy Love, Mountain Brook Flower Shop
Joe O'Donnell, Editor of the *Birmingham Magazine*

COVER & CHAPTER OPENER ACKNOWLEDGMENTS

COVER
> *Table Matters* @ www.table-matters.com
> *Frontera* @ www.fronterairon.com

BREAKFAST AND BRUNCH
> Vulcan Park
> *A'Mano* @ www.amanogifts.com

APPETIZERS AND BEVERAGES
> Sloss Furnaces
> *The Cook Store of Mountain Brook* 205.879.5277

SALADS
> Birmingham Botanical Gardens
> *Harvest Glen Market* @ www.harvestglenmarket.org

PASTA, BREADS AND GRAINS
> Birmingham Zoo
> *At Home* @ www.athome-furnishings.com

SOUPS AND STEWS
> Birmingham Civil Rights Institute and Sixteenth Street Baptist Church
> *Mulberry Heights Antiques* 205.870.1300

MAIN DISHES
> Alabama Theatre
> *Bromberg's* @ www.brombergs.com

VEGETABLES
> The Hillman Building at UAB Hospital
> *Harmony Landing* @ www.harmonylanding.com
> *Andy's Creekside Nursery* 205.824.0233

DESSERTS
> Birmingham Museum of Art
> *Dorothy McDaniel Flower Market* @ www.dorothymcdaniel.com

WINE SUGGESTIONS:
> Smitty Smith—Master Corker, *Overton & Vine* 205.967.1409

NUTRITIONAL PROFILE GUIDELINES

The editors have attempted to present these family recipes in a format that allows approximate nutritional values to be computed. Persons with dietary or health problems or whose diets require close monitoring should not rely solely on the nutritional information provided. They should consult their physician or a registered dietitian for specific information.

Abbreviations for Nutritional Profile

Cal—Calories	Fiber—Dietary Fiber	Sod—Sodium
Prot—Protein	T Fat—Total Fat	g—grams
Carbo—Carbohydrates	Sat Fat—Saturated Fat	mg—milligrams
	Chol—Cholesterol	

Nutritional information for these recipes is computed from information derived from many sources, including materials supplied by the United States Department of Agriculture, computer databanks, and journals in which the information is assumed to be in the public domain. However, many specialty items, new products, and processed food may not be available from these sources or may vary from the average values used in these profiles. More information on new and/or specific products may be obtained by reading the nutrient labels. Unless otherwise specified, the nutritional profile of these recipes is based on all measurements being level.

- Artificial sweeteners vary in use and strength and should be used to taste, using the recipe ingredients as a guideline. Sweeteners using aspartame (NutraSweet and Equal) should not be used as a sweetener in recipes involving prolonged heating, which reduces the sweet taste. For further information on the use of these sweeteners, refer to the package.
- Alcoholic ingredients have been analyzed for the basic information. Cooking causes the evaporation of alcohol, which decreases alcoholic and caloric content.
- Buttermilk, sour cream, and yogurt are the types available commercially.
- Canned beans and vegetables have been analyzed with the canning liquid. Draining and rinsing canned products will lower the sodium content.
- Chicken, cooked for boning and chopping, has been roasted; this cooking method yields the lowest caloric values.
- Eggs are all large. To avoid raw eggs that may carry salmonella, as in eggnog or 6-week muffin batter, use an equivalent amount of commercial egg substitute.
- Flour is unsifted all-purpose flour.
- Garnishes, serving suggestions, and other optional information and variations are not included in the profile.
- Margarine and butter are regular, not whipped or presoftened.
- Oil is any type of vegetable cooking oil. Shortening is hydrogenated vegetable shortening.
- Salt and other ingredients to taste as noted in the ingredients have not been included in the nutritional profile.
- If a choice of ingredients has been given, the profile reflects the first option. If a choice of amounts has been given, the profile reflects the greater amount.

NUTRITIONAL PROFILES

Pg #	Recipe Title (Approx Per Serving)	Cal	Prot (g)	Carbo (g)	Fiber (g)	T Fat (g)	Sat Fat (g)	Chol (mg)	Sod (mg)
25	Baked French Toast	241	6.5	34.2	1.3	8.6	4.4	81	240
37	Peach Blueberry Smoothie	107	2.4	22.2	1.6	1.8	1	6	22
38	Berries with Champagne Syrup	138	1.4	32.7	2.3	0.6	0	0	2
38	Winter Fruit Compote	269	1.1	54.1	4.2	5.9	3.6	15	77
59	Caribbean Salsa	37	1.1	8.2	1.5	0.2	0	0	79
67	Greek Chicken Bites with Herb Cream Dip	55	5.9	2	0.3	2.6	0.6	14	257
87	Pineapple Salad	98	0.6	20.9	1.2	2.1	1.8	0	86
93	Coconut Crab and Shrimp Salad	307	30.5	30	8.2	9.9	3.7	127	642
128	Southwestern Couscous	287	10.6	46.7	7.7	8	1.5	0	378
136	Olive Bread	228	6.3	32.4	2.4	8.7	1.1	0	680
138	Pumpkin Walnut Focaccia with Gruyère	197	6.9	27	1.5	7.7	2.1	9	178
142	Curried Barley with Golden Raisins	294	8.7	52.3	10.4	6.4	0.7	0	351
142	Tabouli	209	3.3	25.6	6.5	10.8	1.5	0	500
169	Baby Lima Bean Soup	203	9	28.8	7.7	6.3	3.7	15	415
169	White Bean Rosemary Soup	216	10.8	28.8	6.1	6.9	2.3	10	779
185	Weeknight Flank Steak	233	31.2	0.6	0.2	10.9	4.4	57	94
193	Rosemary Ginger Pork Tenderloin	269	24	31.8	0.1	5	1.8	65	445
211	Grilled Raspberry Chicken	362	33.3	38.8	1.3	8.3	2.5	83	338
222	Olive and Sage Turkey Breast	356	43.4	2.9	0.7	20.5	2.1	68	798
230	Parslied Clams and Haricots Verts over Fettuccini	431	19.8	63.8	4.3	9.4	5.2	43	379
235	Spicy Grilled Shrimp with Mango Salsa	194	18.4	13.4	1.6	7.9	1.2	166	488
252	Asparagus Bundles	59	2.8	5.9	2.9	3.6	0.5	0	595
255	Garlic-Roasted Green Beans and Shallots with Hazelnuts	132	2.4	9.9	3.6	9.7	1.1	0	398
256	Haricots Verts with Roasted Garlic Butter	67	1.8	9.1	4.3	2.6	1.6	7	157
258	Roasted Beets with Spicy Orange Glaze	160	2.2	23.9	3.7	7	1	0	396
265	Tarragon Sugar Snap Peas	69	3	9.8	3.1	2.2	1.3	5	173
288	Blackberry Mascarpone Ice Cream	332	6.5	52.2	0	12	6.4	85	69

TABLES *of* CONTENT

SERVICE, SETTINGS AND SUPPER

For additional copies of *Tables of Content*
or for order information on our other cookbooks:

Food For Thought

450 recipes along with stories by famous Alabama authors

Magic

356 pages filled with more than 600 recipes

Please contact:
Junior League of Birmingham
Cookbook Committee
2212 Twentieth Avenue South
Birmingham, Alabama 35223
205.879.9861 • 205.879.9868 (fax)
Web site: www.jlbonline.com